Architecture and Design Science

Series editor C M Eastman

Architectural morphology P Steadman
Psychology of architectural design Ö Akın

p Pion Limited, 207 Brondesbury Park, London NW2 5JN

Psychology of Architectural Design

Ömer Akın

SCHOOL OF

CALIFORNIA

PROFESSIONAL

PSYCHOLOGY

LOS ANGELES

p Pion Limited, 207 Brondesbury Park, London NW2 5JN

ISBN 0 85086 120 9

Printed in Great Britain by Page Bros (Norwich) Limited

Preface

This work was started in 1976 in the Department of Architecture at Carnegie-Mellon University. Ten short years and what now seems like countless manuscripts later it has come to a conclusion. The conclusion I am referring to is more like closure than termination. I intend to continue this work in one form or another for years to come. The closure has more to do with the natural cycle of human effort than with any form of exhaustion in avenues to be explored or the desire to explore them.

I am reminded by my own thoughts of Christopher Jones's comment to me nearly sixteen years ago, when I was a recent graduate student in the United States, on the eve of his completion of *Design Methods*. When asked if the work was complete, he responded negatively and added that he simply had to get it out of his system. The completion of this work is somewhat in the same spirit. It is time for me to publish the work. Its completion requires many more years and minds.

After all this time, it is virtually impossible to recount all who have directly or indirectly influenced this work. But some must be recognized. Charles Eastman, my advisor, colleague, and editor of this volume has had the most first-hand input in this work. Others who have just as significantly influenced this work indirectly, through their own work and ideas, are Allen Newell, Raj Reddy, and Herbert Simon. I will always be grateful to these individuals, if not for their influence on this work, then for promoting such high standards of scientific investigation and thought.

The work in its entirety has been done in the main PDP-10 computing environment of the Department of Computer Science. Parts of this work have been supported by ARPA and NSF (contract number MSC 7825824).

My colleagues in the Department of Architecture, in the College of Fine Arts, and my students over the course of the last ten years have evoked more inspiration in me than any one person could possibly muster all on his own. I am grateful for their intellectual company.

Dedication of the work deservedly goes to my wife.

Ömer Akın
Department of Architecture
Carnegie-Mellon University

To Meral

Contents

Contents

Introduction: The architectural design process

"One day the owner of a neighboring garden brought a carpenter to the site and told him to build-up a house. They stopped on a spot where the ground sloped gently downwards. The carpenter had a look at the trees, the ground, the environments, and the town in the valley. Then he proceeded to extract from his cummerbund some pegs, paced off the distances, and marked them with the pegs. He asked the owner which trees might be sacrificed, moved his pegs for a few feet, nodded and seemed satisfied. He found that the new house would not obstruct the view from the neighboring structures... ."

D Grabrijan and J Neidhardt *Architecture of Bosnia* (1957, page 313, author's translation)

Once architecture existed without architects as we know them. In the quotation by Grabrijan and Neidhardt we see architecture embodied in the actions of the carpenter who arrives at the site of a building to be erected and starts laying the foundations in situ. The knowledge used in composing the building comes from the carpenter, who in turn has inherited it from his culture. This is typical of vernacular architecture. Design is not a self-conscious process but rather an integral part of building. Placement of the entrance, use of existing trees, and overall geometry of the building layout are all taken care of in location, based on clearly understood rules of architectural practice indigenous to the site. The carpenter understands the materials and construction techniques available to him. Placement of windows, their sizes, roofing, and finishes all come from a fixed palette. Obviously, to make the building fit a given specific site, exceptions must be made. This is so commonplace that often there are rules that govern the variations from the norm as well as those that define the norm. In this way, exceptions, an important aspect of architecture, can be included in common practice.

Incorporation of the exception into the prototype is also illustrated in the above example. The carpenter moves his pegs to realign the walls he has initially envisioned so as to save the trees that happen to be on the site. Design, even in the form where a preconceived notion is adapted to a specific site, is carried out completely as an integral part of construction. The carpenter uses the actual site and his pegs as a surrogate for the contemporary architect's drawings on paper.

This analogy is at first very clear. However, there are qualitative distinctions between the two processes which are important to understand. Architects as designers have to manipulate abstract representations of the site on paper as well as being self-conscious about how they manipulate these representations. They have to keep track of what is to be accomplished by their designs, how to accomplish them, which design standards to observe, and how to regulate their time and resources.

They also have to observe conventions and regulations beyond their control that govern the delivery of the design to the client. These are necessitated by legal and pragmatic constraints of communication within the profession. In contrast, vernacular architecture requires very little, if any, of these self-conscious aspects of the contemporary design process. The differences between these two processes are also representative of two very different types of design problems. In the case of vernacular design, a prototypical solution exists. The problem, its constraints, and the set of acceptable solutions to it are predefined vis-à-vis prototypes. In the case of self-conscious design, the definition of the problem, its constraints, and solutions (or criteria for solutions) are yet to be determined in the course of the design process. Consequently, designers not only design the objects to be constructed but also the processes that will lead them to descriptions of these objects.

Most contemporary problems in architecture require a self-conscious process. Architects have to decide how design should come about, when to examine the allied bodies of knowledge, and how to bring such knowledge to bear on design. They have to decompose the design process explicitly into smaller phases to make possible the contributions of a large number of participants, such as engineers, planners, landscape designers, and user or client groups. The integration of each participant in this complex process is essential. Professionals and other interest groups can participate in design meaningfully, if they are informed about the relevant decisions and alternatives during the course of the process. A civil engineer's structural analysis is valuable while selecting the structural system and developing the construction documents, not after all design decisions are completely fixed. Likewise, the user's preference and behavioral tendencies are useful during the programming stage.

All of these reasons make it almost mandatory that architects articulate the design process into parts which represent abstractions of the total design problem, appropriate for the purposes of a given participant of the design process, and easily separable from the whole. Architectural conventions developed for practice in the profession support such an analytical form of design. Door-window schedules intended for the builder, shop drawings intended for the manufacturer, perspectives intended for the client, and preliminary drawings intended for the engineer are some examples.

Also, the partitioning of the design process assists the effective and efficient conduct of work through teams of designers in the architects' office. Most design problems require the participation of a multitude of designers with various areas of specialization. This is often a result of the complex multifaceted nature of these problems as well as the sheer magnitude of the tasks involved in meeting construction timetables. Consequently, different aspects of the design product must be worked on by many designers while it is still incomplete or even nonexistent.

1.1 Motivations

A primary purpose of this work is to illuminate further the self-conscious approaches to architectural design and the influences these will have on architectural practice, theory, technology, and education.

Another source of motivation comes from a real opportunity that exists today for understanding the cognitive basis of problem-solving and its applications to the area of architectural design. The opportunity arises from the knowledge and methods recently developed in the area of human problem-solving. Most of these developments are the outgrowths of Simon's pioneering work in the area of decisionmaking (1944) and Newell et al's work on 'heuristics' (1957). The premise of these studies is that mechanisms responsible for the behaviors of problem-solvers, such as designers, managers, and organizations, can be understood by studying their behaviors and by designing information-processing models that account for such behavior (Newell and Simon, 1972).

Traditional approaches to modelling human cognitive performance that predate information-processing theory are based on stimulus–response models. In these studies it is assumed that, at an atomic level, behavior can be explained to the extent that it can be predicted by external stimuli. A one-to-one correspondence between stimulus and response is assumed. What goes on inside the designer's mind after the onset of the stimulus until the onset of the response, however, is not a necessary part of this paradigm. The internal mechanisms that link the stimuli to the responses are considered to be a *black box* into which one cannot and should not pry. Even in more recent studies, design and creativity are occasionally attributed to mystical forces sealed in this black box and claimed not to be fit for study (Lobell, 1975). This belief has been a major deterrent to scientific studies of design and to the development of an explicit theory of the architectural design process.

Information-processing theory, on the other hand, is based on showing the necessity as well as the sufficiency of internal processing mechanisms that logically explain the responses of the system to any given set of stimuli. This results in a more logical, parsimonious, and powerful explanation of behavior than in the stimulus–response type of paradigm. An underlying motivation and mission of the present study is to develop the foundations for an information-processing theory which can be used to bridge architectural practice, research, and education.

To accomplish this aim, several goals must first be met. A model of the cognitive mechanisms of the designer must be developed. Such a model must be detailed enough to represent design behaviors as a function of detailed cognitive operations and information-processing capacities as well as general enough to account for the open-ended behaviors of many designers. Without *detail* the model will not advance the state of the art beyond simple stimulus–response explanations or, rather, nonexplanations. Without *generality* the model will not be valid.

1.2 Background

This study is not the first attempt at an investigation of the design process nor the first application of information-processing theory to the study of architectural design. During the early 1970s four empirical studies dealing with design were published (Eastman, 1970; Foz, 1973; Henrion, 1974; Krauss and Myer, 1970). A second set of studies dealing with the theoretical issues in the area also became available around the same time (Freeman and Newell, 1971; Reitman, 1964; Simon, 1969; 1970; 1973). Last, in more recent years a third set of texts intended for education and based on current findings in this area emerged (Broadbent, 1973; Wade, 1977). Both studies in this last set advanced the earlier work by Jones (1970) on design methods. Although the theoretical basis of most of these studies is in the domain of information processing, each study contributed to the area in a different fashion.

1.2.1 Empirical accounts of design

The study that describes the architectural design process in its broadest sense was undertaken by Krauss and Myer. They observed a team of architects in a Boston office during the design of a school building. The data analyzed in this study cover architects' sketches, discussions, and other documentation produced during an eighteen-month period spanning from programming to construction-document phases of the project. The findings characterize the stages that design goes through, the different design decisions made during these stages, and the seemingly endless iterations that the architect must enact throughout the design process.

Eastman studied the design process as a subset of this broader form of design. The task he gave his subjects corresponds roughly to a one to two hour segment of the design process characterized in Krauss and Myer's work. The task was to improve upon a given bathroom layout on the basis of documented user responses to the layout. Eastman collected and analyzed protocols[1] of several subjects working on the same design problem. His study provides a carefully calibrated account of the operations used, symbols manipulated during design, and the control mechanisms employed by the designer.

Authors of other studies have also looked at the design process at a similar level of detail. Foz and Henrion separately focused on specific properties of the design process. Foz made a series of observations about the use of representation and search in design. Henrion explored the definition, redefinition, and satisfying of constraints in the context of a space-allocation problem. Whereas Henrion's study deals with a well-defined problem and novice designers as subjects, Foz's study deals with

[1] Protocols are recordings of subject's problem-solving behavior which can be subsequently analyzed to identify the invariance in the subject's patterns of behavior (Newell, 1968). Appendix A.1 contains a discussion of protocol analysis.

a complex design problem and uses designers with varying skill levels as subjects. The findings of these two studies are complementary. Foz suggests the ways in which more skilled designers use the many degrees of freedom inherent in the design problem to their advantage and Henrion explains how this process of manipulating design constraints actually takes place.

Other than the fact that they deal with subsets of the same general class of tasks, all of these studies share another attribute. They develop empirical models that account for the behaviors they study. The methods employed in developing these models resemble those used in most scientific observations. First the behavior being studied is observed and recorded. Then a paradigm that can predict this behavior is hypothesized. Next the validity of the paradigm is tested against new empirical observations. Often the foundations of the a priori paradigm come from available theory and the initial observations of behavior. The second set of observations, however, serve a different purpose—that of testing the hypothesis. Therefore, various methods are used in this case: controlled observation of behavior, observation of the simulations fashioned after the a priori model, and comparison of the characteristics of the behaviors predicted by the a priori model against actual behaviors.

1.2.2 Theoretical accounts of design

The second set of studies to be reviewed here are theoretical works exploring the development of a priori paradigms for design. In studying the structure of design problems both Reitman (1964) and Simon (1973) characterize design as an ill-defined problem. Ill-defined problems are those which inherently have little structure in terms of their operational parameters: goals, legal operations, alternatives to be considered, and evaluation functions. Reitman points out that there is little consensus in the architectural field as to what goals should be selected, what methods are acceptable, and what constitutes a sound point of departure for a designer. Simon proposes that to deal with ill-defined problems successfully, the designer has to decompose the problem into well-defined parts. In another study, Simon (1970) points out the dependencies between style and decomposition schemes chosen by designers.

Freeman and Newell's work (1971) departs from the works of these authors in the way it develops a theoretical framework which defines the functional properties of the design process. They propose a formal language[2] for representing functional knowledge about the physical world and demonstrate how this can be used in design. The formal language consists of constructs associating physical objects with their functional requirements and performance properties. Freeman and

[2] A formal language is a notation used to define logically the legal symbol sequences and/or structures that are allowed in a language or symbol system. For more information, see Bachus (1960).

Newell suggest that objects with requirements and performance properties which are complementary to one another can be matched and synthesized into composite objects. These composite objects exhibit new requirements and performance properties and hence are equivalent to design proposals.

Simon, in *The Sciences of the Artificial* (1969), explores the differences between natural sciences and the sciences of design. Simon critically reviews the methods and findings of the two sciences and defines the relationship between them. After considering psychological evidence on the search process and representations applicable to design[3] he proposes a 'curriculum' for design teaching. Later in this text, I shall draw more specifically upon this work.

1.2.3 Design instruction

A third group of studies involved with the documentation of the design process is clearly intended for the educator and the student of architecture. These represent collections of ideas about what design is, how its related areas of knowledge are used and how it should be practiced (Broadbent, 1973; Hanks et al, 1977; Jones, 1970; Wade, 1977). The forms as well as the contents of these works underscore their instructional purpose.

Jones's work, the earliest in this set, describes a collection of many diverse design methods proposed as ways of improving overall design performance. Some of these methods are empirically proven to be superior design aids. Others are transported from theoretical work in decisionmaking and management sciences. 'Brainstorming', for instance, is an example of a method empirically proven to be effective in the idea-generation stage of design. 'Optimization', on the other hand, is a mathematical technique effective in reducing the search space in well-defined problem environments. Jones proposes *strategies* and *tactics* for the designer that incorporate both kinds of methods in the search for a solution.

Broadbent's work represents an inclusive survey of contemporary architectural theory. It deals with issues of process as well as content in architecture and the architect's role in today's technology, culture, and society. It is a comprehensive theoretical work on how architecture should be taught, how it should be practiced as a function of the state of the art in humanities and social sciences. Like Jones' work, it treats the definition of the design process as a prescriptive rather than a descriptive one.

The work by Hanks et al and Wade comes closest to the intent of this book. They approach the design process as a cognitive phenomenon and focus on defining methods and procedures for design. Both sources contain a rich set of abstractions about tasks relevant to real-world

---

[3] Simon uses design in the broad sense of the term encompassing professional areas, such as architecture, engineering, medicine, and administrative decisionmaking.

design contexts. Yet, they depart from this study in their advocacy for prescriptive design techniques like the previous studies.

1.3 Contents
Individually, each study contributes to the modelling of the well-defined portions of the design task. Collectively, they represent inclusive yet noncompatible views of the design process. Understandably, compatibility is hard to achieve with independent research efforts and premature to expect at such an early stage of an emerging field. However compatibility has to be achieved if any of this knowledge is going to be instrumental in positively impacting design fields.

We must recognize that these studies are pioneering studies and each has a partial, yet valuable, contribution. Some remain entirely theoretical and do not test their hypotheses, others develop and test specific hypothesis with little theoretical investigation. The total picture is very hard to complete with individual efforts that study only a segment of the design process. Therefore, it is essential that new research builds upon these findings and strives towards a comprehensive view of design in a form that makes its findings accessible to the architecture community.

It seems that the last set of studies reviewed above come closest in intent to being assimilated by architectural designers. However, none of them go much beyond presenting a catalogue of ideas and a checklist of design methods and issues. Although chronologically these studies represent a trend towards an information-processing view of design, their emphasis is in developing prescriptive definitions of design which lack the theoretical emphasis to unify the independent findings they report. Without a solid foundation of descriptive accounts of design, a sound and comprehensive theory of design is extremely difficult to develop.

1.3.1 What is included?
The primary aim of this work is to contribute towards the development of a descriptive model of design as a foundation for design *research*, *education*, and *practice*. The first goal is to propose a theoretical basis for understanding design. This basis will be developed here from empirical findings specifically undertaken for this purpose as well as the findings from others' work. The studies reviewed earlier are considered the forerunners of this work, and other studies are expected to inherit the results developed here.

A second goal is to calibrate the various components of an information-processing model for design: (a) representations used in design, (b) the problem-solving or search process of design, and (c) the knowledge brought to bear on design. To accomplish this, a number of observation and analysis methods which have not yet been applied to design problems will be applied. One such method is analysis of 'chunk' structures used by deGroot (1965) in studying the relationship between cognitive

representations and chess-playing skills. In chapter 5, this method will
be discussed in detail. Another method dealing with formal codifications
of inference making will be covered in chapter 6.

The third goal of the present work is to evaluate, by means of computer
simulations of human cognitive behavior, the a priori models proposed.
In this context, a simulation of a segment of the design process will be
examined in chapter 6. Computer applications of this kind are intended
to help structure several research objectives. One objective is to define
and structure the process. A second objective is to delineate new areas
of research as parts of an overall framework. A third objective is to
develop well-defined methods to supplement manual methods. The final
objective is to provide support for teaching in the area. A discussion of
each of these objectives in the context of architecture and how this work
contributes towards them is included in chapters 8 and 9.

The fourth and final goal of this work is design education. By proposing
a model that defines the sources of knowledge used in design, a framework
for architectural education is implied. A secondary impact of this is
intended for the area of computer-aided design (CAD) systems. Recent
advances in CAD point to a need for building *friendly* interactive systems.
This requires an understanding of the information input and output to
and from the human designer. Only systems equipped with successful
interface features will bring about the wide use of advanced CAD tools
in the design office. This study offers insights into criteria necessary for
building successful interfaces between automated CAD systems and
designers. Ultimately, this study is directed at an advancement in the
state of the art of our understanding of the design process.

1.3.2 What is not included?

It is neither the intent of this work, nor is it feasible, to cover all relevant
issues with the same degree of emphasis. What is not emphasized in
this book is implied by exclusion from discussion. However, it is
necessary to indicate explicitly some of the popular issues that are *not*
explored here: (a) stylistic goals for the designer in terms of the
designed product, (b) systematic and prescribed methods of problem-
solving, and (c) techniques to improve pedagogy and student motivation.
This work does not deal with defining the product of design to the
extent that it is divorced from the process of design. In fact, I argue
that the product is an integral part of the design process. Consequently,
the working assumption here is that it is inappropriate to build value
systems on design products as things distinct from the process of design.

Also this work is not an attempt to prescribe design methods that are
based on observations other than empirical. Some methods commonly
prescribed for design are the tools of systematic and rational thinking.
Optimization, for example, is such a method which has been repeatedly
misunderstood by designers. Designers have developed a habit of

overlooking the usefulness of optimization in well-formulated subparts of the design problem and grossly misrepresenting its capabilities as a global evaluation metric. The design problem as formulated in real life does not lend itself to the well-defined format of optimization nor is it possible to quantify all the variables applicable in design in ways suitable for optimization. Hence, I will not propose any design methods that are based purely on their analytical merit.

This work will also exclude from discussion issues of motivation, expediency, and group dynamics in design and in teaching environments. To the extent that these assist better teaching they are useful. However, the intent of this study is not to provide a better design guide or a manual for design teaching. Instead my aim is to improve our understanding of the design task so that better design or design teaching comes about as a consequence of this understanding. In this way individual readers, having the option to prescribe their own methods, will do so in agreement with their own purposes and cognitive parameters.

1.3.3 Intended audience
Three kinds of readers are the intended audiences for this study: the reader who is interested in the practical implications of the work for architectural education, the *academic*; the reader who is interested in the implications of the findings for architectural practice, the *practitioner*; and the reader who is interested in the research techniques as well as the findings, the *researcher*. The academic is primarily the student and teacher of architectural design. The practitioner is the person who applies design knowledge daily in his or her profession, such as the architect and the planner. The researcher uses these findings to develop new areas of investigation or simply to expand them beyond their current scope.

1.3.4 Method of investigation
This work constitutes a scientific study of the design process.

Having stated the method in its strongest form, let me now step back to qualify it. Any study with a serious intent to unravel some aspect of a fact or phenomenon has "the central task to make the wonderful common place: to show that complexity; correctly viewed, is only a mask for simplicity; to find pattern hidden in apparent chaos" (Simon 1969, page 1). Scientific and nonscientific studies both share this intent. The greatest distinction between scientific and nonscientific studies, however, is in the methods employed in each for accomplishing the end. Scientific studies find pattern in regularity through careful observation and flawless reasoning. The question of method lies in the terms 'careful observation' and 'flawless reasoning'. The recognition that reasoning can be flawed and observation can potentially be careless is significant. This is reflected in the methods of the sciences which rely on a consensus about the admissibility of observations and reasoning used towards the discovery of truth. The intentions of these methods is to develop theories about truth that are testable by others and general to all instances included in the truth.

In spite of a lack of unequivocal consensus about the philosophical tenets of Western scientific method[4] its practice continues to help the multiplication of knowledge in many fields and disciplines; and its methods are more powerful than ever. An empirical view would conclude that the bulk of these methods fall in the category of *hypothesis and test*. New theories are first hypothesized as general relationships. Then by testing through experimentation and finally through application of their predictions to as yet nonexistent events, they are either verified or refuted.

Fields of study outside the realm of natural sciences such as psychology have also adopted this method in its general form. To describe the theoretical bases of cognitive mechanisms available to man, psychologists as well as computer scientists have developed a priori hypotheses about their respective areas of study. Then they have tested the validity of these hypotheses by comparing them against human behavior observed under experimental conditions. Finally, they have applied these hypotheses to the prediction of behavior.

The final step in this process has traditionally been the most difficult and ambitious one. Although, in the natural sciences, theories are not only applicable but are often beneficial in their application (such as predicting the effect of gravity on free-falling bodies, electrical conductivity of copper, strength of a wooden beam), it is less feasible to do the same with cognitive theories of human behavior. Often these theories are simply paradigms for simulation of behavior, rather than tools for predicting behavior in real life. Recently, applications in artificial intelligence, especially in the area of robotics, have moved the field forward in the direction of the natural sciences.

1.3.5 Outline of book

The outline of this book will closely follow the methodological pattern applied in artificial intelligence. This pattern can be characterized through a three-step process: (1) proposition of an a priori paradigm, to explain human cognitive behavior, (2) calibration and verification of the paradigm in the context of empirical observations, and (3) testing of the predictive power of the paradigm through computer simulation. The chapters which constitute the basic organization of the contents are categorized into several groups each of which corresponds to a step of the method outlined above. Chapters 2, 3, and 4 are a description of the a priori

---

[4] The debate on the nature of scientific induction, theory, and empirical observation is an ongoing one in the philosophy of Western science and is unlikely to end any time soon. In fact this debate seems to be the primary raison d'être for the field of study.

model representing the designer's cognitive mechanisms. Chapters 5 and 6 are a review of the empirical observations and calibrate the model proposed. In chapter 7, I demonstrate the application of the model through computer simulation. Chapters 8 and 9 are a summary of the overall findings of the work.

More specifically, chapter 2 provides a general review of the theory of information processing with special emphasis on information-processing models of problem-solving and complex behavior. Chapter 3 is a general introduction to the notion of process, problem-solving, and the assumptions underlying this study of architectural design. Chapter 4 is a description of the a priori model of the design process hypothesized.

In chapters 5 and 6, I take the major aspects of the a priori model of design: search, representation, and inference making, respectively, and elaborate upon them. Chapter 5 is a description of the core of processing knowledge in design, that is, the search for solutions and the heuristics that guide this search. The structure of memory and recall with complex architectural stimuli are explored in chapter 6. Attributes and organization of memory for architectural stimuli are discussed.

Chapter 7 is concerned with the mechanisms of inductive reasoning. Their relevance for design is explored through empirical observation and computer simulation. Chapter 8 provides a summary for the whole book. Chapter 9 contains a retrospective discussion of the major issues considered in the book: design process, the finite nature of architectural knowledge, the tools of problem-solving in design, and the teaching of design.

1.4 Suggested readings

1 Broadbent G, 1973 *Design in Architecture* (John Wiley, New York)
2 Krauss R I, Myer R M, 1970, "Design: a case history" in *Emerging Methods in Environmental Design and Planning* Ed G T Moore (MIT Press, Cambridge, MA) pp 11-20
3 Hofstadter D R, 1979 *Godel, Escher, Bach: An Eternal Golden Braid* (Vintage Books, New York)
4 Foz A, 1973, "Observations on designer behavior in the parti" in *The Design Activity International Conference* volume 1, Printing Unit, University of Strathclyde, Glasgow, pp 19.1-19.4
5 Moore G T, 1972 *Emerging Methods in Environmental Design and Planning* (MIT Press, Cambridge, MA)
6 Popper K R, 1972 *Objective Knowledge* (Oxford University Press, Oxford)
7 Simon H A, 1969 *Science of the Artificial* (MIT Press, Cambridge, MA)
8 Wade J W, 1977 *Architecture, Problems, and Purposes* (John Wiley, New York)

Theory of information processing

"An information processing theory is not restricted to stating generalities about Man. With a model of an information processing system, it becomes meaningful to try to represent in some detail a particular man at work on a particular task. Such a representation is no metaphor, but a precise symbolic model on the basis of which pertinent specific aspects of man's problem solving behavior can be calculated. This model of symbol manipulation remains very much an approximation, of course, hypothesizing in an extreme form the neatness of discrete symbols and a small set of elementary processes, each with precisely defined and limited behavior. This abstraction, though possibly severe, does provide a grip on symbolic behavior that was not available heretofore. It does, equally, steer away from physiological models, with their concern for fidelity to continuous physiological mechanisms, either electrical, chemical or hormonal."

A Newell and H A Simon *Human Problem Solving* (1972, page 5)

Information-processing theory (IPT) provides for us an abstract symbolic medium within which we can represent, measure, and understand 'man's problem-solving behavior'. Through IPT a body of knowledge applicable to many areas of problem-solving has been developed. This knowledge consists of methods of examining, calibrating, and describing problem-solving behavior through psychological experiments, formal and computer simulations. Throughout this book frequent references to this body of knowledge will be made. Related methods will be discussed in the context of architectural design tasks. Consequently, it is important first to understand the foundations of IPT.

Two comprehensive texts, one by Lindsay and Norman (1972) and the other by Newell and Simon (1972), cover the principles of human cognitive behavior and information processing. Lindsay and Norman's book emphasizes perception and elementary information-processing. Newell and Simon's book deals with cognitive behavior in the context of problem-solving, using such tasks as cryptarithmetic, logic, and chess problems. The latter book is the more appropriate one for our purposes and has more to offer in terms of applications to architectural design.

Newell and Simon postulate that humans operate as information-processing systems (IPS). They define an IPS as "a system consisting of a *Memory* containing symbol structures, a *Processor*, *Effectors*, and *Receptors*" (figure 2.1). Receptors gather information from the environment and effectors manipulate the environment through motor behavior. Memory contains individual symbols, or tokens, that stand for objects and other symbols and their relations. The processor is basically a symbol manipulator that: (a) converts the information provided by receptors into a code that is internally consistent with the symbol structures of the system, (b) transforms internal symbols and their relations, and (c) converts internal symbols into code that can be transmitted to the external world or the environment by effectors. Newell and Simon propose that the processor consists of *atomic processes*, a *working memory*, and an *interpreter* that determines the sequence in which the processes are performed as a function of the symbol structures present in the working memory.

Atomic processes represent the basic functionalities of the processor. When these are activated in particular sequences, the functions that the processor is responsible for are performed. For example, the function of maintaining information in memory—retrieval of a 'chunk'[5] from memory—hinges upon a set of atomic processes: finding the address of a chunk in memory, going to that address, obtaining the contents of the 'chunk', moving these contents to working memory. Working memory, like the sketchpad of the architect, provides the representational medium in which these operations take place. The interpreter determines the sequence in which these atomic processes are executed so that the functions of the processor are performed properly. As a whole, the IPS provides a sound hypothesis. Through computer simulations Newell and Simon also have shown how the IPS accounts for human behavior in a variety of task contexts and how problem-solvers solve a given problem over time.

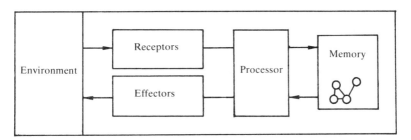

Figure 2.1. Information-processing system (source: Newell and Simon, 1972, page 20).

2.1 Codifying human problem-solving
Like all real-world phenomena, problem-solving constitutes a continuous series of events along the time dimension. It starts at a particular point in time, goes through many intermediate stages, and ends either with a solution or resignation at a later point in time. Often there are causal relationships that associate these individual events sequenced over time. Since continuous representations are much more difficult to analyze, codification systems used for studying such processes approximate the problem-solver's behaviors as sequences of discrete events. To develop a good representation of the design process, however, one must select

[5] Chunks are psychologically defined units of prepackaged information stored in memory. This subject will be discussed in detail in chapter 6.

those static states that are most informative and explicitly specify the transformations necessary to establish the causal relationship between each state and its predecessors and successors.

2.1.1 State space representations

To understand the taxonomy of such discrete event representations we must consider the notion of a *space*, or a *problem space*. Analogous to the definition of space in set-theoretic terms, a problem space consists of a set of predefined discrete entities. The basic entity in a problem space representation is a *state*. A state is the totality of all information relevant to the problem-solving process and available to the IPS at any given instance. This information usually includes all dependent and independent variables of the problem, their values, criteria of evaluation, constraints of the problem, and the goals of the IPS.

As an example, let us consider a simple problem called the *15-puzzle* (Neisser, 1976). Figure 2.2 provides a graphical representation of an *initial* state, some probable *intermediary* states, and the final or *goal* state for this problem. The object of the problem is to reach the final state from any other given state by moving[6] the numbered cells of the grid into the position of the blank grid represented as a dark square in figure 2.2. Each intermediary state generated on the way to the solution state of the 15-puzzle problem can be described alternatively by specifying the positions of all numbered squares in a four-by-four grid. Observe that one can achieve this through representations different from the one shown in figure 2.2, such as coordinates to designate the position of each of the numbered squares in the grid (table 2.1). The x and y coordinates used in table 2.1 correspond to the columns and rows of the grids in figure 2.2. The numbers in the left-most column represent the labels of individual squares of the grid. Each column of a pair of coordinate numbers represents a unique problem state, which corresponds to one of the matrixes included in figure 2.2.

The set of all possible problem states of the 15-puzzle problem constitutes the total problem space. Even in the case of a relatively simple problem like the 15-puzzle this is a very large space. With 16

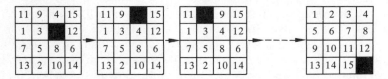

Figure 2.2. 15-puzzle problem (source: Neisser, 1976).

---

[6] This operation illustrates the next important ingredient necessary for defining a problem space: *actions*. This category will be considered in greater detail in the next section which deals with transformations between problem states.

grid squares and 16 possible values to assign to each, there are a total of 16! or about 2.09×10^{13} possible problem states. Hence, by definition, the problem space includes all possible initial states, intermediary states, and goal or solution states of a problem. In this particular problem only one state out of all possible states, represents the goal state. This is when all the integers are organized in a left-to-right top-to-bottom ascending order with the blank grid occupying the bottom-right position. This state is represented in the right-most grid in figure 2.2 and the right-most pair of coordinate values in table 2.1.

Table 2.1. Alternative state space description for the 15-puzzle problem, based on coordinate designations.

Squares of the grid	Initial state			Intermediary states						Goal state	
	x	y		x	y		x	y		x	y
1	1	2	→	1	2	→	1	2	→ ... →	1	1
2	2	4	→	2	4	→	2	4	→ ... →	2	1
3	2	2	→	2	2	→	2	2	→ ... →	3	1
4	3	1	→	3	2	→	3	2	→ ... →	4	1
5	2	3	→	2	3	→	2	3	→ ... →	1	2
6	4	3	→	2	3	→	2	3	→ ... →	1	2
7	1	3	→	1	3	→	1	1	→ ... →	2	2
8	3	3	→	3	3	→	3	3	→ ... →	4	2
9	2	1	→	2	1	→	3	2	→ ... →	1	3
10	3	4	→	3	4	→	3	4	→ ... →	2	3
11	1	1	→	1	1	→	1	1	→ ... →	3	3
12	4	2	→	4	2	→	4	2	→ ... →	4	3
13	1	4	→	1	4	→	1	4	→ ... →	1	4
14	4	4	→	4	4	→	4	4	→ ... →	2	4
15	4	1	→	4	1	→	4	1	→ ... →	3	4
■	3	2	→	3	1	→	2	1	→ ... →	4	4

2.1.2 State transformations

Alterations of the contents of a state within the state space of a problem are called state *transformations*. Each problem state can be transformed into a next state using the transformations that are by definition declared to be *legal* for the problem being solved. For instance, in the 15-puzzle problem the only transformation allowed, thus legal, is 'switching the position of any numbered grid-square that is adjacent to the blank grid-square with the position of the blank grid-square".

The success of problem representations relies on their functional appropriateness for state transformations. A 'good' representation can facilitate transformations in such a way that the solution of the problem is obtained efficiently. For example, in the 15-puzzle problem, transforming a problem state requires that the problem-solver has knowledge about the adjacencies between the grid-squares. More specifically he or she needs to identify all or at least one grid-square that is adjacent to the blank grid-square. To find adjacencies in the representation provided in table 2.1 one has to compare, on the average, two pairs of grid numbers twice before a single adjacency can be found. Finding many adjacencies, essential for the efficient resolution of the problem, will require relatively greater effort. But the adjacency information is trivial to obtain in figure 2.2. For the visually oriented IPS, figure 2.2 provides a much more powerful representation.

2.1.3 Reaching the goal state

For each problem state the IPS has the choice of applying one of a multitude of legal transformations. The success with which a goal state is reached depends on the application of the correct sets of transformations. Random selection can make an otherwise trivial problem practically impossible. Searching in the 15-puzzle problem space randomly, requires the application of as many transformations as there are individual problem states, or 2.09×10^{13}. In this mode the problem-solver who can continuously make a move every second around the clock for 663 457 years could expect to explore all possible states only if he or she is lucky enough to avoid generating each state more than once. On the other hand, a carefully selected sequence of transformations leads the skilled problem-solver to the goal state in a matter of minutes.

Let us reconsider the problem space of the 15-puzzle problem from the viewpoint of the problem-solver's decisions at any given point in time. There are an average of 3 transformations possible at each state. This figure is obtained by averaging the number of possible moves available as a function of the position of the blank grid-square: 8 squares with 3 possible moves, 4 squares with 4 possible moves, and 4 squares with 2 possible moves. This defines a search space of 3^n search paths[7] where 'n' is the number of total transformations necessary to complete a path. Typically, experience shows that reaching a solution from any typical initial state will require about 50–60 successive transformations. Thus there are at least 3^{50} alternative paths or 7.179×10^{23} distinct ways to the solution.

Goal-directed search can drastically cut down the number of necessary transformations. Consider the example included in figure 2.3. Let us assume that the IPS has set up the goal of moving one square in the initial problem state (say number 1) to its final positions designated in the solution state. To fulfill this goal, new goals or subgoals have to be defined. That is, to move square number 1 to position (1,1), the square presently occupying position (1,1) must first be moved away. In this

---

[7] Each path is a particular sequence of transformations joining the initial state to a final state.

fashion a series of subgoals can be identified to accomplish the original
goal efficiently:
    To move number 1 to coordinate position (1,1):
        first move number 4 to (3,2),
        then move number 9 to (3,1),
        then move number 11 to (2,1).
    This technique resembles a general purpose method called *heuristic
search*. Heuristics are rules of thumb which, through experience, are
known to simplify search in a given problem space. Although they may
not guarantee a solution, they reduce the number of things to be
considered, thus bringing the problem-solver closer to a goal state.
Consider the example illustrated in figure 2.3. By means of rotating any
sequence of numbers on the 15-puzzle matrix that form a continuous
loop or ring that contain the blank square and the numbered square
designated to move, it is possible to move any square to any position
on the ring. This procedure defines a complex process which is
equivalent to a combination of a number of transformations and allows
the moving of any square to the other position on the matrix efficiently.
Through this heuristic the IPS can look ahead and reduce the amount of
search to be done to accomplish its goal.
    Heuristic search is only one of many search methods used in complex
task contexts. In chapter 5 we shall review some of the other methods
of search, especially those of particular interest to architectural design.

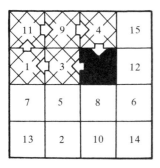

11	9	4	15
1	3		12
7	5	8	6
13	2	10	14

Figure 2.3.   A method for reducing search in the 15-puzzle problem.

2.2 Architecture of the human memory
Let us now move our attention away from the problem space, to the
capabilities of human cognition.

    Regardless of the type of problem tackled, the cognitive processes
used in solving problems have to conform to the constraints of the
architecture of the human mind. This topic has been investigated too
many times to permit an exhaustive review, here. However, citing the
findings of a few significant studies will serve our purpose. It has been

repeatedly demonstrated that functionally the human memory is a dual system (Newell and Simon, 1972; Posner, 1973). On the one hand, there is the *long term memory* (LTM) which is the repository of knowledge worth remembering. On the other hand, there is the *short term memory* (STM) which interfaces LTM with the external environment and serves as a temporary repository of information for cognitive processes that manipulate information[8]. It is not clear whether the STM is a component that is distinct from LTM or simply a temporally activated portion of the LTM. Regardless of what the structural relationship between the two memories is, functionally they seem to be distinct from each other and their information-handling capacities are drastically different.

Consider the case of trying to learn a telephone number. If the number has seven figures, typically we group the numbers into two sets: one of three and the other of four digits, respectively. If the first three digits match an already known exchange then this is simply remembered as a referent of this information existing in LTM. For number sequences that do not resemble or match previously learned ones, some mnemonic relationship is conjured up to aid learning and recall[9]. When mnemonic devices are used successfully or simple rote learning is employed repeatedly, the information may be remembered for a long time to come. The duration of accurate remembrance depends largely on the number of times the information is rehearsed or recalled from memory, subsequently. This obviously is neither the only way one learns telephone numbers nor the only sequence of events that would take place while doing so. However, many of the characteristics of the dual-memory system are illustrated in this example.

It is the STM that stores the new number sequence temporarily as it is being learned. The necessity of processing the number in smaller groups and the high probability of failure in learning numbers with digits greater than nine, indicate that the STM is limited in terms of space (table 2.2). Furthermore, the increased chance of failure to learn if the encoding is not done quickly and without complete concentration illustrates the fact that the STM is limited in terms of its temporal span as well.

LTM stores the encoded information along with all that is learned up to that point in time. The problem here is not simply an issue of space

[8] In this sense the STM and LTM are analogous in their functions to those of the working memory and memory, respectively, as cited earlier from Newell and Simon (1972).

[9] Learning in this case consists of finding the appropriate mnemonics in order to store the number in LTM. For example, given the digits '2448' one can use the following mnemonic device to assist recall: 'first digit is 2', 'second digit equals twice the first digit', and 'second two digits form a number that is twice the number formed by the first two digits'.

but one of organization so that the information stored can be retrieved when needed, with ease, and in a matter of seconds. This illustrates the importance of the role of STM as the memory component responsible for packaging incoming information. There seems to be no limit to how much the LTM can store and for how long. As long as encoding and occasional rehearsal takes place, the LTM seems to handle very large amounts of information as well as increase the span of STM almost indefinitely (Ericsson et al, 1980). In addition the LTM serves as the source of all the mnemonics one needs in encoding and retrieving new information.

There is a great deal more to what we know about the architecture of the human mind. This brief and simplified overview provides a starting point for understanding a model capable of replicating and predicting the behavior of designers. A far more detailed account of the human cognitive system can be found in Lindsay and Norman's (1972) and Newell and Simon's (1972) work.

Table 2.2. Parameters of short term and long term memories (STM and LTM, respectively).

Memory	Storage capacity	Temporal span	Operational role
STM	*limited* 7 + 2 units of information can be held at any given time.	*limited* information will erode, if not rehearsed after two seconds.	*active* primitive processes are applied; incoming, outgoing information is (un)packaged.
LTM	*unlimited* there is no measured limit to the amount of information that can be stored.	*unlimited* once learned, no erosion in contents with occasional rehearsal; acquisition takes 5 – 10 seconds per unit of information.	*passive* provides the database for cognitive operations; information organization is also one of its functions.

2.3 Design and problem-solving

To apply this knowledge to the area of architectural design, several assumptions have been developed as outlined below. Since the premise of this study is that IPT constitutes a viable paradigm for the study of design, these assumptions are built upon the findings reviewed above. It is not the aim of this book, however, to expand and justify these assumptions. They are simply used as axioms that define the point of departure for the present investigation.

Assumption 1. There is clear phenomenological evidence that all design takes place through individual decisions that reinforce and build upon each other to achieve a total comprehensive design-proposal. This proposal is the objective of the design process. Then, *design is a form of problem-solving where individual decisions are made towards the fulfillment of objectives.*

Assumption 2. A fundamental argument stemming from the central role of cognition and the structured nature of cognitive activity is that goal-driven systems and their cognitive behaviors can be explained through causal relationships. Consequently, our products in design are not random responses, but clearly articulated products based on thought. Then, *the designed product is a direct consequence of the preceding cognitive activity and not some arbitrary process that is independent of such activity.*

Assumption 3. Depending on the knowledge acquired by the cognitive system and the context of the problem at hand, different circumstances will lead to radically different behaviors. However, this does not negate the existence of invariants in the underlying cognitive mechanisms used by different individuals. This has already been demonstrated for many problem-solving tasks, such as chess, syllogistic reasoning, theorem proving, and the 15-puzzle task. Then, *although designers' knowledge and behaviors may vary, their basic information-handling capabilities such as encoding, manipulation, and recall of information, are essentially similar to the capabilities observed in other task contexts.* This does not mean that the information-processing functions of all individuals are identical, regardless of their backgrounds. On the contrary, the evidence provided in this work supports the hypothesis that behaviors of different individuals performing the same task or the same individual performing different tasks are different. The temporal interface between the ever-changing context in a problem and the knowledge of the problem-solver account for the unique behaviors that result each time a problem is encountered.

2.4 Design versus problem-solving

To use the knowledge available in the area of problem-solving in the study of design, we must examine the similarities as well as the differences that exist between them. Architectural design shares some properties with problem-solving.

1 Design problems have an *initial state*, usually described in the 'design brief' or 'program'.

2 Design problems go through *states* that are represented by internal and external symbols, such as notes, diagrams, and sketches.

3 Each state is *transformed* into other states using operations that are sometimes explicitly represented in the form of knowledge. For example, the formula TREAD + RISER = 17″ can be used to transform a set of stairs without precise dimensions into one with dimensions.

4 Many *search* strategies are used by designers to minimize the large numbers of transformations necessary for reaching solution states.

5 At the end, a set of working drawings are produced that describe a *solution* to the problem specified in the brief.

The resemblance between problems like the 15-puzzle and design problems practically ends here. Many researchers have pointed to the properties that separate simple and well-defined problems from complex and ill-defined ones. Both Reitman (1964) and Simon (1973) discuss the nature of ill-defined problems in detail. Here it is sufficient to review those properties of design that differentiate it from problems like the 15-puzzle, without discussing explicitly what constitutes 'ill-definedness'.

A *design problem* is typically specified in a brief. However, many documents, customs, and human experiences that are natural extensions of the brief cannot be completely specified. Consider a client who wants a house designed for the use of his family. The range of information that is applicable to the specification of the problem is extremely broad in scope, and some vital information needed during design is usually not available in any form other than patterns embedded in the life-styles and values of the users. In the case of the anonymous user, the sources of information needed are even more obscure. Because of these constraints, a design problem, its scope, and ground rules are never fully specified. Often these specifications are made *during* design and are correlated with the types of solutions desired or anticipated. In the case of design, the *deterministic* relationship that exists between the well-defined problem description and its solution is a *dialectic* one.

Types of *representations* and *transformations* possible in well-defined problems are known a priori. Redefinition of these ground rules is not necessary and not allowed. In contrast to this, in design, discovery of new rules is desirable, even though a large set of conventions is available as part of the culture of design. Creative design solutions are often linked to the redefinition of conventional interpretations of design, and creativity is a ubiquitous goal for the designer.

Goal states of design problems are usually inadequately specified at the onset. There are no explicit evaluation functions that can be applied to a state that will result in the unequivocal identification of it as a solution state. Each designer applies his or her own specialized tests to determine whether or not a design is acceptable. Most designers are satisfied because of lack of time rather than anything else. Hence, when given the same design problem over again these designers tend to develop further their previous solutions or come up with entirely new solutions, rather than regenerating parts of an earlier solution. This typically is not the case in well-defined problem domains[10].

There is also a dimension of *complexity* that differentiates design from well-defined tasks. For example, a state representation in design includes

[10] Simon (1969) discusses how this is reflected in the kinds of solutions developed for well-defined problems (that is, optimization) as opposed to ill-defined ones (that is, satisficing solutions).

many more variables and more complex relationships between these variables than does the 15-puzzle problem. At times, hundreds of objects, each with dozens of descriptive attributes, have to be included in the state representation of a design problem. Similarly, transformations applied to these involve much more elaborate procedures than the alteration of a couple of coordinate numbers, as is the case in the 15-puzzle.

2.5 Summary
In this chapter we reviewed the basic principles of IPS, examined a simple task context using these principles, and discussed properties of architectural design in comparison with simpler tasks. Although the behaviors manifested in each case are significantly different, it is possible to apply a common descriptive taxonomy to design as well as to simpler tasks. This taxonomy consists of three major parts: a system of references for *representing* the problem and its variables, a body of *knowledge* that facilitates the transformation of problem states, and *search* techniques that enable the matching of problem-solvers' resources with the task at hand.

Design behavior differs from simpler well-defined problem behavior in many ways. The most salient difference seems to be the degree of structure. Whereas the representational and transformational repertoire of well-defined tasks can be defined a priori, no such bounds can be imposed on the design task. Goals and evaluation criteria in manual design also lack a priori definition. The solution to a design problem is usually defined culturally, through insight and experience and evaluated via example and analogy during the process of design.

In the next two chapters an information-processing model that accommodates design behavior and provides a framework for exploration will be proposed.

2.6 Suggested readings
1 Feigenbaum E, Feldman J, 1963 *Computers and Thought* (McGraw-Hill, New York)
2 Lindsay P H, Norman D A, 1972 *Human Information Processing* (Academic Press, New York), chapter 1
3 Miller G A, Galanter E, Pribram K H, 1960 *Plans and the Structure of Behavior* (Henry Holt, New York)
4 Newell A, Simon H, 1972 *Human Problem Solving* (Prentice-Hall, Englewood Cliffs, NJ (chapters 1, 13, and 14

2.7 Exercises
2.1 Specification of a problem space for a given task consists of three things: (a) a set of representations adequate to codify all information relevant to any state of the problem that may be reached while attempting a solution, (b) a set of operationally defined rules for transforming any one state to a successive one, (c) a set of procedures that describe the

sequence of application of these rules, for efficient search. First solve, then specify the problem space for the following problems. Use the examples given in this chapter as a guide to develop your answers.
(a) Given a three-by-three orthogonal grid of nine dots, draw no more than four straight and connected lines, that pass through all dots. More than one line *can* pass through any one dot,
(b) Given three pegs, peg-1, peg-2, and peg-3, and five discs of five different sizes all organized on peg-1, (with largest disc on the bottom and smallest on the top); move all discs to peg-3 by moving them one by one from one peg to any other peg. At no time should a bigger disc be placed on a smaller disc.

2.2 Specify a small design problem. Collect a protocol using this problem. In other words, ask someone to design for you and record his or her verbalizations. Use a tape recorder, video recorder, or simply take notes to codify the processes and their sequence accurately. Remember to ask the designer to think aloud and keep track of the sequence of drawings generated during design. Analyze the protocol and specify the problem space for this design task.

3

Studying complex processes

> "Artistic creation, which was a clearly definable intellectual activity, based on explicable and learnable rules of taste, for both courtly classicism and the enlightenment now [in the eighteen century German romanticism] appears as a mysterious process derived from such unfathomable sources as divine inspiration, blind intuition and incalculable moods. For classicism and enlightenment the genius was a higher intelligence bound by reason, theory, history, tradition and convention."
>
> A Hauser *The Social History of Art* (1951, page 612)

Throughout the history of art the position of artists towards their goals and their products has been constantly redefined. The two opposing views in the above quotation, those of German romanticism and classicism, are typical of the prevailing extremes in the state of the art. Today's artists use intuition as well as reason in their creative work. Similarly, whether we consider architects as artists or scientists, they are constantly required to use their intellectual as well as emotional resources while designing.

This total involvement is not an ethical question. It is a necessity. Without a coalition of all of his or her resources, the designer has very little chance against the complexity of even the simplest of design tasks. This is a result of the open-ended nature of the premises, methods, and objectives of the average design problem. Unlike the well-defined context of most problems that fall within the scope of the natural sciences, design sets no limits on the range of acceptable solutions and methods for developing these solutions (Reitman, 1964). Consequently, designers often find themselves in circumstances where they have to bring the totality of their conceptual, perceptual, and motor ability to bear on a problem over long periods of time.

What are these abilities that designers summon to their work? What are the cognitive mechanisms that underly their abilities? How do these interact with the design problem? What skills are responsible for the managing of these mental functions? What constitutes learning in this context and how does it take place? How can we study our own abilities and intervene in our own design process? To begin to answer these questions, we must first examine the designers' problem-solving[11] behavior and construct a model of their cognitive mechanisms.

[11] Problem-solving is used traditionally to mean behavior that is characterized by well-structured task contexts where the constraints of the problem and the resources of the problem-solver are explicit. Here this paradigm will be used to model a far more complex task. The analogy between design and problem-solving is drawn not to equate the two but to use the framework of the second as a tool to explore the first. For brevity, design shall be referred to as problem-solving, with the recognition, however, that it is an especially complex form of problem-solving.

3.1 Systems, behavior, and internal mechanisms

There are causal dependencies between internal structures and external behaviors of all systems. Ordinarily, how a car runs can be explained through its mechanical condition; how a school teaches can be explained through its programs, administration, and teachers; how a traffic intersection works can be explained through its roads and physical properties. Often the dependencies between structure and behavior are predictable. Let us consider an example of a relatively simple system where many such dependencies can be observed with the naked eye, such as a thermostat that regulates a heater.

Let us assume that all we know about this system is (a) the thermostat is connected to the heater, (b) there is a manual switch which regulates the heater, and (c) the heater comes on and goes off (figure 3.1). Let us also assume that we have observed and recorded the behavior of the system over a period of time and have obtained the hypothetical data shown in table 3.1. The question marks under the column entitled "thermostat" in the table indicate the fact that simple visual observation has yielded no information about the state of the thermostat. If we use this tabulation to infer a causal relationship between the components of the system, then we must conclude that the switch alone does not turn the heater on. Although there is perfect correlation between the off-state of the switch and the heater, the on-state of the switch does not predict the behavior of the heater. This implies that a factor other than the switch, most probably the thermostat, is affecting the state of the heater, particularly when the switch is on. Since we do not have any other knowledge about the thermostat we may assume that its behavior is similar to that of the switch. That is, like the switch, it has on and off states, that is, it is closed or open. Notice that this assumption creates

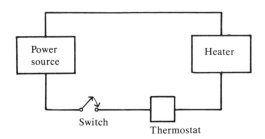

Figure 3.1. A hypothetical heating system.

Table 3.1. First observation of the heating system.

if switch:	then heater and	thermostat:
on	on	?
off	off	?
on	off	?

a system which can logically account for the states of the heater: that is, the heater is on only when both controlling devices are 'on' (table 3.2).

However, unlike the switch, the mechanism that opens or closes the thermostat is not apparent. How can we characterize the internal control mechanism of the thermostat? In the tabulation there is no causal relationship that implies anything about this. So the answer must be sought in other environmental factors that might trigger the control mechanism of the thermostat, such as a heat-sensitive component.

One can test this hypothesis by making more observations. Suppose that we measure the temperature around the thermostat and observe its state at regular intervals and obtain the tabulation in table 3.3. These observations would support our hypothesis about the heat-sensitive control mechanism. In other words, when the temperature is above 80° F the thermostat opens and when it is below 80° F it closes.

Although such a finding would have us believe that we have determined what causes the thermostat to change its state, we still would have no explanation about how this actually happens. Short of opening up the thermostat and examining its internal parts or taking sophisticated measurements, readings, and recordings from the outside, it is nearly impossible to describe with certainty the internal make-up of the thermostat. The next best thing in such circumstances is to develop an abstract model representing the internal organization of the system which is *sufficient* and *necessary* for explaining and predicting its behavior. For all practical purposes, especially when major surgery of the system is not possible, such models are as useful as actual hardware descriptions.

The first step in developing such models is to hypothesize alternative models that account for the behavior of the system. For example, in the case of the thermostat, the heat-sensitive device inside it can operate in alternative ways. We can claim that a heat-sensitive metal in the

Table 3.2. A hypothetical observation of the heating system.

if switch	and thermostat:	then heater:
on	closed	on
off	closed	off
on	open	off
off	open	off

Table 3.3. The second hypothetical observation of the heating system.

if temperature	and switch	and thermostat:	then heater:
< 80° F	on	closed	on
< 80° F	off	closed	off
> 80° F	on	open	off
> 80° F	off	open	off

thermostat expanding to open the main internal circuit of the thermostat at temperatures above 80°F would accomplish this end [figure 3.2(a)]. Alternatively, we can claim that the increase in the temperature closes a minor circuit and this circuit in turn causes a magnetic field through a coil which moves a switch that actually opens the main circuit [figure 3.2(b)]. Or we can claim that the expanding metal itself breaks contact and opens the circuit directly [figure 3.2(c)].

All these explanations would give us the behavioral predictions recorded in table 3.3. Consequently all models are *sufficient*. Whether any one of the models is *necessary* (or more necessary than others) is a question that is harder to answer. The best answer we can come up with, given what we know about the system, is a relative one. That is, the second model is less parsimonious than the first one because of the extraneous magnetic mechanism it contains. And the third model is less reliable than the first one because of the fact that the heat produced in the

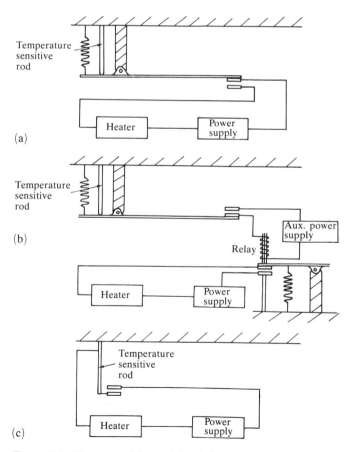

Figure 3.2. Three possible models of the thermostat.

circuit will keep the temperature of the expanding metal high enough to confound the behavior of the system. Therefore, until a more parsimonious and more robust explanation is developed the first model is the *necessary* and *sufficient* explanation we must adopt.

This example illustrates how we can develop *necessary* and *sufficient* models of internal mechanisms, through careful examination of alternatives that account for external behaviors. We accomplished this by first determining what the behavior of the thermostat was; then how this behavior was affected by the environment; and finally what the internal mechanisms that support this behavior must be like. In the remainder of this chapter, I shall illustrate how this method, with minor modifications, can be applied to architectural design. In the remainder of the book, using the same principles of inference, I shall develop a model to represent design behavior. First, however, we must develop some working assumptions about the architectural design process.

3.2 An example of architectural design

Architectural design is sometimes used to refer to the rather complicated process in which a team of professionals develop design proposals. At other times it is used to refer to a process through which an individual architect develops a conceptual solution. These two processes have many similarities and commonalities and they both embody significant portions of an all-inclusive definition of design. The focus of this study is the latter task. However, it is expected that there will be significant carry-over from the knowledge gained in the individual's case to the

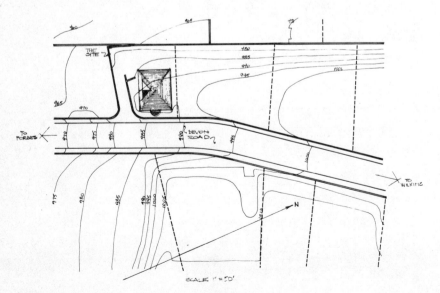

Figure 3.3. Site-plan used in the design protocol.

group design circumstance. One of the reasons for this is that the carry-over in the reverse direction is not necessarily possible.

Let us now consider data from an experiment which will be reviewed in detail, later. In this task, a practicing architect is asked to design a carriage house on the site of a detached garage adjoining a single family house located near Carnegie-Mellon University, in Pittsburgh (figure 3.3). The brief[12] used in presenting the problem to the architect describes the needs of the occupant who is single, blind, and a teacher at the School for the Blind (table 3.4). It is required that the existing house on

Table 3.4. Program used in the design protocol.

Brief for a single-person dwelling
(based on an interview with the client)

The problem is to design a garage with occupancy for one person over it or around it in some way. The site is on a lot currently occupied by a house and its garage. The site of the existing garage is donated by the owner of the house to the Association for the Blind. The new building will replace the existing garage. The area to the right of the garage is the private back yard of the house which will continue to be used by its present owners. The new garage has to handle two full size cars and 600 ft^3 of storage space for the use of the owner of the house.

The purpose of the donation is to provide a permanent place of residence for guests and teachers related to the School for the Blind on Craik Street. Different persons are expected to occupy the residence over a long period of time. All users are assumed to be blind and they are most likely to be teachers at the School for the Blind.

The objective of the design is to provide a rich personal environment for the blind user of the residence. Currently we have access to the person who will be occupying the building as soon as it is completed. Possibly in three years another person will move in in her place.

The user will live here, eat here, and sleep here. She will use it as a base of operations for her teaching activity in the School for the Blind. She is well educated; has braille machines and other technical equipment for recordings etc. She teaches blind persons of all age groups.

Since she has been blind for most of her life the sensory experiences of blind persons and nonvisual aesthetic considerations must be regarded in designing this building.

The owner of the house has also set up a trust fund for the building and its maintenance. The total fund is $60000, as an endowment. This fund should be used in such a way that after paying for the design and construction of the building there should be enough money left to yield sufficient yearly interest to meet the maintenance costs of the house. For instance a $35000 building would leave $25000 in the fund, from which a yearly interest of $1250 can be obtained. This amount should be sufficient to cover the steady-state maintenance costs of the house.

Please design a preliminary scheme which will be presented to the Association for the Blind and the donor of the fund, for their approval.

[12] 'Brief' refers to the notion of 'facilities program' upon which the building design is based.

the site will continue to be occupied by the client and the new residence will be located on the site of the existing garage, preserving the existing two-car garage function for the use of the owner of the property.

An architect worked on this problem, without stopping, for about four hours and developed 1:8 scale plans, sections, and elevations as part of his proposal (figure 3.4). The session was recorded in its entirety on videotape to allow subsequent analysis. An episode from the architect's design behavior is shown in the form of a verbal protocol[13] in table 3.5. This episode corresponds to a segment immediately after the examination of the program documents and the slides of the site by the architect.

At this point, the architect has developed three alternative solutions based on alternative points of entry into the proposed dwelling. Alternative 1 locates the dwelling unit above, on the second floor of the existing garage; alternative 2 is a proposal to locate a dwelling unit below, on the basement floor of the existing garage; and alternative 3 places the dwelling unit in place of the existing garage structure. Alternative 3 is readily disqualified because it makes it very difficult to meet a major requirement of the program: maintaining the double-garage function for the use of the owner.

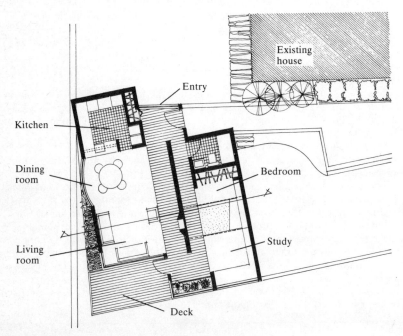

Figure 3.4. Solution developed by the architect.

[13] See appendix A.1 for a discussion of protocol analysis.

The episode starts with the architect's evaluation of alternative 1. Then he moves to general programmatic estimates of rooms and room sizes. Finally, he reveals his decision about which alternative to pursue and how. In the remainder of the session, after this episode, the architect continues to work on alternative 1 which becomes the basis of

Table 3.5. A sample from subject 1's protocol.

[The subject has just considered placing the residence he is designing under the existing garage (figure 3.4). This seems like an alternative solution among others that he is currently considering.]

1 Probably the expense would be considerable to do that [designing under the existing garage].
2 It would solve the entry problem.
3 It would also save some money from building the structure, the physical outside walls.
4 We probably will have to rebuild the structure of the garage
5 which might defray some costs.
6 So I have an idea to do something.
7 [Experimenter shows slide 9 of site.]
8 [Experimenter shows slide 10, last slide of site.]
9 Would it be possible to go back and look at the slides later?
10 [Experimenter] Sure, any time
11 So there is quite a bit of flexibility in the house.
12 There is a number of different approaches we could take.
13 It's going to be one person living here.
14 And that one person would probably need a living area, dining area, kitchen, bath, bedroom, and perhaps a study for the equipment.
15 So it is essentially a one-bedroom unit.
16 Which could be put in easily, not easily but in 625 ft^2 [which is the size of the available site].
17 OK. I think what I would like to do is to sketch some organizational ...
18 [Experimenter] I will start the video now.
19 [Experimenter] You can use some of the paper and drafting equipment here.
20 [Experimenter] Just use whatever you're most comfortable with.
21 Start out with ... [mumble] ... [subject starts drawing].
22 OK. We have ... [draws south wall of the site].
23 we have a site ... that is ... [draws west wall of site].
24 existing garage ... that ... [draws outline of existing garage].
25 walk through right here ... [draws curved retaining wall].
26 There are some trees here [draws trees to the south of driveway].
27 I think the first thing I am going to try is ...
28 I think ... I often found that the first ideas are; often are the best ...
29 After examining several ideas [they] are the best.
30 So I'll first experiment with the idea of trying to enter right here [draws line to indicate entry from the corner].
31 Leave the existing garage where it is.
32 take the roof off [redraws the garage outline].
33 and add the building over.
34 Problems being right at that point [points to curved corner].
35 [Experimenter] Would you elaborate that?

the final proposal he ultimately develops. In the remainder of this chapter we shall study this episode in detail to illustrate the various taxonomic and information-theoretic interpretations of the architectural design process.

3.3 Architectural design knowledge

Knowledge comes in many forms. Particularly in a problem domain as open-ended as architectural design, many diverse forms of knowledge can be observed. To review the basic categories of knowledge found in the design episode in table 3.5 we must first review several concepts commonly used in knowledge acquisition and knowledge-engineering literature and establish a common terminology for our purposes.

3.3.1 Procedural versus declarative knowledge

Recent work in knowledge engineering distinguishes two broad categories of knowledge: declarative and procedural. *Declarative* knowledge is all that we know which describes how things are (Anderson, 1981; Sussman, 1973). This is accomplished through *objects* (office, light, building, pen, car, lawn, entrance, table), their *attributes* (functional, solar, expensive, attractive) and the *relations* between them (green car, attractive building, open entrance, dysfunctional but attractive building). *Procedural* knowledge, on the other hand, is all that describes and predicts actions or a plan of action (Lenat, 1983a; 1983b; Anderson, 1981). All knowledge of 'how-to's' (How to ride a bicycle? How to solve a problem? How to make stairs? How to draw plans?) are examples of procedural knowledge. Although the distinctions between the two categories of knowledge are tautologically obvious, it is not immediately clear why they are needed.

While studying behaviors of students learning to use postulates and theorems in solving basic science problems Neves and Anderson (Anderson, 1981) focused considerable attention on the representations of procedural versus declarative forms of knowledge. After carefully studying problem-solving behaviors of their subjects Neves and Anderson developed a computer program that simulates such behavior in their subjects. An interesting characteristic of this program is that it can represent scientific laws in the form of declarative formula, as well as procedural instructions.

For example, let us consider an example from the field of physics. Given a steel cable with a tensile load of P and cross-sectional area of A; to compute the axial stress on the cable, we can use the formula (Marcus, 1977, page 94):

$$f_t = \frac{P}{A},$$

where
f_t is the computed axial stress, ksi
P is the applied axial tensile load, kips
A is the applicable cross-sectional area, in^2.

This formula embodies a relationship between three variables and is simply represented as a declarative statement. To use this knowledge in a problem-solving task requires additional procedural knowledge. If we know the values of P and A, then we can apply algebraic knowledge and calculate the value of f_t. If we know, however, the values for f_t and P and would like to find the value of A, then we can rewrite the formula as $A = Pf_t$ and calculate A. Furthermore, if we do not know the value of A, but can calculate it from other information we have, then we may structure the application of the formula differently. Consequently, before the declarative formula can be of use, an understanding of how the goal state is linked to the initial problem state must be present and a set of transformations to accomplish this must be developed. This is the procedural form of knowledge which complements the declarative form.

Neves and Anderson's work also reveals that as problem-solvers become more skilled in their tasks, they rely more on procedural and less on declarative knowledge. Although novices seem to derive all of their procedures from declarative knowledge, experts rely directly on procedural knowledge independent of declarative formula. Then it is sound conjecture that one aspect of the expertness of experts is a result of the translation of declarative knowledge into procedural forms. Neves and Anderson proceed to show this in the context of problem-solving.

These deliberations also raise numerous new questions about knowledge representation. How do different forms of knowledge influence memory span or ability to store information? How do they influence efficiency in problem-solving? What degree of cooperation is needed between different forms of knowledge? Yet they also illustrate the significance of the distinction that must be made between these two forms of knowledge if we are to understand the effect of knowledge on problem-solving.

3.3.2 Specific versus general knowledge

A second important distinction to be made is between *specific* and *general* purpose knowledge. Borrowing from psycholinguistics we shall call the general form of knowledge *schemata* and the specific form *instances*. Schemata represent knowledge that is equally applicable to many different circumstances or individual instances. For example, when the architect comments (lines 14 and 15, table 3.5), "one person would probably need a living room, dining area, kitchen, bathroom, ... study", he is drawing this from a general knowledge source about the occupancy needs of a single-family dwelling. At the same time, he is adapting this knowledge to the specific instance at hand: the single and blind teacher.

He articulates the study area as a separate room to accommodate the special equipment called for in the program[14]. This suggests that both general knowledge about things, such as *any house*; as well as ways of adapting them to specific conditions, such as *a carriage house for a single blind teacher*, are parts of the designer's general knowledge.

Declarative as well as procedural knowledge can come in general as well as specific forms. Primarily for historic reasons I shall use the terminology included in table 3.6 to refer to these key knowledge types.

3.3.2.1 *Things*: *tokens and schemata*

A primary use of descriptive knowledge is to codify 'things' not only as distinct entities but also through normative references to identify classes of entities. This allows for the distinction between general and specific cases of 'things'. For example, when the designer says 'entrance', does he mean a particular entrance or any entrance in general? In the design episode shown in table 3.5, a residential unit, its entry area, its structure, its rooms, its plan organization, its site are repeatedly referred to vis-à-vis general concepts without identifying particular, existing, or proposed objects. These are representations of a *general* kind and will be called *schemata*. Specialized references, on the other hand, used to identify specific objects, such as the existing garage, the entry to the garage, and so on, are called *tokens*. All tokens and schemata used in the episode in table 3.5 are listed in table 3.7.

Table 3.6. A taxonomy for knowledge representations.

	Specific knowledge	General knowledge
Declarative 'things'	tokens	schemata
Declarative 'relationships'	attributes	rules of inference
Procedural	transformations	heuristics

Table 3.7. Things: descriptors representing elements used in design.

Tokens	Schemata
Existing garage (t_1), structure of t_1, area of t_1, existing site (t_2), north wall of t_2, west wall of t_2, east wall of t_2, existing trees, bank for access (t_3), corner of t_3, entry to t_1, organizational diagram for t_2.	Residential unit (s_1), entry of s_1, structure of s_1, outside walls of s_1, living room, dining area, kitchen bathroom, bedroom, study, equipment, one bedroom unit, organizational diagram, site-plan.

[14] In a second experiment where the program called for a college professor with no special equipment needs the designers did not articulate the study area as a separate component of the program. This indicates that the 'study' is a special part of the building program which sets it apart from the standard single-person dwelling.

3.3.2.2 Relationships: attributes and inferences

Another category of information constituting declarative knowledge is the relationships or associations between things. For example in lines 1, 3, and 5 of table 3.5, the knowledge about the relationship between cost and the construction of a structure are used to make inferences and evaluate design ideas. The statement in line 1 is indicative of the architect's belief that 'building under an existing structure is costly'. This shows a general purpose relationship between schemata which will be called an *inference rule*. When applied to specific cases, such inferences signify *attributes* which are specific to instances and tokens at hand: "the expense [of the proposed underground structure] would be considerable" (line 1). Hence, attributes are specific knowledge representations that refer to relationships between tokens.

Some examples of attributes and rules of inference used in the episode are shown in table 3.8.

Table 3.8. Relationships: attributes and rules of inference.

Line[a]	Attribute	Rule of inference
1	"Probably the expense would be considerable to do that."[b]	It is expensive to build under existing structures[c]
2	"It would solve the entry problem."[b]	Physically separating two functional distinct entrances resolves potential conflicts between them.[c]
3	"It would also save some money from building the structure, the physical outside walls."[b]	
14		"one person would probably need a living area, dining area, kitchen, bath, bedroom."
15	"So it is essentially a one-bedroom unit."[b]	

[a] Line in table 3.5.
[b] "that" and "it" refer to alternative 2 that is, building under the existing structure.
[c] Paraphrased to articulate the inference rule implied in the protocol.

3.3.2.3 Procedural knowledge: transformations and heuristics

The primary information embodied in procedural knowledge is the specification of action. Consider lines 27 and 28 of table 3.5 where the designer states "I think the first thing I am going to try is ... I think ... I often found that the first ideas are often the best ... after examining several ideas ... [they] are the best". This is a commonly used rule of thumb that specifies a certain action with the intent of narrowing down

the choices one has. In chapter 4 the term *heuristics*[15] will be introduced
to represent normative forms of such rules.

Heuristics is the general form of procedural knowledge. It is usually
adapted to specific situations and rarely appears in data as generalizations,
such as the one cited above. A term which has been used to represent
specific problem-solving intentions is *transformations* (a term already
defined in chapter 2). For example, in lines 30–34 the designer
elaborates the steps needed to accomplish one of his solution ideas.
This is a premeditated sequence of transformations that is adapted to
the specific case the architect is considering. One can only speculate
about the form of the heuristics which has generated this particular set
of transformations[16]. The transformations and heuristic devices used in
the episode in table 3.5 are listed in table 3.9.

Table 3.9. Procedural knowledge: transformation and heuristics.

Line	Transformation	Heuristic
9	"Would it be possible to go back and look at the slides later?"	
12	"There is a number of different approaches we could take."	
17	"OK. I think what I would like to do is to sketch some organizational ..."	
28		"I often found that the first ideas are; often are the best."
30	"So I'll first experiment with the idea of trying to enter right here."	
31	"Leave the existing garage where it is."	
32	"take the roof off."	
33	"and add the building over."	

3.4 Analysis of design protocols

To analyze the architect's behavior and to arrive at a necessary and
sufficient model of design, we must first come up with conventions of
representing his behavior. The concepts defined above provide a
taxonomy suitable for such a representation. In addition a representation
that approximates continuous behavior in time, is necessary. The state-space
representation described in chapter 2 is the most suitable for this
purpose. Through states and transformations which alter states to

---

[15] Heuristics are rules of thumb that improve the problem-solver's efficiency in
finding solutions by identifying 'promising' alternatives and eliminating those
alternatives less likely to yield solutions (Feigenbaum and Feldman, 1963).

[16] This issue is further elaborated in chapter 4.

generate new ones, it is possible to simulate virtually any continuous behavior with any grain of resolution desired. By employing a fine grain of resolution, one can animate the architect's behavior in a 'true to life' fashion. Alternatively, it is possible to observe larger patterns of behavior by leaving greater durations between states and obtaining a more 'grainy' animation of behavior.

Let us now consider the data illustrated in table 3.5 using the state-space notation. What constitute the states and transformations in this segment of the protocol? Each information state characteristically consists of relationships defined between things, such as 'expense', 'existing garage', 'entry', 'problem', 'considerable', and so on. These concepts are sometimes used as schemata: 'a garage', 'an entry', 'a problem', and at other times, they refer to specific instances, such as, 'the existing garage', 'the expense of building under the garage'.

To represent this formally, let us assume a convention illustrated by the following formula:

$$T, [t_1, (t_{11}, t_{12}, ...), ...], [t_2, (t_{21}, t_{22}, ...), ...], ...[t_n, (t_{n1}, t_{n2}, ...), ...],$$

where

T is a schema entitled 'task',
t_1 is the task of building over the garage, an instance of T,
t_{11} is the subtask of building the outer walls in task t_1,
t_{12} is the subtask of building the ceiling structure in task t_1,
t_2 is the task of building under the garage, an instance of T,
t_{21} is the subtask of building the outer-walls in task t_2,
t_{22} is the subtask of building the ceiling structure in task t_2,
t_n is any other task which is an instance of T,
t_{nl} is any subtask of t_n.

Alternatively, we can represent the same information graphically as shown in figure 3.5. In fact, the multiple associations that may be formed between schemata in LTM are best communicated in graphic form. Such a composite representation of many schemata and instances is sufficient to codify any number of relationships and concepts manifested in the protocol segment.

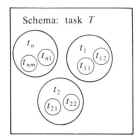

Figure 3.5. Graphic representation of schemata.

The subject's statements in table 3.5 show his assessment of how much 'expense' is needed for accomplishing task t_2. However, it is not possible to know whether this is an accurate estimate, a 'guestimate', or simply a guess that has resulted from a keen sense developed through years of experience. In general, the only thing we can safely say is that the subject has an inference mechanism (however crude or refined it may be) that takes a task such as t_2 and transforms it into a prediction about the cost of undertaking task t_2, that is, its expense, e_2. Let us represent the specific form of the inference rule as

$$TE_2$$
$$t_2 \rightarrow e_2,$$

where TE_2 stands for the transformation operation[17] that produces the new information state containing e_2. Let us include e_2 as part of a new state shown in figure 3.6(a). Notice that a new schemata, expense (E), is a necessary metaconcept which must be included to enter e_2 in the table. The architect does not really assign a precise value to e_2 in this statement or anywhere else in the protocol segment. The only value assigned to e_2 is a relative one, 'considerable'. That is, e_2 is predicted to be greater than normal or what would be expected under normal circumstances. This represents a comparison between e_2 and e_3 (the cost normally expected as a function of the funds available) or e_1 (the cost expected in the case of task t_1, if we assume t_1 to be the normal solution to the problem). This comparison obviously yields a disagreement ($\rightarrowtail\!\!\dashv$) in favour of the 'normal' expense as opposed to an agreement ($\longleftrightarrow$).

Applying this kind of interpretation to the rest of the statements in table 3.5 we can show that the architect makes the inferences illustrated in figure 3.6. The statement "It would solve the entry problem" [figure 3.6(b)] indicates that the subject has transformed task t_2 into a physical configuration schema C_2 via transformation TC_2; and ultimately into its functional implication f_2 via CF_2. Subsequently, this functional implication (f_2) is compared against a normative schema of 'entrance' (f_n) with agreeable results.

The architect continues his assessment of t_2 in the next statement: "It would also save some money from building the structure" [figure 3.6(c)]. In this statement there is a stronger cost comparison implied between t_1 and t_2, this time in favor of t_2; whereas the next statement implies a similar comparison with the results operating in the reverse direction: "We probably will have to rebuild the structure of the garage [because of building underneath the existing foundations] which might defray some costs" [figure 3.6(d)]. In the final statement of this segment the subject concludes this train of thought with a self-assessment indicating his

---

[17] From now on, the term 'operation' will be used to refer to actions that are responsible for state transformations.

"Probably the expense would be considerable to do that."

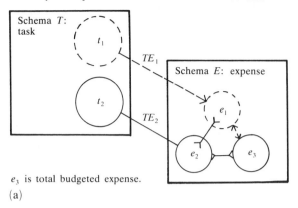

e_3 is total budgeted expense.

(a)

"It would solve the entry problem."

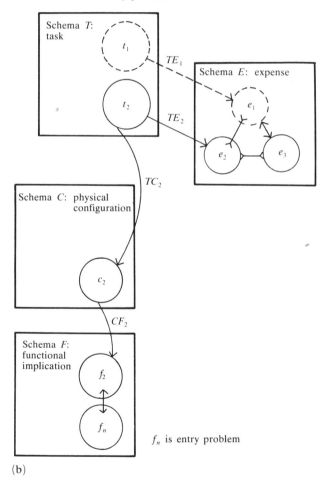

f_n is entry problem

(b)

Figure 3.6. Schema-spaces are various lines of protocol (see table 3.5): (a) line 1, (b) line 2, (c) line 3, (d) lines 4–5, (e) line 6. (Figure continued overleaf.)

"It would also save some money from building the structure."

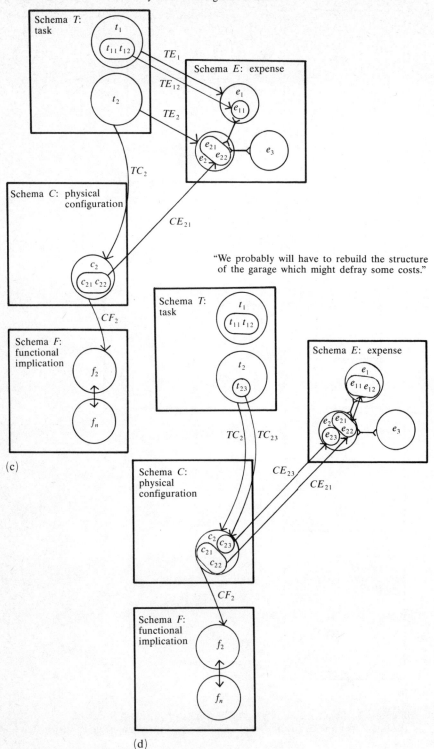

"We probably will have to rebuild the structure of the garage which might defray some costs."

(c)

(d)

Figure 3.6. (continued).

satisfaction with what is accomplished: "So I have an idea to do something" [figure 3.6(e)]. This suggests that he knows what the appropriate design goals are and how to set up a plan of action to accomplish them. This in essence is a schema of the design process itself, labeled P in figure 3.6(e).

In this short segment of the design process the designer is seen as primarily interested in understanding the problem and identifying the most plausible solutions for it. Although this is typically the case at the onset of most design episodes, this is not representative of the actual development of design solutions, formally or conceptually. In the last half of the segment in table 3.5, we observe the beginning of a process which deals more directly with physical design. Figure 3.8 (below)

"So I have an idea to do something."

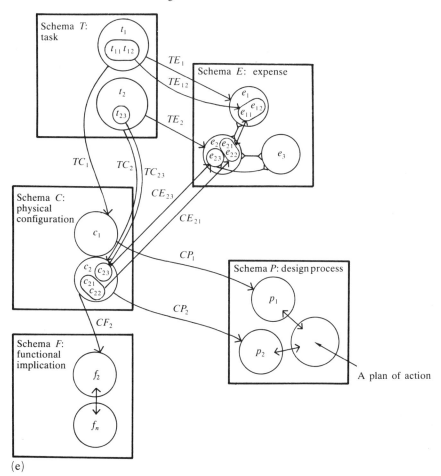

(e)

Figure 3.6. (continued).

shows the states and transformations as manifested in this portion of the protocol. Here we encounter not only states dealing with conceptual schemata but others that pertain to graphic representation.

In addition to the previous states, here the designer uses the drawing operation to carry out his explorations (figure 3.7). The first statement of this section indicates the designer's interest in drawing the site plan in diagrammatic form, "OK, We have ... we have a site ... that is ..." [figure 3.8(a)]. This broken verbalization pattern is indicative of the fact that the designer is engaged in motor activity (drawing) in addition to speaking. And the interface between the two modes of communication is responsible for the cryptic utterances. Next the subject draws the west and south retaining walls of the site which constitute the strongest reference points of the site. Once these boundaries have been established he begins to draw the remaining portions of the outline of the existing garage: "existing garage ... that ... " [figure 3.8(b)]. At this point he is concerned with the external context of the garage and its implications for access to the site: "walk through right here" [figure 3.8(c)].

From experience, entry is a fundamental consideration for design. Thus the designer spends the rest of his time discussing and justifying the approach he has chosen to take towards the point of entrance and the particular entry sequence implied in his site drawings. First, he points out the existing trees that line and reinforce the path of entry: "There are some trees here" [figure 3.8(d)]. Then he justifies the value of building above ground which is consistent with the entry sequence

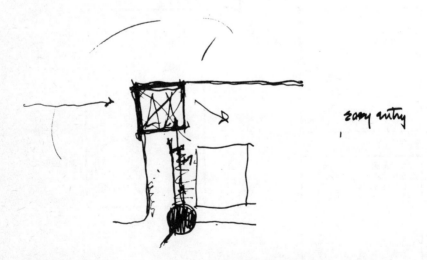

Figure 3.7. Subject 1's sketches corresponding to the protocol segment analyzed in figure 3.6.

"OK, We have ... we have a site ...
that is ..."   "existing garage ... that ..."

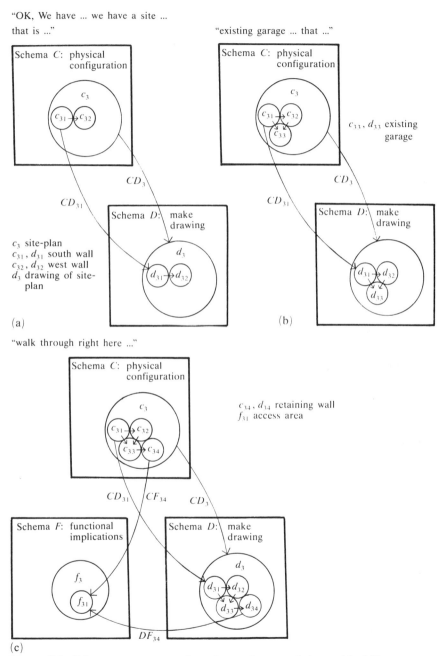

(a)   (b)

"walk through right here ..."

(c)

Figure 3.8. Schema-spaces at various lines of protocol (see table 3.5):
(a) lines 22–23, (b) line 24, (c) line 25, (d) line 26, (e) line 27 and line 30,
(f) lines 28–29, (g) line 31, (h) line 32, (i) line 33, (j) line 34. (Figure continued
overleaf.)

"There are some trees here."

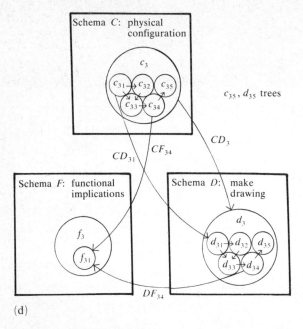

c_{35}, d_{35} trees

(d)

"I think the first thing I am going to try is ..."
"So, I'll first experiment with the idea of trying to enter right here."

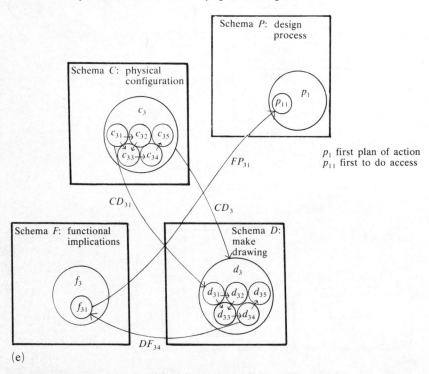

p_1 first plan of action
p_{11} first to do access

(e)

Figure 3.8. (continued).

"... I think ... I often found that the first ideas are often the best ...
... After examining several ideas ... are the best."

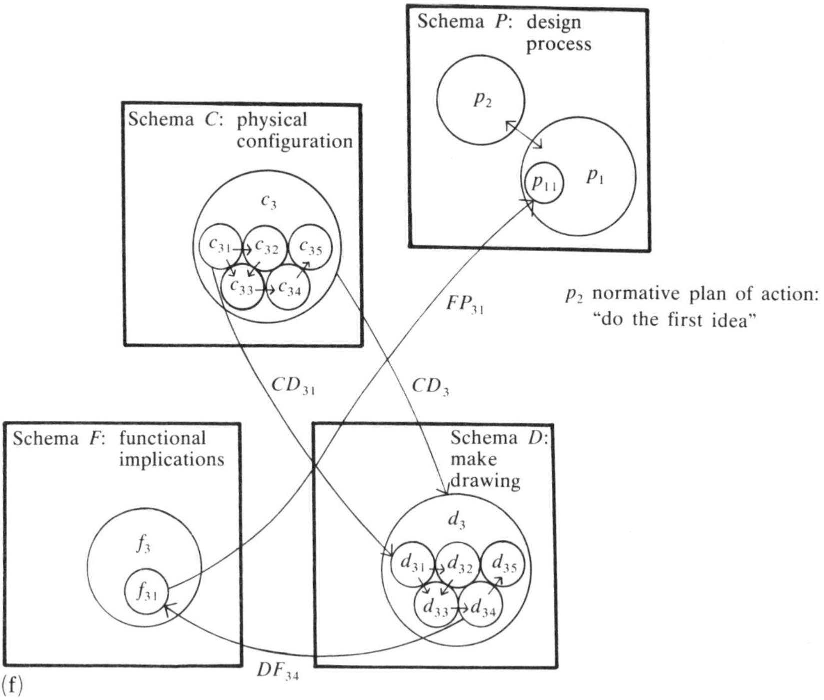

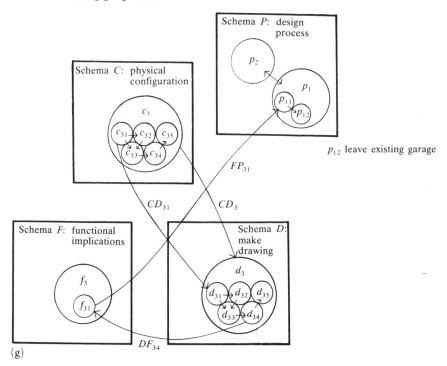

Schema P: design process

p_2

p_{11} p_1

Schema C: physical configuration

c_3

c_{31} → c_{32} c_{35}

c_{33} → c_{34}

FP_{31}

p_2 normative plan of action: "do the first idea"

CD_{31} CD_3

Schema F: functional implications

f_3

f_{31}

Schema D: make drawing

d_3

d_{31} → d_{32} d_{35}

d_{33} → d_{34}

(f)

DF_{34}

"Leave the existing garage where it is."

Schema P: design process

p_2

p_1

p_{11}

p_{12}

Schema C: physical configuration

c_3

c_{31} → c_{32} c_{35}

c_{33} → c_{34}

FP_{31}

p_{12} leave existing garage

CD_{31} CD_3

Schema F: functional implications

f_3

f_{31}

Schema D: make drawing

d_3

d_{31} → d_{32} d_{35}

d_{33} → d_{34}

(g)

DF_{34}

Figure 3.8. (continued).

"take the roof off"

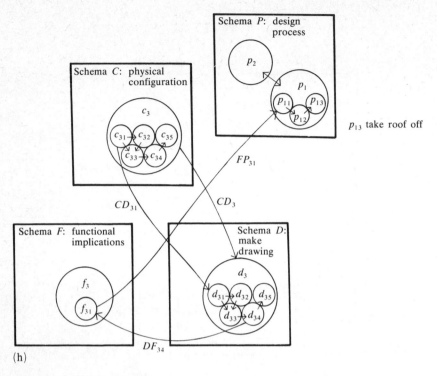

p_{13} take roof off

(h)

"and add the building over"

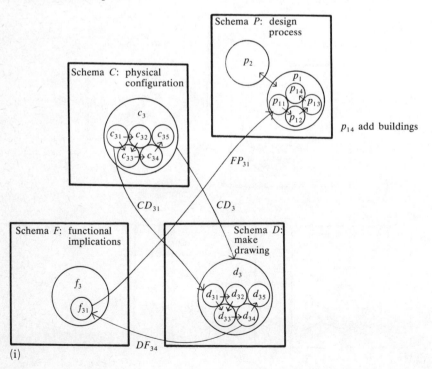

p_{14} add buildings

(i)

Figure 3.8. (continued).

implied in his site drawing: "I think the first thing I'm going to try is ...
I think ... I often found that the first ideas are often the best ... So I'll
first experiment with the idea of trying to enter right here" [figure 3.8(e)].
Finally he enumerates the implications of choosing this alternative;
"Leave the existing garage where it is [figure 3.8(f)], take the roof off
[figure 3.8(g)], and add the building over [figure 3.8(h)]. Problems being
right at that point [figure 3.8(j)]". He points out that the area marked
with a circle in figure 3.7 will cause problems.

   This train of thought provides a plan of action underscoring each
subtask necessary to accomplish task t_1. Figure 3.9 illustrates this point
by reencoding the schema entitled 'task' to indicate all subtasks
necessary to accomplish task t_1. In this encoding, task t_1 is designated
by a more detailed schemata showing all subtasks of t_1: establishing
access into the building, leaving the existing garage where it is, taking
the roof off, and adding the new building on top.

"Problems being right at that point."

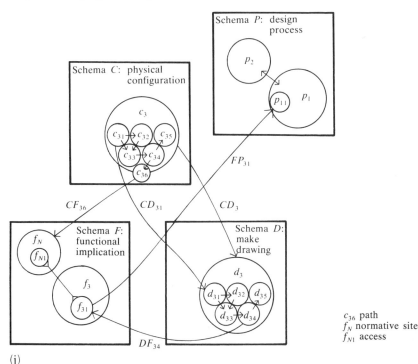

(j)

Figure 3.8. (continued).

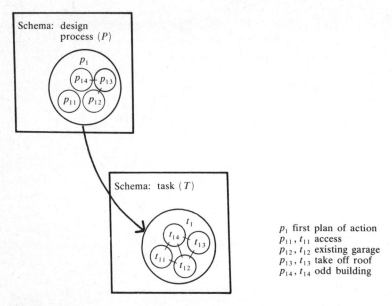

p_1 first plan of action
p_{11}, t_{11} access
p_{12}, t_{12} existing garage
p_{13}, t_{13} take off roof
p_{14}, t_{14} odd building

Figure 3.9. Schema: design process (P) and task (T).

3.5 State transformations in architectural design

The above analysis underscores several forms of transformations consistently used to alter problem states during the course of the episode. These correspond to several general categories of operations at least insofar as the investigations in this work have shown. These operations are:

1 *Projection of information* from existing information through inference, interpolation, or deduction.

2 *Acquisition of information* from the external environment (slides, drawings, notes) as well as from memory (assumptions about cost, access).

3 *Representation of information* either after acquisition or after internal processing to assist memory retention and help the other operations.

4 *Confirmation of information* that is newly acquired or projected to verify its consistency against existing information.

5 *Regulation of flow of control* from one operation to the next to reduce the search space of the designer as a function of the present state of the problem.

Projection of information, operating through inference making, is evident in all transformations that result in forming associations between schemata and their instances. As new information is gained and encoded, the designer examines and assesses what he has accomplished in relation to his goals and what he intends to do next. For example, "probably the expense would be considerable to do that ... " [figure 3.6(a)] is an instance of reasoning about the probable cost of building alternative 2. During the act of inference-making the designer takes a given piece of information, adds to it what he knows, and arrives at new or modified information. In the above example he takes alternative 1, develops cost information based on his own experience and asserts the statements in figure 3.6(a), "probably the expense would be considerable to do that," as the new pieces of information inferred from his cost analysis.

Although each inference is somewhat different from the others in terms of its source and the level of confidence associated with it, they all have some common features. First, each inference is a step in an overall process of developing appropriate information that builds towards a goal. Each inference does not directly contribute to how the actions of the designer are steered towards a solution. Yet they play a critical role in developing the substance that is essential in doing so. Second, each inference draws from an area of knowledge that is relevant to specific professional areas of expertise, such as cost (lines 1, 3, and 5 in table 3.5), occupancy (lines 2 and 25), construction (lines 4, 31, 32, and 33), programming (lines 14 and 15), and feasibility (lines 15 and 16). Finally, each inference produces a new previously unspecified piece of information that declares the truth of an object, concept, relationship, or procedure relevant to these areas of knowledge. For example, the architect states that a solution would cost more and involve less outside wall construction in lines 1 and 3 of table 3.5. This information is entirely new in the context of the problem at hand.

Acquisition of information is also evident in the designer's behavior. Questions, visual scanning, and other sensory input are the overt behavioral evidence that support this assertion. These constitute the data that enable the activation of the other operations. Before and after each statement in table 3.5, the designer examines a slide, drawing, or text and in response makes inferences and statements about what he plans to do. At times he draws lines on paper which are done in response to previously acquired information and in turn become new information to be acquired and reacted to by the designer.

Representation of information is also a necessary operation in design. The term 'representation', as used here, refers to all overt or covert behaviors aimed at encoding of information, such as writing, drawing, marking, learning, memorizing, and so on. A major external representation effort takes place in lines 21–26 in table 3.5, where the designer starts his site analysis (figure 3.7). In this particular case the subject represents his ideas graphically on paper. There are many other instances where no manual representation takes place, yet we know that the subject encodes information in memory to be recalled later.

Representations are as much for evoking design ideas by providing stimuli with which to react as they are for assisting memory and recall. Often these reactions are critical in refining or further developing design ideas. When the designer draws a Venn diagram for the first time to indicate graphically the relationships between parts of the program, this usually implies the decomposition of the problem into manageable parts or the identification of design opportunities and difficulties. Such realizations invariably provide the data the designer needs for guiding his subsequent behaviors. External representations are necessary, if not for these powers of evocation, then for the sake of providing aids to memory.

Confirmation of information can be demonstrated through the comparative links formed in the graphs of figures 3.8. As a new piece of information is assimilated into a schema its agreement ($\longleftrightarrow$) and disagreements ($\longmapsto\!\!\!\longleftarrow$) are noticed and expressed. All new information, whether found outside the designer's memory or developed by him during the course of the task, gets represented some place. Often we see the designer encode these overtly on paper; at other times we can infer that he has simply saved them in memory (that is, the two tasks t_1 and t_2 are referred to many times but they are never explicitly spelled out on paper). The process of encoding new information requires that its consistency or potential conflict with existing information be examined. Otherwise the designer is forced to work with conflicting and inconsistent information.

Although implicit manifestations of this function are in abundance, the only explicit evidence of confirmation in table 3.5 is in line 34 where the subject asserts that there is a problem with the solution he is currently developing. He points out that the area marked with the circle in figure 3.7 will cause problems. This is a clear indication of his value judgment about the potential of this solution for failure. In other instances of inference making, that is, where most costly solutions are considered to be undesirable, evaluation takes place in a less explicit way (lines 1, 3, and 5).

Regulation of control is one of the least frequently observed operations in the above protocol. However, it constitutes an essential part of the design process. It allows the designer to use his resources effectively, that is with reasonable time and effort. Some regulation behavior deals directly with the question of "what to do next?" (lines 6, 9, 12, and 17). Others help identify goals about desired solutions (line 14); rules of thumb to facilitate the design process (lines 28 and 29); and the subgoals of more general strategies for design (lines 30 – 34). At times this function becomes much more explicit. Designers state clearly and directly the knowledge they use in working towards particular design goals. Figure 3.8(f) provides a perfect example. The architect decides to study alternative 2, because it occurred to him first. We showed in chapter 2 that the necessity of planned nonrandom problem-solving behavior is obvious even in the case of well-defined tasks such as the 15-puzzle problem. This is even more critical in the case of design, where the goals and means of search are less explicit and the problem much more open ended.

3.6 Knowledge and behavior in design

Let us now explore the relationships between the categories of knowledge discussed in section 3.3 and behavioral processes exhibited by the designer discussed in section 3.5. Newell and Simon have developed a representation which allows the consolidation of the various transformations shown in figures 3.6 and 3.8 into a single graph called a problem behavior graph (PBG)[18]. Very simply, a PBG is a graph which shows all states and transformations applied by the problem-solver in the course of solving a problem. By drawing a PBG consisting of nodes that correspond to problem states, and links that correspond to transformations applied to the states, one can succinctly represent the designer's behavior as well as the knowledge he brings to bear on the design problem vis-à-vis these transformations.

Figure 3.10 (see over) represents the PBG for the design episode in table 3.5. The nodes included in the top three lines of the graph indicate significant information states which were generated prior to this episode. These are the initial problem description given to the designer and the first two of the alternative solutions developed[19]. All states generated in the episode are labelled S_1. The corresponding utterances of the designer are consecutively numbered from 1 to 35, to correspond to the utterances in table 3.5. The transformations applied to each state are labelled B_k.

The transitions from one state to the next are determined as much through their information contents as through the transformations applied. Consequently, there are dependencies between the contents of the states. This is why the successive states are not strung along a linear path, but form a tree-like structure. For example, after the site has been drawn in lines 21–26, the next behavior pattern, that is, 'planning what to do next', develops from the original idea of alternative 1 and consequently it is connected to the state representing alternative 1 rather than to the state in line 26.

Other than providing a map of the designer's actions, the PBG allows the collective representation of many variables inherently important for the analysis of problem-solving and their interdependencies. It also provides a medium in which alternative models of the designer, his knowledge sources, and transformations, can be studied.

[18] Newell and Simon (1972) provide a detailed description of the PBG.
[19] These alternatives are further discussed in chapter 4.

Problem statement

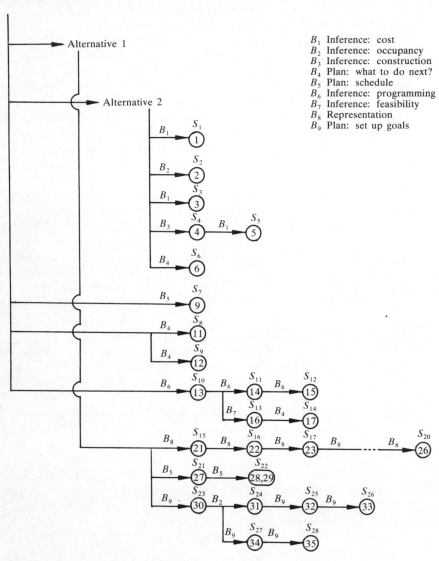

B₁ Inference: cost
B₂ Inference: occupancy
B₃ Inference: construction
B₄ Plan: what to do next?
B₅ Plan: schedule
B₆ Inference: programming
B₇ Inference: feasibility
B₈ Representation
B₉ Plan: set up goals

Figure 3.10. State-space representation.

3.7 Summary
Modern science has at its disposal tools and methods that are suitable
for exploring mechanisms that underlie behaviors of complex systems.
Current advances in psychology and computer science have extended the
applicability of these tools to the human cognitive system. It is possible
in many problem-solving domains to explain and even to predict human

behavior with accuracy. It has also been demonstrated that the same tools are applicable with modifications and extensions to complex task domains such as natural language, mathematics, medical diagnosis, and architectural design.

A cursory exploration of the basics of the architectural design task and review of current research on design indicate that the same tools, when applied to design tasks, would lead to previously unavailable explanations and predictions about the design activity. In this chapter we reviewed three categories of knowledge applicable to design: knowledge of things, their properties, and plans of action for manipulating this information to achieve goal-directed behavior. This provides a plausible framework for the process of architectural design. Next we shall explore these mechanisms in the course of a more detailed analysis of the design process.

3.8 Suggested readings

1 Akin Ö, 1984, "An exploration of the design process" in *Developments in Design Methodology* Ed. N Cross (John Wiley, New York) pp 189–208
2 Eastman C E, 1973, "Automated space planning" *Artificial Intelligence* **4** 41–64
3 Newell A, 1970, "Heuristic programming: ill-structured problems" in *Progress in Operations Research, Volume 3* Ed. J A Arnofsky (John Wiley, New York), chapter 1, pp 360–414
4 Reitman W R, 1964, "Heuristic decision procedures, open constraints and structure of information processing problems" in *Human Judgments and Optimality* Eds M W Shelly II, G L Bryan (John Wiley, New York) pp 282–315
5 Simon H A, 1973, "Structure of ill-structured problems" *Artificial Intelligence* **4** 181–201

3.9 Exercises

3.1 Assemble the parts of the mechanical system indicated in figure 3.11. Maintain the designated relationships between these components and their physical dimensions. While solving this space-planning problem, develop a record of your problem-solving process by keeping your notes, drawings, and thoughts in chronological order.
(a) Identify the *tokens*, the *attributes* of these tokens, and the *transformations* you have used while solving this problem.
(b) Identify and represent the *schemata*, *rules of inference*, and *heuristic devices* that correspond to the tokens, properties, and plans you identified, respectively.

3.2 Discuss how closely the results of exercise 3.1 represent your design behavior.

3.3 Write a critique of self-introspection as a research method in studying the design process.

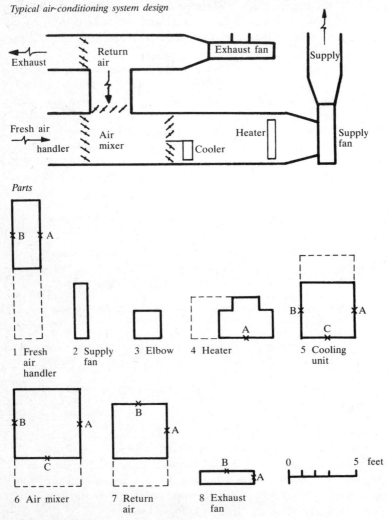

Typical air-conditioning system design

Parts

1 Fresh air handler   2 Supply fan   3 Elbow   4 Heater   5 Cooling unit

6 Air mixer   7 Return air   8 Exhaust fan

0   5 feet

Required relations

1   Element 2 oriented toward supply.
2   Element 2 < 5 ft from supply.
3   Element 3 adjacent to side 3 of element 2.
4   Element 3 adjacent to side 2 of element 4.
5   Point A on element 4 < 1 ft from point B on element 5.
6   Point A on element 5 < 1 ft from point B on element 6.
7   Point A on element 6 < 1 ft from point B on element 1.
8   Point A on element 1 < 3 ft from outside air.
9   Side 4 on element 7 adjacent to side 1 on element 6.
10   Point B on element 7 < 1 ft from point B on element 8.
11   Point B on element 8 < 3 ft from return air.
12   Side 1 of element 8 oriented toward return air.
13   Visibility from door to point C on element 6.

Figure 3.11. Space-planning problem (from Eastman, 1973).

An information-processing model of design

"The natural sciences are concerned with how things are. Design on the other hand is concerned with how things ought to be, with devising artifacts to attain goals. We might question whether the forms of reasoning that are appropriate to natural science are suitable also for design. One might well suppose that introduction of the verb "should" may require additional rules of inference, or modification of the rules already embedded in declarative logic."

H A Simon, *The Sciences of the Artificial* (1969, pages 58–59)

Any scientific investigation starts with a hypothesis that defines a relationship or sets of relationships between things. 'Grass is green' establishes an association between the color green and grass, thus proposing a hypothesis we can consider. Although the nature of the relationship between two things may differ from one association or hypothesis to the next, this relationship can be simply represented as $A \rightarrow B$, where A and B are the associated elements and '$\rightarrow$' is the associative link. Investigations in design also make use of relationships that are structurally identical to associative constructs of the type $A \rightarrow B$ (discussed in section 3.3.2.2). The only distinction, as Simon pointed out above, is that in design the associative link '$\rightarrow$' implies 'should' instead of 'is'.

Although this may seem to be an insignificant distinction at first, its implications for design knowledge are significant[20]. Consider scientists who are concerned with the truth of a given hypothesis. Their task is bounded by the declarative knowledge to which they have access, the declarative hypothesis in which they are interested, and the rules of reasoning they have at their disposal which enable them to compare the hypothesis against their knowledge. Their task is clear. They rely on paradigms that are well understood. They can measure success and failure. They can predetermine a course of action for investigation. And perhaps most importantly, they can communicate these to others with almost the same clarity as they can to themselves.

Now consider designers concerned with the truth of a hypothesis that predicts what ought to be. An immediate implication of this is that they have an open-ended context within which to test this hypothesis. For example, 'grass ought to be green' as opposed to 'grass is green' implies that there is a context within which grass must be green. This context may be one we know of (in an ideal suburban front lawn); one we expect will be possible (in a suburb in the Sinai Desert); or one we desire the existence of (year round, on the surface of the moon). The

[20] This distinction is similar to the one we made earlier between declarative and procedural forms of knowledge in section 3.3.1.

mere suggestion that our hypothesis becomes a future state or a prediction opens the door to the possibility of future contexts yet to be determined.

In addition, designers are faced with the problem of ephemeral hypotheses. If it is only a wish, is it not entirely conceivable that designers can assert with equal confidence that 'grass ought to be red'? Can they not conceive of or find a context within which grass may indeed grow to assume a red color? The objective of the design problem and the design itself have a dialectic relationship, forcing designers to solve not only the problem at hand but also the problem of how to solve it, simultaneously. In short, designers usually face a problem without clearly defined objectives, methods, or evaluation criteria.

However, there are things that are shared by many design problems and designers which characterize these processes and suggest the existence of normative methods and knowledge. These things have to do with the designer's cognitive mechanisms, information-processing capacity, and culture shared with other fellow designers. The purpose of this chapter is to define a paradigm which codifies these and employs the IPS proposed by Newell and Simon (figure 2.1) in the process.

4.1 Architecture of an information-processing system for design: DIPS

In developing an information-processing model for design, design information-processing system (DIPS), it is useful to examine design at various levels of abstraction: its component parts and their relationships through their most general properties as well as their most detailed and articulated descriptions. Consequently, the contents of this chapter are organized from general to specific. More precisely, it spans three levels of abstraction ranging from a derivative of the general purpose model of IPS illustrated in figure 4.1, to a more detailed version illustrated in figure 4.2, and finally to a set of flow diagrams that further articulate processes and knowledge structures illustrated in figure 4.13 (below).

In its most general form (figure 4.1), DIPS operates on two environmental sources of information: the *problem* being studied and the *solution* being developed. The *receptors* facilitate the acquisition of the information needed from these environmental sources, and the *effectors*

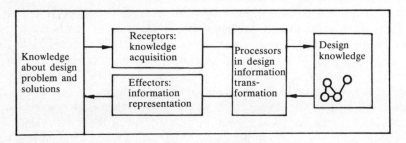

Figure 4.1. Design information-processing system.

encode information developed internally in the environment. The task of the *processor* is to transform the information that is acquired with the assistance of the *memory*. The memory, as in figure 2.1, constitutes the long-term knowledge necessary in design. The transformations performed by the *processor* have the effect of altering the contents of the memory as well as the environment with the intent of solving the problem described in the environment.

Let us now focus on these general attributes of DIPS under three headings: external representations, design processes, and organization of memory (figure 4.2).

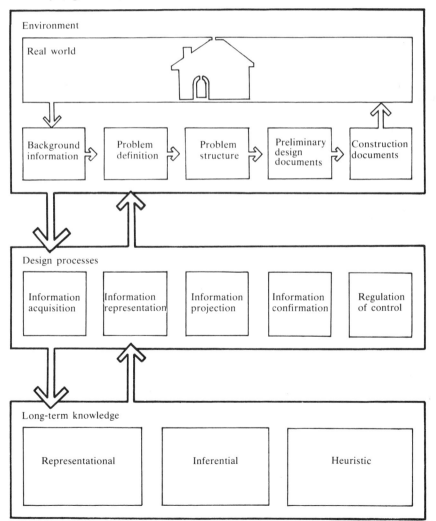

Figure 4.2. Design information-processing system in detail.

4.2 External representations in design

Design is a lengthy process often with many professions and different skill areas as its necessary participants. Clients, users, engineers, building contractors, social scientists, planners, and many others participate in the transformation of design information. With the broad range of backgrounds, motivations, and methods these participants bring to this process, it is very difficult to reach a consensus around any one design solution. In reality, compromise often replaces perfect agreement.

The complex interactions between the designer and the design problem complicate the matter even further. To support the proper communication of these actors in the design process, conventions governing the exchange and transformation of information are necessary. Although clearly delineated categories do not exist, identifiable forms of information constitute a basis for these transactions. Designers communicate with the client using certain kinds of drawings and with the contractor using entirely different kinds of drawings. The information necessary for a preliminary cost estimate for the client is very different from that needed as part of the contractual agreement between client and contractor. Consequently, it is important to understand these forms of architectural information before examining the processes and knowledge applied in the context of such information.

Architectural information has been codified not only for the purpose of studying the design process but also to regulate and organize the interaction between its participants. Most national professional organizations in the Western world[21] define the stages of work that constitute the professional responsibilities of the architect. These classifications tend to conform to standard tasks that have evolved over decades of practice: programming, site design, building design, construction documents, bidding and negotiation, fitting out, construction, and post-occupancy evaluation. Some notable exceptions to this do exist and will be reviewed later.

This list represents an accurate account of what needs to be done by the architect. However, it does not signify a linear design process. The individual services identified above appear during different stages of a typical design process, in various sequences, and are repeated singly or in combination with other services. For example, site design can become a part of programming when the needs of the users are examined. Yet it must also be a part of the construction-document stage. Similarly, programming does not stop, sometimes until well after the completion of the construction documents. Designers may find themselves reexamining their predictions about patterns of use, even after construction is complete.

A more detailed and representative classification is offered by Davis and Szigeti (1980, see figure 4.3). This classification not only disaggregates

[21] NCARB National Council of Architectural Registration Boards, AIA American Institute of Architects, RIBA Royal Institute of British Architects.

the tasks cited above into smaller parts, but also places these parts into a general chronological order. An independent codification of the design-delivery process provided by Eastman (1978) accounts for a portion of this process, that is, parts 2–5 (figure 4.4, see over). Both classifications are in almost perfect agreement, at least about those aspects of design covered by both. Whereas Davis and Szigeti consider the tasks from the viewpoint of the chronology of design development and delivery processes, Eastman considers them in terms of the information transformations that occur during design. Consequently, Eastman's classification is more suitable for our purposes.

As part of DIPS, I propose a classification that resembles Eastman's and one that further disaggregates the first two stages, as shown in figure 4.1. This classification is included in the top box of figure 4.2, entitled 'environment'. The first category that defines part of the environment of an architectural problem, *background information*, is the

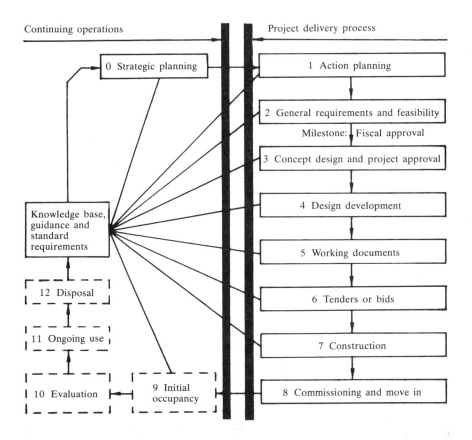

Figure 4.3. Project-delivery process (from Davis and Szigeti, 1980).

general body of knowledge that is shared by design professionals. This
is knowledge that is not specific to any one design problem, but is part
of the general culture of design which exists within the field of architecture.
There are basically two kinds of knowledge included in this category:
(1) *conventions*, the immeasureable and temporal consensus that exists
among individuals who share beliefs because of similar experiences, and
(2) *codes*, facts documented in professional standards books, archives,
and other regulatory records. By definition, conventions are usually not
documented and cannot be studied outside empirical observations.
Documentations of vernacular architecture instantiating this category,
such as the one in the quotation by Grabrijan and Neidhardt in chapter 1
are rare occurrences. Codes, on the other hand, represent written
standards of a society and are abundantly documented in building codes,
graphic standards, and building ordinances.

The next category in figure 4.2 is labelled *problem definition*. This
category is congruous to the facilities program that aids the communication
between the client or user and the designer. The program document
specifies the needs and resources of a specific client and forms the basis
for any given design problem. A large portion of this information is
implicitly connected to the first category: background information, such
as ergonomic principles of design, structural integrity, and occupancy
standards. Less general aspects, such as site, budget, building program,

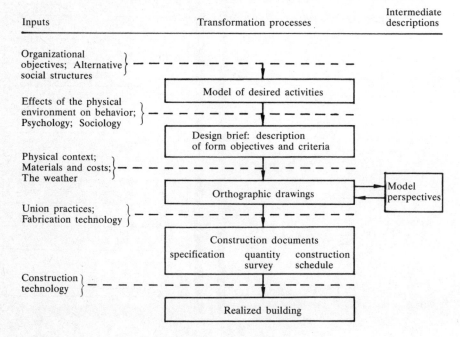

Figure 4.4. Design-delivery process (from Eastman, 1978).

and user characteristics, have to be specified and documented separately for each problem. Some of this information is readily available when design starts. Others, such as user characteristics and site selection, have to be developed as design progresses.

Problem structure, the third category in figure 4.2, stands for the individual architect's formulations of what is commonly known as problem definition. This is largely a function of the individual designer's process and may include alternative problem formulations each of which can potentially lead to a successful solution. For example, the designer we examined in chapter 3, while formulating a solution to the carriage-house problem, considers three alternative entry solutions and leaves many others outside his deliberations. One could argue that different, yet acceptable, entry solutions could be developed using the existing house, a part of it, or the backyard. These alternatives were not even considered by the designer. This may be because of the designer's belief that issues of privacy and separation between the existing and the new residents outweigh the merits of generating many more alternatives. In other words, some possible formulations of the problem are carried out as a function of the designer's biases, whereas others are excluded, a priori.

The final two conventions for codifying architectural information included in figure 4.2 pertain directly to the design solution: *preliminary design documents* and *construction documents*. The first are necessary for communicating the design in its preliminary form to the client(s) and to other professionals who take part in the design process, such as engineers, planners, regulatory agencies, and user groups. A wide range of graphic and visual techniques including drawings, charts, diagrams, models, and slides are commonly used in this stage of design. In the case of large-scale and complex projects, preliminary design is carried out in two steps: schematic design and design development; each representing a full cycle of design specification, and the latter being more detailed and closer in content to construction documents.

Construction documents are the basis of contractual agreements between the designer, the client, and the builder. They are normally prepared by the architect. These documents consist of the specification of the final product in a detailed fashion, including information about materials, construction processes, and performance specifications for the final product. This representation is the best understood one among architectural professionals.

4.2.1 External memory (EM)

From an information-processing point of view, these conventions used in representing the problem environment of the designer aid the designer's memory as well as his or her communications with others. Many of the representations used in each category are *external memories* in the true sense. They extend and augment the capacity of the designer's memory.

This is not a simple relationship to show in the form of a functional model. Information, represented externally and in forms that are fundamentally different from internal forms of representation, cannot be readily integrated with the latter. Newell and Simon (1972, page 580) discuss the different ways in which external memories can be incorporated in information-processing systems:

"1 It [external memory] can act as a repository for elements of the space that are not current but can be reached by recall mechanisms rather than by operators that generate new knowledge.

2 It can be wholly external to the knowledge state, so that operators that access the memory and search it have the same status as any other operators in the problem space. When successful they generate new knowledge that becomes part of the knowledge state.

3 It can be incorporated into the processing at a node, in such a way that all the relevant information in the external memory is in fact available.

4 It can be an extension or adjunct to the current knowledge state, with some of its information available, but not all. We will call a knowledge state, along with any such adjuncts, the *extended knowledge state*."

The first three alternatives simply assimilate the external memory in the problem space. That is, all the information potentially brought to bear on the problem is considered to be readily accessible by the problem-solver. This is clearly not the case in design. The architect has much searching to do to find and select the information needed from books, documents, people, and the physical environment. Therefore, the fourth, "extended knowledge state", alternative is the one best suited for design.

The term "extended knowledge state" alludes to the fact that this form of memory contains a great deal more than the information that is immediately accessible to the designer. And this information requires nontrivial processing before it can be accessed and assimilated. Newell and Simon describe this in the following terms (1972, page 585):

"If an external memory is being used in a routine way, but is not totally available, even when relevant, how should one view it. We can introduce the notion of an *extended knowledge state*, which contains additional information that is available to the problem solver at a node in the problem space, but not all the information that is in the external memory. For such a concept to be operational, rather than just a relabeling of the phenomena, we must be able to define the accessing functions used by the problem solver, so that we can describe what information is actually available to him. Thus, instead of describing the current knowledge state of the subject as the contents of memories X and Y, we describe it as the contents of memory X plus what can be obtained from memory Y by retrieval program P."

It is the need for this program P that is of interest to us. What this essentially means is that interface with external memories is not through 'hard-wired' connections but through further information processing. This aspect of the designer's process was called *information acquisition* in chapter 3. In the following sections I shall review this, alongside the four other processes responsible for transforming problem states in design: information representation, information projection, information confirmation, and regulation of control (see section 3.4).

4.3 Design processes
Before I begin discussing each of these primitive processes in detail, let me first define a taxonomy suitable for operationally representing these primitive processes. One of the simplest and most versatile taxonomies suitable for this purpose is flow diagrams. Flow diagrams are two-dimensional graphs with *nodes* and *links* connecting the nodes. Depending on one's preference, the nodes or the links can be used to represent either the states or the transformations in a process. The state-space representations used in chapter 3 for transcribing designers' behaviors are examples of flow diagrams.

Miller et al (1960) used a similar notation they called the TOTE unit (see figure 4.5), in representing the fundamental unit of behavior in problem-solving. A TOTE (test–operate–test–exit) unit stands for a

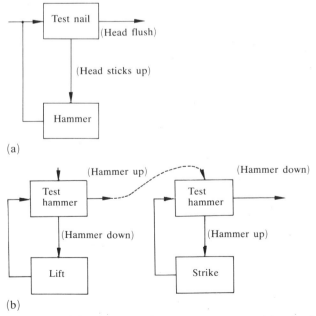

(a)

(b)

Figure 4.5. (a) The TOTE (test–operate–test–exit) unit; (b) the composite TOTE (from Miller et al, 1960).

simple control mechanism that characterizes simple behaviors like the hammering of a nail in the form of a flow diagram. Figure 4.5(a) illustrates the three basic components of a TOTE unit: test, operate, and exit. *Test* determines whether or not the purpose of the TOTE is accomplished, for example, whether the head of the nail is flush or not. If the head of the nail is flush, the whole process stops and control is passed to *exit*. If not, control is passed to the 'hammering' *operation*, which can accomplish the purpose of the TOTE and automatically return control to test.

This mechanism, basic enough to represent simple functions, is also powerful enough to be adaptable to more complex situations through the redefinition of its tests and operations. For example, if we substitute a test that measures the length of the nail remaining outside of the wood, we can have the TOTE unit simulate a system that can insert nails partially as well as fully. Or if we substitute the operation 'pull nail' for 'hammer' and reverse the direction of the test, the TOTE will become a nail-removal mechanism. Furthermore, one TOTE can be connected to other TOTEs, forming compound processes as shown in figure 4.5(b).

In short, the TOTE paradigm provides a suitable framework for representing the normative forms of behavior, including human behavior, simply and with precision. Here a similar flow-diagram format shall be used; one consisting of tests and operations chained to each other by links that simply indicate the passage of control. In the fashion of TOTEs, combined to form compound processes, an attempt will be made to illustrate how the individual processes used in design can be interconnected to form larger processes such as the detailed version of DIPS in figure 4.10 below.

Let us now review in detail each of the five primitive design processes defined earlier in chapter 3.

4.3.1 Acquisition of information

While designing we often rely on our LTM. When this is inadequate we try books, drawings, on-site observations, interviews, documents, and other survey methods to gather the relevant information. All of these, including the searching of one's own memory, are forms of information acquisition. Acquisition occurs most often during the problem-structuring phase and through three main modes: (a) visual search, (b) verbal inquiry, and (c) search of memory contents.

Visual search includes the inspection of texts, maps, sketches, photographs, or the real world itself. No designer prefers to substitute the examining of secondary sources (such as slides or photographs) for the actual inspection of a building site. But often designers have to rely on secondary sources for pragmatic reasons, particularly in the problem definition stage. Verbal inquiry is necessary when the information needed is not documented. For example, the preferences of the client and availability of materials are issues that have to be verified through inquiry. Usually the designer and the client meet numerous times to exchange information and opinion throughout the course of the design process. The designer's own memory is also a frequently used source for information. In fact, in most cases the designer will consult his or her own memory before turning to external sources. In cases where external as well as internal (cognitive) sources are inadequate, the designer is forced to rely on inference capabilities alone, to create new information.

Let us now use the flow-diagram format to represent this process operationally [figure 4.6(a)]. The first node in the diagram, labelled 'B' simply indicates the point in time when this process is activated[22]. This corresponds to the point at which the designer decides to examine

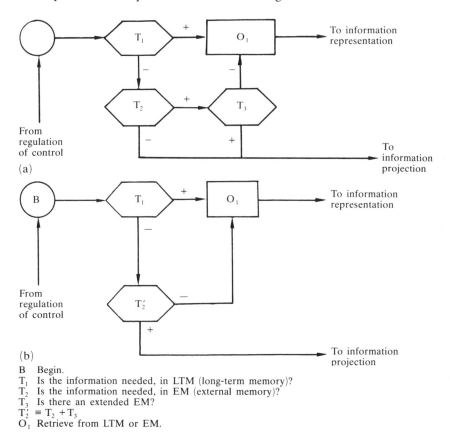

(a)

(b)

B   Begin.
T_1 Is the information needed, in LTM (long-term memory)?
T_2 Is the information needed, in EM (external memory)?
T_3 Is there an extended EM?
$T_2' \equiv T_2 + T_3$
O_1 Retrieve from LTM or EM.

Figure 4.6. (a) Flow diagram of information-acquisition process; (b) a possibly more parsimonious version of the flow diagram.

[22] For consistency, in the flow diagrams we shall review in this section, all such nodes initiating the flow of control will be shown as circles and as the points of input.

the contents of EM or LTM to retrieve information. Somewhere between this and the point at which the designer leaves this process he or she typically does one of three things:

1 Find the information sought in LTM.

2 Find the information sought in EM (this may involve other processes as implied by the parameters of searching the EM).

3 Develop a working assumption about the information not found in EM or LTM (this may also involve other processes).

If we leave aside the question of the sequence in which memories are searched, this flow diagram represents all tests and operations necessary to accomplish these three things[23]. The tests T_1, T_2, and T_3 in figure 4.6(a) verify the presence of data in various memory structures by answering two questions: "is the information in LTM or EM?" or "is there an extended EM?" These we can assume to be primitive operations that the human cognitive system performs routinely and automatically. Information-processing studies show that such routine processing can be decomposed into more primitive operations that last tiny fractions of a second. Because of the wider scope of our interest here, the smallest cognitive operation we shall consider will be at the level of the tests and operations included in figure 4.6(a). Generally, these correspond to standard cognitive operations, such as retrieval, encoding, and testing. The retrieval operation is a relatively straightforward function of the human cognitive system. Especially after the source, if not also the 'address', of the information has been determined through the tests applied, the retrieval of information is 'routine' in most cases.

The diagram in figure 4.6(a) models the information-acquisition process as defined earlier. The question we must entertain here is whether this model is sufficient and necessary. In other words, does this process account for subject's behavior fully; and is it possible to represent the same process more parsimoniously? The question of sufficiency will be examined in detail in the next chapter, so let us focus here on the question of necessity. There are two ways in which we may be able to improve the parsimony of the process as represented in figure 4.6(a): (1) can any of the tests or operations be combined or eliminated altogether, and (2) can the tests or operations be reordered so as to eliminate steps?

The answer to the first question is yes. Tests T_2 and T_3 are sequential and their outputs overlap sufficiently to allow integration. To show this we can redraw the flow diagram, replacing T_2 and T_3 with T_2' [figure 4.6(b)]. Yet it is not clear whether or not this integration achieves greater parsimony. Since within T_2' the presence of extended external

---

[23] The tests are indicated as diamond-shaped nodes, the operations as rectangular nodes and the flow of control between these nodes as labelled pointers: plus (+) when the test yields a positive result, minus (−) when a negative result, and neutral when generating from an operation node.

memories must be checked to identify the goal to be achieved, the number of tests in actuality remains the same. Combination of tests T_2 and T_3 does not result in elimination of any redundancy. Although it is quite possible that an analysis of T_2' may reveal that it could be more parsimonious than T_2 and T_3 combined, at the present level of detail it is not possible to verify this.

Similarly, the answer to the second question posed above does not yield to further parsimony. The model will work just as effectively when the sequence of tests are $T_2 \rightarrow T_3 \rightarrow T_1$; $T_3 \rightarrow T_2 \rightarrow T_1$; or $T_2' \rightarrow T_1$. This does not circumvent any steps, unless there is a different probability of finding a piece of information in LTM as opposed to EM. By placing the test with higher probability of yielding a positive result in the front end of the sequence, one can conserve processing steps. Thus, although figure 4.6(b) may prove to be more parsimonious under certain conditions, there is not sufficient evidence at this point to refute the parsimony of the flow diagram in figure 4-6(a).

However, if we were given a specific problem it might be possible to fine tune this flow diagram and achieve greater parsimony. For example, a close examination of the protocols in chapter 3 indicates that most of the information used by the designers is retrieved from LTM. Whereas in real life, where the designer encounters new or complex architectural programs all the time, reliance on the EM is greater and the sequence of tests T_1, T_2, and T_3 may have to be altered to model such behavior. This implies that, in general, the flow diagram in figure 4.6 (a) lends itself to a larger set of cases and thus proves to be more robust than the 'parsimonious' model in figure 4.6(b).

The transfer of control from this process to others takes place either through a successful acquisition of the desired information, or through a failure to do so coupled with the recognition of the need to transform the problem state. In the first case, control is passed to the *information-representation* process for encoding the new information. In the second case, the information has to be transformed, either to gain access to the extensions of EM or to develop assumptions about the information needed. In any event, the LTM is used to advance inferences through the *information-projection* process which shall be discussed later. For the time being, it will suffice to know that this process allows transformations, for instance, of the form:

(a) if information about 'how the blind use sunlight' is needed and this is not available in LTM, then imagine yourself to be blind and infer that you would be oversensitive to the other senses and direct your design to the tactile, olfactory, kynesthetic, and auditory information; alternatively:

(b) if more information about the specification of facilities for the blind is needed and is available in EM, then examine contents of graphic standards or call local organizations for the blind for more information;

if all else fails, then blindfold yourself for extended periods of time
and rely on experiences gained.
After the generation of the new information through the projection process,
control once more must be passed on, this time to the information-
representation process so that the new information can be assimilated in
the present problem representation.

4.3.2 Representation of information
Representation of information also takes place through multiple modes:
(a) written text or spoken word, (b) graphics, and (c) memory systems
(STM and LTM). Within each mode a designer has a wide range of
choices in setting up the form, content, and access schema for the
information in storage. Texts usually play an important part in the early
conceptual development of designs and specifications of construction
documents. Many technical attributes of materials, construction techniques,
and user activities are best represented through text. Graphics typically
deal with spatial descriptions: topologies, object descriptions, shapes and
their relationships, such as in Venn diagrams and flow diagrams. In
design development, graphical representations are preferred over others
because of their compatibility with physical object descriptions.

Storage and retrieval of information into and from human memory is
a process which is only partially understood. Storage is usually
manifested vis-à-vis encoding of the to-be-stored information and its
recall from LTM. Most graphic encodings serve the double purpose of
external storage as well as assisting internal storage through rehearsal.
Rehearsal is a prerequisite for the longevity of information in LTM.
This implies that the information that is rehearsed must have been
stored in LTM earlier. It also implies that the STM in encoding and
decoding information influences the form of knowledge. In chapter 6
these influences will be elaborated. Let us now discuss the process of
information representation itself. The flow diagram (figure 4.7) of

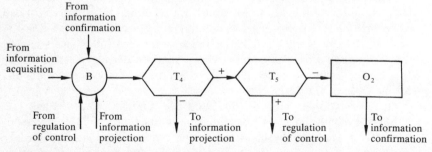

B Begin.
T_4 Is the new information consistent with existing representations?
T_5 Is the new information already present in existing representations?
O_2 Encode new information in external memory or long-term memory.

Figure 4.7. Flow diagram of information-representation process.

the information-representation process consists of two tests, T_4 and T_5, and one operation, O_2. T_4 and T_5 both ask the question about consistency between the information to be represented and the representation at hand or in memory. For the purposes of successful problem-solving this is a critical question. Hunt, in his book, *Artificial Intelligence* (1975), reviews the interaction and agreement between problems and representations selected in solving them. In discussing the representation of problems for the computer he observes (pages 208 – 209)

"Thinkers do not deal with problems directly; they deal with representations of problems. This fact is so commonplace that we do not realize its importance until we attempt to construct a problem-solving program. The program, of course, does not deal with the physical world. It deals with a symbolic representation of the world, on the assumption that there is a translation between symbols and operations on symbols in the computer and states and actions in the external world. The whole of applied mathematics can be looked upon in the same way. Numbers and operations on numbers are used to represent the physical world and actions in it. We first solve the numerical problem and then translate the solution into physical terms. Sometimes the translation is an obvious one. This would be the case, for instance, if we were asked to find the average weight of a football team. We would assign a number to each individual player, corresponding to his weight, do the appropriate arithmetic, and produce an answer. Sometimes the translation is more subtle. Consider the problem of finding an optional route for a school bus. Given any particular route we can calculate the mileage traveled and the time each child spends on the bus. We become uneasy when we attempt to define 'best route' by combining these variables. Should an additional bus be purchased if the average transit time is greater than 15 minutes with only one bus, or should we wait until the transit time is greater than half an hour? How does the price of the bus affect this decision? How do we balance the average transit time for all students against maximum transit time for an individual student? In this example we can measure the individual variables but are uncertain about the meaningfulness of combining operations. In many 'real life' situations the crucial variables themselves may elude measurement. It has been claimed by a number of observers that the failure of United States military policy in Vietnam was because of this. Policy decisions in this conflict seem to have been based upon mathematical models of the 'cost-effectiveness' of the use of different tactics and weapons systems. Effectiveness was measured in terms of the number of target personnel killed, equipment destroyed, and similar quantifiable variables. No satisfactory way was found to measure the social and psychological reactions of either the hostile North Vietnamese or the allied South Vietnamese to the different

military measures. The result was a stunning setback for United
States foreign policy despite many victories in local actions.

The first question we want to ask about a representation, then, is
whether it is a sufficiently accurate model of reality. A second
criterion of the utility of a representation is that it should be one that
the problem solver finds easy to use. 'Easy to use' is a concept
which implies something about the problem solver as well as the
problem. For example, an arithmetician equipped with a slide rule
will find an analog representation of numbers useful for multiplication,
while one equipped with an abacus will use a digital representation.
In artificial intelligence we are often concerned with differences
between those representations which are natural for a human
problem-solver and those suitable for machine problem solving."
In the conclusion of this discourse, Hunt states that representations are
heuristic devices for looking at problems and that good representations
suggest good problem-solving methods (page 212). Thus, newly acquired
information has to be represented in the right form if design is to be
successful. This is supported by the observation that, as new information
is developed by the designer, he or she moves from Venn diagram to
cost analysis, from plan to section, from elevation to perspective,
seeking the best representation in response to incoming information.
Shifting representations can stem either from the incompatibility between
the new information and the present representation, or from the
saturation of representations being worked on so that new information
has no place to go but onto a new representation.

The aim of the two tests T_4 and T_5, in figure 4.7, is to verify these
two conditions. Test T_4 inquires about the compatibility of information
with the representation for which it is designated, and test T_5 compares
the information with the contents of its point of destination. Both tests
pertain to information-retrieval operations that are, although complex,
routine for the cognitive system. Ordinarily, we can expect any designer
to respond to the following questions in a matter of seconds: 'Can you
indicate this entry sequence in elevation E_1?' 'Can you show structure
in plan P_1?' 'Is there a bathroom present in plan P_1?' Where E_1 and P_1
stand for the two drawings (one, the elevation, and the other, the floor
plan), tests T_4 and T_5 are equivalent to the processes that are responsible
for answering these two questions, respectively. The operation O_2 is the
complement of the retrieval operation O_1 we reviewed earlier. O_2 consists
of either the motor behavior of making symbols that stand for the
information at hand: drawing, painting, sketching, model making, or the
packaging, addressing, and storing of information in LTM (this subject is
discussed in detail in chapter 6), or both.

4.3.3 Transformation processes in design

Up to now we have examined only those processes that contribute to the input – output functions of DIPS. Normally, these do not involve any transformation of information. Obviously the information once included in the internal memories of DIPS must be used in a purposeful way to assist in developing design solutions. Since the design process has been represented as a state-space paradigm, there must be ways of transforming new information from one state to the next until a solution state is developed. In other words, DIPS has to manipulate the information that is acquired and represented in its various memories in ways that, after many rounds of transformation, will lead to design solutions.

Many researchers studying human cognitive processes have designed computer programs that simulate such transformations for solving spatial puzzles, mathematical, logical, and physics problems (see Baylor, 1971; Lenat, 1976; Newell and Simon, 1972; Simon and Simon, 1978). In all of these programs a set of finite and formally defined *primitive processes* are used to simulate more complex transformations. Here a similar approach is taken. The architect starts from a set of external representations and performs transformations on these representations to develop the final solution. Thus the process of information transformation in design will be represented through three primitive processes already identified during the analysis of the design protocol in chapter 3: projection of information, confirmation of information, and regulation of control. Let us now review each of these.

4.3.3.1 *Regulation of control*

It is apparent that the designer's search space is as vast as search spaces go. Because of the open-ended nature of design problems, the number of potential alternative choices faced by a designer are too large even to estimate. Consequently, it is necessary to reduce the size of this space during design. This is the primary goal of the process of regulation of control. Ultimately, as the size of the solution space is reduced to a handful of choices, the design solution comes within reach and the task of the regulation process becomes more manageable.

Automated and formal methods of decisionmaking use mathematical tools, such as linear programming and statistical analysis techniques for reducing search spaces. Studies on human problem-solving, however, show that while performing complex tasks subjects use less rigorous methods which have been categorized under the general umbrella of 'weak' methods or *heuristics*. Heuristics help focus the attention of the problem-solver on a portion of the search space which is likely but not guaranteed to contain a solution. In this way the problem-solver can effectively regulate the search without eliminating potentially 'good' solutions from consideration. Also, when heuristics are applied, the designer does not have to commit extensive resources to pruning of the search tree, thus avoiding the risk of wasting time.

One of the primary heuristics used in design is means – end – analysis (MEA). Simon (1969) argues that this is in fact the primary technique of search used in design. In MEA the selection of a method to be used in transforming the problem state at hand is based on the expectations of the problem-solver about the result(s) the method is likely to produce and the constraints implied by the present problem state. Depending on the prior knowledge of what results are desirable and expected, the designer selects the appropriate method of search. MEA, itself, in its generic form constitutes the *control switch* for many other methods of search, such as generate-and-test, hill-climbing, induction, and pattern matching[24]. For our purposes the most suitable form of the regulation process is one that is fashioned after the MEA paradigm (figure 4.8). This allows the inclusion of the other methods of control as individual operations within the body of MEA.

Figure 4.8 shows the anatomy of the MEA process in the form of a flow diagram. Tests T_6 and T_7 represent parts of a larger composite test responsible for matching the methods of search with the goals of DIPS. In general, the goal of the regulation process is to reduce the size of the search space. Test T_6 determines if this goal has ben achieved and if the attention of the designer should be shifted away from its current focus. In the case where the result of T_6 is false, Test T_7 determines if there is any other available method suitable for achieving the goal of the regulation process.

The general goal of the regulation process assumes a more specific form as the results developed by the other primitive processes become available. For instance, the information-representation process may develop the need for selecting a new format for codifying a new piece of information. When control is passed to the regulation process with

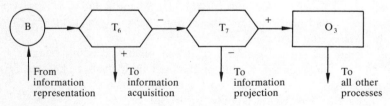

B   Begin.
T_6 Is the problem space reduced by the heuristic method applied?
T_7 Is there an applicable heuristic to reduce the problem space?
O_3 Apply heuristic method.

Figure 4.8. Flow diagram of the regulation-of-control process.

[24] There are methods of search which have been proposed and codified, especially by Reitman (1964) and Newell (1970), for ill-defined problem contexts. Later, in chapter 5, we shall review these methods of search.

this goal in mind, the heuristic methods relevant to the selection of new representations are activated and a selection is made.

When, as a result of tests T_6 and T_7, a heuristic method that can reduce the search space is identified, operation O_3 is activated. Otherwise one of two things takes place.

1 If the problem space is sufficiently reduced, then attention is shifted to external memories to identify what must be done next.

2 If there is no heuristic method applicable then control is passed to the information-projection process. This is equivalent to activating a generate-and-test (GAT) strategy: as new information projection takes place, it alters the present state of the problem then the new information is tested for its consistency against existing information and control returns to the regulation process, completing one full iteration of the GAT cycle.

Thus the sole operator in the regulation process O_3 is actually a compound operation (even a compound process) in itself. For this reason the diagram in figure 4.8, simplified for clarity, is misleading. It does not show what O_3 may potentially involve. For example, when the GAT cycle is activated by O_3, this will involve the other primitive processes; especially projection and confirmation. To understand the real implications of the regulation process, a detailed account of the methods used in design must be provided. Although this will be done in chapter 5, to illustrate how operation O_3 really works, let us now review in some detail an example of a complex search method which can be activated by the regulation process: hill-climbing.

Newell describes hill-climbing (HC) as a specialized form of a GAT (figure 4.9). The problem-solver selects a strategy for the transformation of the problem state q and applies it to the problem state at hand, obtaining a new solution X'. Then X' is compared with the best solution generated so far, X. If X' is better than X, then X' replaces X, otherwise the problem-solver discards X' and applies q once more to the present problem state. The process continues in an iterative fashion until the best solution at hand cannot be improved any longer.

Problem statement
Given a comparison of two elements of a set $\{X\}$ to determine which is greater;
a set of operators $\{q\}$ whose range and domain is $\{X\}$ [that is, $q(X) = X'$, another element of $\{X\}$].
Find the greatest $X \in \{X\}$.

Procedure

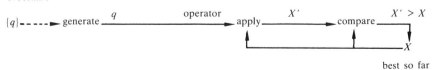

Figure 4.9. Hill-climbing (from Newell, 1970).

Using this as the control mechanism in design involves the processes of projection ('apply' in Newell's terms) and confirmation ('compare' in Newell's terms) of information as integral parts of the regulation process. That is, when activated, HC involves these two processes as subparts of regulation of control, and a hierarchical relationship is established between these processes. The passage of control between these primitive processes must be determined by the regulation process, which itself is another primitive process. This contradicts the structural make-up of DIPS. Ideally, all primitive processes are to coexist as modular units and interact through simple input–output mechanisms internal to each one. As the task of one process is complete, control is expected to pass to another process and so on. The HC, like the GAT and like many other complex methods of problem-solving, engages the other primitive processes as subprocess under the umbrella of the regulation process. This violates the principle of modularity.

The solution to this apparent contradiction in DIPS is also inherent in its modular structure. Consider the most drastic conflict that may result from this. Let us assume that the normal course of actions during HC dictates that after comparison of X' and X, control must be passed to the projection process. During the undertaking of this comparison let us also assume that the confirmation process recommends that control be passed to the representation process. This will create a conflict in the DIPS control structure. What will the regulation process do next? Will it pass control to projection or to confirmation? The resolution of the problem is possible if the conflict is treated as *new information* and is simply fed into the confirmation process, requiring that it be resolved as the case might be with any other case of inconsistency between data. It is assumed that the conflicts that arise in processing are no different from conflicts that arise from the data which are a part of the problem-solver's agenda. Since most ill-defined questions in design bear resemblance to these more informal and conflict-ridden questions of processing, their resolution should not present qualitatively different problems for DIPS.

The relationship of the thermostat to the heater in the example provided in chapter 2 is a good metaphor for the relationship of the regulation process to the other primitive processes. As the thermostat senses excess heat or lack of it in the environment, it activates the heater or shuts it off. The regulation process similarly develops the agenda for the other processes and activates them in accordance with the 'plan' implied in the heuristic methods available to it. In turn, these processes alter the problem state through their behaviors (just like the heater altering the temperature of the environment) resulting in new actions in the regulation process (or the thermostat for that matter).

4.3.3.2 *Projection of information*

The workhorse of all transformations in DIPS is the projection-of-information process. The paradigm it represents is inductive reasoning disguised in the informality of everyday inference making. Later, in chapters 6 and 7, this process will be elaborated in detail. For now, an example will suffice. In the protocol episode we examined earlier the designer states, "It [entering the carriage house at a level below the existing ground level] would solve the entry problem" (table 3.5). Here the designer goes from a physical configuration, that of placing the new construction under the existing garage to an assertion about expected performance: that the physical configuration solves the entry problem. How is this possible? How does the spatial relationship of two functional levels (one a garage and the other a residence) translate into a functional idea?

It is clear that the evaluation is only possible after transforming the physical relationship into a functional idea. Otherwise the evaluation would be of a physical sort, such as 'this is too vertical' or 'this is like a basement' as opposed to functional assertions such as 'this solves the entry problem' or 'this responds to privacy'. Here we must conclude that one set of relationships (physical) are transformed into another (functional). This functional description is then assessed to satisfy a general functional requirement, that is entry. Consider the following statements:

$$\text{new construction (NC)} \xrightarrow{\text{is under (U)}} \text{existing garage (EG)}, \qquad (4.1)$$

therefore,

$$\text{new construction (NC)} \xrightarrow{\text{is coplanar with (C)}} \text{major street (MS)}, \qquad (4.2)$$

therefore,

$$\text{new construction (NC)} \xrightarrow{\text{is accessible from (A)}} \text{major street (MS)}. \qquad (4.3)$$

To understand the logical steps that allow these inferences to occur, let us consider some spatial tautologies. Figure 4.10 represents three planar areas and their relationships that are analogous to the two floor areas, the major street, and the relationships that exist between them.

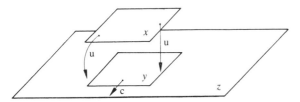

Figure 4.10. Planes *x*, *y*, *z*, with relationships: u(above or below), p(coplanar).

Here we can observe that

if $y \xrightarrow{u} x$, then $y \xrightarrow{\sim c} x$,

if $z \xrightarrow{u} x$, then $z \xrightarrow{\sim c} x$,

if $y \xrightarrow{c} z$, then $y \xrightarrow{\sim u} z$,

where u is defined as 'is under', and c is defined as 'is coplanar with', and $\sim$ means 'is not'.

Notice that although c and $\sim$c relationships are reflexive the u and $\sim$u relationships are not. A general consistency that underlies these observations is that u and c are inversely related. That is, when x is under y, x is also not coplanar with y; and when x is coplanar with y, x is also not under y. An equivalency between relationship u and $\sim$c as well as between c and $\sim$u holds as a general rule. We can express this principle as a formal rule of substitution:

if $x \xrightarrow{u} y$, and u $= \sim$c, then $x \xrightarrow{\sim c} y$,

or

if $x \xrightarrow{c} y$, and c $= \sim$u, then $x \xrightarrow{\sim u} y$.

Another general consistency we can observe in a universe of only two possible positions in the z-dimension, as shown in figure 4.10, is a formal rule of transitivity:

if $x \xrightarrow{u} y$, and $z \xrightarrow{u} y$, then $x \xrightarrow{c} z$.

That is, if planes x and z are both under plane y and at the same distance from it, then x and z must be coplanar. Applying these rules of transformation to statement (4.4) we can obtain statements (4.5) and (4.6).

$$NC \xrightarrow{U} EG, \text{ and } MS \xrightarrow{U} EG. \hspace{2cm} (4.4)$$

Using the rule of transitivity we obtain

$$NC \xrightarrow{C} MS. \hspace{2cm} (4.5)$$

Assuming equivalency between coplanarity (C) and accessibility (A), in this particular case, we can substitute A for C and obtain the predicate we are trying to derive:

$$NC \xrightarrow{A} MS. \hspace{2cm} (4.6)$$

In all of these transformations we start with a present state and work towards a goal state. Often the present state can be expressed as a relation of the kind NC $\xrightarrow{U}$ EG. The goal state, on the other hand, can be a combination of constants and variables. That is, the designer may wish to know more about something as a part of the goal (for example, whether or not a location is good for the new construction), or more about the accessibility into the building as planned. We can express these as:

$$\text{NC} \xrightarrow{C} X, \text{ and } \text{NC} \xrightarrow{A} X, \qquad (4.7)$$

where C and A indicate spatial and access relationships, respectively, and X is a variable. Studies of syllogistic reasoning (Clark and Chase, 1973) and conceptual inference making (Shank, 1975) suggest that the mechanics of this process consist of finding rules of transformation in LTM that either match the *premise* (initial state) or the *implication* (goal state) or both. Figure 4.11 shows how this takes place. First, LTM is searched to find if there are rules that match the implications desired. For example, both the rules of substitution (4.6) and transitivity (4.4) match the implication: NC $\xrightarrow{A} X$. This test is undertaken by test T_8 in figure 4.11. Since in this case the result is ambiguous, the designer

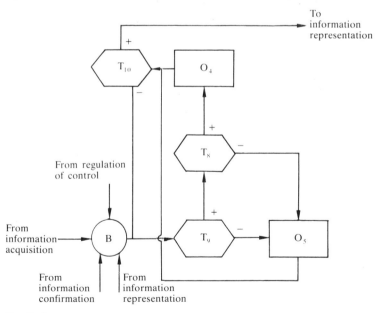

B   Begin
T_8 Are there premises that are applicable?
T_9 Are there implications that are applicable?
T_{10} Is the new predicate developed?
O_4 Change implication given.
O_5 Change implication desired.

Figure 4.11 Flow diagram of information-projection process.

applies a second test, $T_9^{(25)}$. Here LTM is searched to find if there is a rule that also has a matching premise. For example such a search, because of the isomorphism that is apparent, will find a match between:

$$x \xrightarrow{u} y, z \xrightarrow{u} y \text{ and } NC \xrightarrow{U} EG, MS \xrightarrow{U} EG .$$

Since this is actually a match with the rule of transitivity the rule is applied (operation O_4) and the new relationship (4.5) is inferred:

$$NC \xrightarrow{C} MS.$$

This now can be substituted in the current premise. Next, test T_{10} checks if the desired implication is achieved. The substitution rule provides a perfect match, hence it is applied and the new premise (4.7) is generated:

$$NC \xrightarrow{A} MS,$$

which passes test T_{10} and the projection process successfully terminates. Control is returned to the representation process, for the encoding of the new relationship.

In the likelihood that there is no rule in LTM which matches the implication, the implication of the goal can be altered. This is equivalent to the designer modifying the goal (operation O_5). If, for example, the goal of the designer was to determine whether or not the access at the level below the garage will be more costly than all other access alternatives, then it is likely that the designer will be unsuccessful. That is, he will try to find a match with the predicate:

$$NC \xrightarrow{F} X,$$

where F is the cost of access. Short of doing a detailed site analysis, he will find no match that applies to the current site and the location of NC. Consequently, he will have to alter the goal to a more realistic one, such as:

$$NC \xrightarrow{A} X,$$

which is the premise of the earlier example.

4.3.3.3 *Confirmation of information*
Each implication generated in the projection process does not necessarily turn out to be consistent with previously acquired knowledge. For example, consider statement (4.3):

$$NC \xrightarrow{A} MS : \text{new construction (NC) is accessible (A) from major street (MS).}$$

(25) Observe that combining T_8 and T_9 into a composite test, T_8' can make the configuration of the flow diagram in figure 4.11 more parsimonious.

Although this premise helps the designer conclude that the accessibility of the new construction is satisfactory from the ground level, elsewhere he has concluded that the cost of the new construction is excessive. In spite of the fact that its economics are entirely unfavorable, from a point of view of utility to users this alternative can lead to a favorable evaluation. Detecting such inconsistencies is the primary purpose of the information-confirmation process. To avoid generation of inconsistent representations, the validity and consistency of newly projected information must always be verified in the context of existing information.

First, the plausibility of each new implication must be checked against all known information with which it can potentially be in conflict. The primary purpose of the confirmation process is to find previously acquired information, that may potentially be in conflict with newly acquired information, and to check for consistency between them. If no conflicts are found, then the new information is stored as a part of the existing information; otherwise, either the new or the old information must be altered, by means of the projection process.

Let us now show how the flow diagram in figure 4.12 represents the confirmation process. The first thing that happens is the retrieval of information against which new information must be compared (Operation O_6). This is equivalent to identifying all potential conflicts between two chunks of information. For example, if the new information relates to large spans and unusual materials and construction techniques, then its implications must be verified against cost information. If, on the other hand, the new information designates something about layout, then it must be assessed in terms of constraints relating to orientation, proximity, circulation, and access. In the case of multiple constraints, the comparisons have to be done successively and exhaustively.

Next, test T_{11} is applied. This test shows whether there is a conflict present between new and existing information. If there is no conflict, test T_{12} [26] determines whether other categories of information exist

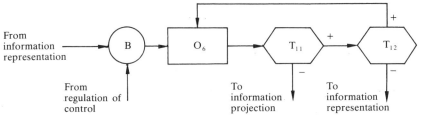

B Begin
T_{11} Is the new information in agreement with existing information?
T_{12} Any other existing information against which new information must be checked?
O_6 Retrieve existing information potentially in conflict with the new.

Figure 4.12. Flow diagram of information-confirmation process.

[26] Observe that combining tests T_{11} and T_{12} into a composite test, T'_{11} has the effect of greater parsimony in the representation of the process in figure 4.12.

against which to compare the new information. If so, the cycle repeats; if not, control is passed to the representation process so that the new information can be codified either in LTM or EM. If, on the other hand, test T_{11} finds a conflict, then the conflict must be resolved by modifying either the new information or the existing information in question. This, of course, calls for the activation of the projection process, once the new information is requested.

4.4 Process sequences
Above the five primitive processes of design have been defined and illustrated. Although each process is adequate in performing a specific task, none of them alone is sufficient to account for the totality of the design process. The integration of these individual processes into a whole is necessary before we can determine how DIPS accounts for design. It must be obvious by now that having represented these processes in flow-diagram form with inputs and outputs connecting each one to the others, makes it easy to assemble them into a single flow diagram (figure 4.13).

Although this composite flow diagram provides a comprehensive and accurate picture of DIPS, it is not easily understandable. Let us

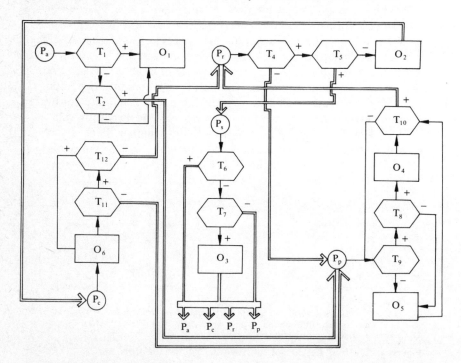

Figure 4.13. DIPS (design information processing system): flow diagram showing all five primitive processes.

disaggregate figure 4.13 into a new form where each process is shown as simple nodes labelled P_r, P_a, P_c, P_s, P_p, to correspond to representation, acquisition, confirmation, regulation of control (search), and projection, respectively. The lines connecting these nodes are interpreted as directional links showing the flow of control from one to the next (figure 4.14).

To demonstrate that this paradigm adequately accounts for design behavior, we have to convince ourselves that (a) there is a formally describable set of behaviors predicted by DIPS, (b) there is a formally described set of behaviors observed during design, and (c) there is a significant agreement between these two sets. Let us now apply these criteria against the structure indicated in figure 4.14.

Figure 4.14 allows certain strings of successively applied processes to be possible while excluding others. As indicated in graphic form, some, but not all, processes have direct connections between. Table 4.1 shows in matrix format all processes to which control is permitted to pass from other processes. Pluses represent connections from the processes labelled in the left-hand column to those labelled at the topmost column. And the zeros represent the absence of connections. This means that control can be passed in certain sequences, for example, $P_a \rightarrow P_r \rightarrow P_s \rightarrow P_a \rightarrow P_p \rightarrow P_r$ or $P_p \rightarrow P_r \rightarrow P_c \rightarrow P_p \rightarrow P_r$ and *not* in certain other sequences, for example, $P_c \rightarrow P_a \rightarrow P_c \rightarrow P_s$ or $P_p \rightarrow P_c \rightarrow P_r$.

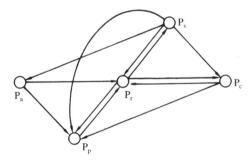

Figure 4.14. Directional links showing flow of control.

Table 4.1. Legal process transitions.

From	To				
	P_r	P_a	P_c	P_s	P_p
P_r		0	+	+	+
P_a	+		0	0	+
P_c	+	0		0	+
P_s	+	+	+		+
P_p	+	0	0	0	

The connections allowed in DIPS are a smaller set than all possible connections that could potentially occur between the five processes. On the assumption that all possible connections between the five processes exist, and given any one of the five choices, there are four more choices left: five times four choices allows twenty paired combinations in total. Hence, with five processes there are a total of twenty possible pairwise connections. The matrix in table 4.1, on the other hand, restricts this to twelve pairs (hence the total of twelve pluses shown in the matrix). On the average, then, this means that there are 2.4 choices available after each process at any given time.

With five processes and a chain of processes N-long, the number of unique process sequences can be calculated using the formula:

$$P_i = NK^{w-1} ,$$

where
P_i is the number of unique process sequences possible,
N is the total number of processes
K is the average number of links from any one process,
w is the number of processes included in a chain.
Table 4.2 shows the magnitude of P as a function of K, for $N = 5$. Thus, by definition, DIPS severely limits the number of legal sequences that are allowed by limiting K to 2.4.

The next set of questions we have to answer are how can we characterize designers' behaviors in the terms defined by these process sequences, and how well do these sequences account for the observed behavior? In the following chapters, I will attempt to answer these questions.

Table 4.2. Number of unique process sequences (P) as a function of the average number of links from any one process (K) and the number of processes included in a chain (total number of processes, N, is 5).

w	P_1 (for $K = 4$)	P_2 (for $K = 2.4$)	P_3 (for $K = 1$)
1	5	5	5
2	20	12	5
3	80	29	5
4	320	69	5
10	1 310 720	13 209	5

4.5 Suggested readings

1 Akın Ö, 1978b, "How do architects design?" in *Artificial Intelligence and Pattern Recognition in Computer-aided Design* Ed. J-C Latombe (North Holland, New York) pp 65–104
2 Akın Ö, Reddy R, 1977, "Knowledge acquisition for image understanding research" *Journal of Computer Graphics and Image Processing* **6** 307–334

3 Akın Ö, 1982b, "Representation and architecture" in *Representation and Architecture* Eds Ö Akın, E Weinel, Maryland: Information Dynamics Inc, 111 Claybrook Drive, Silver Springs, MD 20902, pp 1–26

4.6 Exercises

4.1 Select a personal experience in which inference making is explicitly used to make a decision.

(a) Write out a chain of rewriting rules illustrating a possible sequence of inferences characterizing this experience. State the rules in if–then form.

(b) Construct a different chain of inferences connecting the initial rule to the final rule of the answer to 4.1(a) using a different set of rules in between.

(c) Discuss the generality and parsimony of these rules in each case.

4.2 Write a chain of rewriting rules to illustrate means–end-analysis for the following tasks

(a) selecting the mode(s) of transportation from your home to the White House, Washington, DC.

(b) selecting the new finishes for the redecoration of your room. Assume that a rich uncle is subsidizing the cost of redecoration up to $1 000.

Search in Design

"What, in fact, is mathematical discovery? It does not consist in making new combinations with mathematical entities that are already known. That can be done by anyone, and the combinations that could be so formulated would be infinite in number, and the greater part of them would be absolutely devoid of interest. Discovery consists precisely in not constructing useless combinations, but in constructing those that are useful, which are in infinitely small minority. Discovery is discernment, selection."

H Poincaré *Science and Method* (1952, pages 50–51)

What Poincaré has proposed for scientific discovery is equally applicable for discovery in design. By discovery I mean the act of finding solutions, or partial solutions, to design problems. It should be clear even to the beginner in design that a solution cannot be obtained by systematic and exhaustive combination of all architectural components at one's disposal. Such an undertaking is beyond the means of feasibility. Because there is not a single set of constraints which can be taken a priori, each design constraint presents a new design problem, in turn, leading to new constraints to be considered. The solutions for each subproblem introduce new considerations for the overall problem. As Poincaré points out, solutions lie on paths which can be followed only through discernment or selection. The purpose of this chapter is to describe some of these paths.

5.1 Codifying the design process

In exploring the design process, the primitive processes defined and substantiated in chapters 3 and 4 will be used as a taxonomy. That is, the behaviors of designers under observation will be codified using the primitive processes and the sequential patterns they create. The method of observation to be used is protocol analysis (see appendix A.1). Since this technique has been discussed earlier, let us begin with the experiments used in this exploration.

The intent of the experiments was to study design in its unabridged and realistic form. Therefore, four architects and teachers of architecture were asked to participate as subjects in the experiments. All subjects were asked to design a single-person dwelling. Video recordings of each session were made. The design problem was specified using two alternative programs developed in an earlier experiment. Two of the subjects designed on a sloped site overlooking an industrial park near the Allegheny River in Pittsburgh, PA (figure 5.1). The client for this problem was a single male college professor. The other two subjects designed a carriage house over an existing garage, located in a residential area in the city of Pittsburgh (figure 3.3) for the use of a blind teacher.

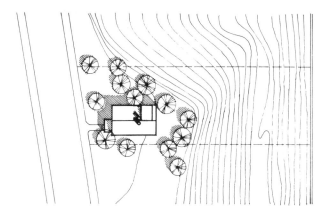

Figure 5.1. Site-plan used in the design protocol.

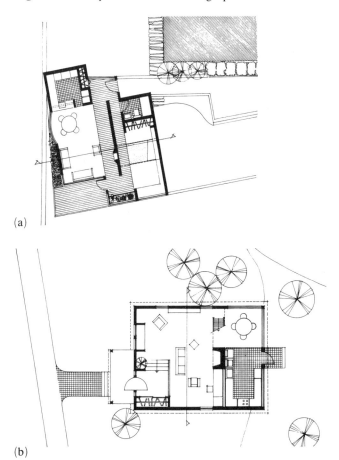

(a)

(b)

Figure 5.2. Solutions to the (a) blind teacher and (b) university teacher problems.

Figure 5.2 shows an example solution in both problem categories generated by subjects 1 and 3, respectively.

The protocols consisted of two kinds of data: recordings of subjects' verbalizations and the notes and sketches they made during the experiment. To use the terminology defined in chapter 3, both types of data can be interpreted as representing two distinct categories of information: (a) focus of attention of subjects during the design process on *tokens* (defined in section 3.3.2.1) and their *attributes* (defined in section 3.3.2.2) and (b) the primitive *processes* (defined in section 3.3.2.3) of design the subjects used in manipulating these tokens and attributes within their focus.

5.1.1 Codifying the designer's focus of attention

Focus of attention of subjects is used here as an intuitive notion referring to the act of mental concentration. This focus can be characterized in reference to the subject's verbalizations and sketches which explicitly identify specific parts of the design. Often these parts correspond to *tokens* or *schemata* which are distinguishable elements of buildings: columns, rooms, windows, doors, and so on. At other times relationships between these tokens and their *attributes* are focused on, such as, the orientation of the bedroom, furnishings of the dining room, and adjacency of the kitchen to the dining room, and so on.

Whenever drawings or utterances referring to the tokens and their relationships were observed in the protocols it was assumed that the subject's attention was focused on these parts of the problem. Interpreted in this fashion, the data suggested generalizable patterns that follow from the subject's behaviors. At times the attributes of tokens seemed to have a hierarchical relationship to the tokens. Orientation, adjacency, size, and shape were attributes frequently observed within the span of the designer's focus on a single token, say bedroom, bathroom, or dining table. At other times a hierarchical relationship between tokens was implied by spatial definition: bedroom being part of the 'private' half of the house, the private half being part of the whole house, and the house being part of the site.

To show the overall pattern of the subjects' focus of attention a representation called problem description graph (PDG) was used, see figure 5.3. The information needed to construct a PDG is the part–whole relationship that relates tokens and their attributes. This information was extracted from the protocols in their temporal order of occurrence. The following procedure was used to develop the PDG:

1 Assign all tokens or attributes that are not nested in any other part, to the top level, or level 1, in the PDG.

2 Assign each remaining token or attribute that is nested inside others already assigned to a level of the PDG to the next lower level. Initially, any token or attribute can receive an assignment to more than one level.

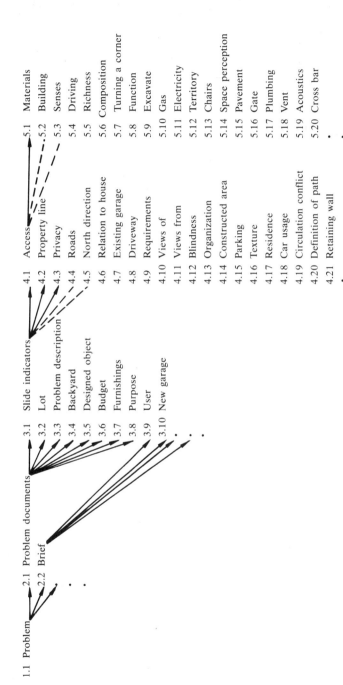

Figure 5.3. Problem description graph; for brevity only a small portion of the nodes and links are included.

3 When all tokens or attributes are assigned, make a singular assignment
for each token to the lowest level of assignment they have received so far.
Figure 5.3 illustrates a partial PDG for subject 1. The nodes indicate
the tokens or attributes and the links indicate part–whole relationships
between them. The numbers assigned to each link show the sequence in
which the subject actually focused his attention on the nodes. The PDG
provides a precise codification of the decomposition of the designed
object and the sequence in which the subject focuses on each part.
Let us now examine the same data from the viewpoint of the search
processes used in design.

5.1.2 Codifying the primitive design processes

The behavior of the designer can be codified using a taxonomy very
different from the one defined above. The primitive processes of design
already defined in chapters 3 and 4—acquisition (P_a), representation (P_r),
projection (P_p), confirmation (P_c) of information, and regulation of
control (P_s)—are best suited for this purpose. This taxonomy, unlike
that of the designer's focus of attention, permits the representation of
the design process at a very detailed level, accounting for processes
at the order of 4 seconds on the average, each of which corresponds to
the 'tactics' used by designers. To codify the data in this form, however,
a set of operationally defined rules of data transcription are necessary.
The following criteria were developed for this purpose.
1 When the subject asks a question, visually examines an external
source, or simply remembers a general fact from memory, for example
'house costs are running in the neighborhood of $40.00 per square foot'
it is assumed that he or she is *acquiring* information.
2 When the subject draws, writes, or simply verbalizes a piece of
information which is used later in the protocol it is assumed that he or
she is *representing* information.
3 When the subject transforms a given piece of information into a
different format, for example, 'so 40 into 25 000', or 'we can say it's a
two-car garage', he or she is *projecting* information.
4 When the subject comments on the validity or correctness of a piece
of information, for example, 'it would take an assessment of the
property to determine correctness of the assumption', it is assumed that
he or she is *confirming* the consistency of this information with respect
to other things known. At times the subject terminates some trains of
thought abruptly, for example, 'Well, in the $1250.00 is ...' or 'Well, could
be figured in relation to ...'. It is assumed that at such times, he or she
has discovered some inconsistencies in reasoning as a result of the
confirmation process.
5 When the subject comments about what must be done next with
respect to the task being performed, such as 'But what must I do, for
lack of information, is to accept that cost of design to be $35,000.00', it

is assumed that he or she is *regulating control* over behavior, to narrow the scope of the search space. Not all instances in this category assume explicit form.

Using these criteria, portions of each protocol can be codified as sequences of one or more instances of these five primitive processes. When evidence for one process exists immediately after the evidence for another one is found in the data, with no interruptions in between, these two processes are assumed to be connected. Any one of three conditions is considered to be an interruption:

1 *Discontinuous data*: complete inactivity exceeding five seconds (corresponding to a break in the data and implying a similar discontinuity in the subject's train of thought).

2 *Unexplained data*: behaviour that does not correspond to any of the criteria outlined above.

3 *Nonconformity to the a priori model*: the connection between the two processes does not match the set of legal process connections: that is, P_a to P_r, P_c to P_r, P_s to P_r, P_p to P_r, P_s to P_a, P_s to P_c, P_s to P_p, P_r to P_s, P_r to P_p, P_a to P_p (figure 4.14 of chapter 4). This is attributed to erroneous categorization of data during transcription.

The data were first broken into segments of linear lists of primitive processes using conditions 1 and 2 alone. On the average, a total of 164.2 such process sequences were observed in each protocol. Only 24 or 14.6% of these violated condition 3. After using condition 3 for further dissection of these process sequences a total of 222.1 process sequences were codified, 24.5% of these were singular processes and were disqualified from analysis. The remaining 75.5% met all the conditions listed above and are summarized in graphic form in figure 5.7. From here on these graphs shall be called process sequence graphs (PSG) and their implications for search will be discussed in the following sections.

Now let us consider the question of validity of this method of transcription for the data. What is the likelihood that the process sequences codified in this way indeed constitute behavior predicted by DIPS in the model indicated in figure 4.13. To answer this question let us consider the matrix in table 4.1 which indicates the frequency of all process transitions observed in the subjects' protocols. Entries with zeros in this matrix show those process transitions which are not legal as determined by the connections between primitive processes of figure 4.13.

Ideally, all transitions between these processes observed in the protocols should correspond to those cells of the matrix in table 4.1 which are not marked by zeroes. Similarly, the zero cells should correspond to no observed transitions whatsoever. However, the actual observations deviate from this prediction: 140.2 observations (mean) fall in the predicted categories while 24.0 (mean) do not. These correspond to the type 3 discontinuity defined above. Ideally, for a total of 164.2 observations these means should have been 164.2 and 0.0, respectively. Such a distribution corresponds to all observations falling in categories as predicted by the a priori model in figure 4.13. On close examination, however, observed means did not deviate significantly from these a priori means[27]. In spite of some deviation from the predicted norm, the observed frequencies are probabilistically consistent with the a priori model. This suggests, furthermore, that the agreement between the distribution of the observed sequences and the predicted process sequences is not caused by chance, and the agreement between the model and the data cannot be explained by random coincidence.

5.2 Global search methods

It is useful at this point to distinguish between those methods of search that apply to the entire protocol as opposed to those that are localized to relatively short segments. This is because methods that reside over the total design process have different characteristics from those applied only locally. They allow the nesting of local methods within, relinquishing control to local processes from time to time, but nevertheless regulating the overall pattern of search. For example, the overall pattern of shift of focus of attention can be explained only through designers' global objectives and not those specific to limited segments of the protocol. Alternatively, it is possible to argue that these global behaviors are manifested as a result of the methods applied locally and their sequence of application. If the first explanation is true, then we must expect a degree of independence between the points of inflection in the global behaviors of the designer and the patterns of behavior generated through local methods. If the second explanation is true, then we must expect to see a degree of correlation between local and global patterns of behavior. As will be clear later, the evidence in this study supports the first assertion.

Let us now explore each category more carefully. Global strategies of search are those patterns that can only be detected through the examination of the complete protocol. A useful device for accomplishing this is the PDG. By following the (part–whole) links in the graph (figure 5.3) in chronological order, one can retrace the designer's search patterns that apply to the whole protocol, as well as to the individual tokens and their attributes.

5.2.1 Depth-first search

First of all, we see that subjects traverse the PDG in *depth* as well as in *breadth*. Initially, they spend some time examining each of the handful of top nodes and only their immediate siblings. After they have

[27] The means were compared statistically using the *t*-test both for legal ($t = 0.5747$, $N = 5$) and for illegal ($t = 2.0395$, $N = 5$) transitions.

completed this breadth-wise search, they take each parent node and dwell on all of its siblings nearly exhaustively.

Depth-first search can be characterized as the allocation of designer's attention to the siblings of a parent[28] node before moving to the next parent node of the same depth in a tree-like search space, such as the one in figure 5.3. For example, consider the PDG of subject 1 in figure 5.3. In depth-first search, the nodes in this tree would be visited in the following sequence: 1.1 problem, 2.1 problem documents, 3.1 slide indicators, 4.1 access, 5.1 materials, 5.2 building, 4.2 property line, 4.3 privacy, and so on. This implies that the designer does not move to a next major issue, or another parent node such as the 'brief', before exploring all siblings of the current issue, 'problem documents', 'lot', 'problem description', and so on. In terms of the potential success of a search process, the depth-first strategy has some important implications. As a search method in tree-like or lattice-like networks, depth-first search (a) does not guarantee optimal search of the tree, (b) does not insure finding a solution, and (c) does not insure a balance of emphasis between multiple issues of equal priority that may be implied by the levels of the tree structure. On the other hand, it is a popular method especially for human problem-solvers (Hunt, 1975).

This is a conclusion which cannot be readily applied to designers. To eliminate segments of the search space not likely to contain a solution, it is necessary to compare the potential success of each path in the PDG. This is tantamount to considering alternative approaches, or traversing the problem space, in breadth. Taking a particular aspect of the problem and consistently studying it in lieu of others (as dictated by search in depth) eliminates any possibility of this comparison taking place. Imagine the designer who studies the question of construction alone: developing system details, door–window schedules, material and finish selections, without any consideration for the structural requirements, user-occupancy needs, or site conditions that may influence the selection of construction materials and methods. What are his or her chances of completing the design in a reasonable time period? The designer's efforts with the most optimistic of assumptions may exhaust all that can possibly be considered in the area of building construction; only to find, on moving to another major component of the design problem, say site conditions, that many of the decisions about material selection are infeasible because of soil conditions. Investigation of major components of the design problem early in the process is necessary to insure an acceptable level of consistency between various design decisions.

Depth-first search becomes even more inefficient if the branches of the search tree being examined contain cyclic paths or are very large.

---

[28] A *parent* node is a node from which several branches connect to lower nodes. These lower nodes are called the *siblings* of the parent node.

An in-depth investigation of such a design problem may render a design infeasible. This will occur when the information needed for the investigation is either *open-ended* (such as construction methods and materials) or *nondecomposable* (as in the dialectic relationship that exists between occupancy and physical environment or cost and aesthetics). The designer using only depth-first search will oscillate endlessly between the two ideas or will be lost in an almost infinitely large branch of the tree.

Last, even if we have a problem where cyclic and open-ended conditions do not exist, depth-first search still presents a major obstacle in achieving optimality through a sequential decisionmaking process. As one selects a construction method, then a structural span, and then a room layout, each decision working off from the constraints of the earlier decisions, it is virtually impossible to insure optimality. Each new decision has to work with a narrow set of alternatives defined, often arbitrarily, as a function of earlier decisions. To achieve optimality, earlier decisions must be made with cognizance of the decisions to follow. This requires parallel investigation which is not possible in depth-first search.

Studies of experts' search behavior, however, seem to work against this theoretical bias. Newell and Simon (1965) observed that master chess players used a modified depth-first strategy. Hunt (1975) also reports on subjects' preference for depth-first over breadth-first search. The anomaly is perhaps not as puzzling as it sounds. These counterexamples come from experts working in problem domains which are obviously very well understood. It is evident that experts, having traversed the same problem domain countless times, have developed specialized knowledge that enables them to deal with interdependencies between different parts of the PDG without explicitly visiting each top node in a breadth-first manner. That is through their a priori knowledge of different branches of the tree they can compensate for the inherent difficulties of depth-first search. One way of doing this is to anticipate the constraints that occur elsewhere in the tree. In design, however, problems vary considerably, from one instance to the next reducing the designers degree of 'expertise' in relation to the domain of each problem. Consequently, as we shall observe below, depth-first search is not the only type to be observed in design.

5.2.2 Breadth-first search

Upon embarking on the design task, subject 1 immediately allocates his attention horizontally rather than in-depth (figure 5.3). This represents *breadth-first search*. The sequence in which the nodes are visited using a pure breadth-first strategy are: 1.1 problem, 2.1 problem documents, 2.2 brief, and so on; 3.1 slide indicators, 3.2 lot, 3.3 problem description, 3.4 backyard, and so on; 4.1 access, 4.2 property line, 4.3 privacy, and so on; 5.1 materials, 5.2 building, and so on. Although this is not the pattern of behavior which dominates our data, the breadth-first strategy is used by all subjects to advantage.

Consider a design problem for which strong typological solutions exist. The speculative high-rise office building, for example, can be successfully resolved by selecting a solution type from a handful of archetypal plan organizations that respond to a few critical constraints of the problem: maximum rentable floor space and minimum investment. A depth-first search of the same problem domain would undoubtedly result in much greater effort being expended towards reinventing some of these archetypes. This requires a thorough knowledge of the performance of many building types in terms of the efficiency of circulation, structure, energy use, and construction materials. But in breadth-first search, little time is needed for each one of these categories initially. Once the suitable type is identified, all of the remaining effort is allocated to that type. This means that the designer has to study each problem component in a lateral sequence, not allowing himself or herself the opportunity to search any one component in great depth, before identifying a solution type and constraining the problem further.

The advantages of breadth-first search over depth-first search are largely a result of the greater likelihood of finding a solution in a shorter time, especially when there is a large repertoire of prototypical solutions available. In fact, the dominant pattern of behavior in the PDGs of the protocols analyzed here indicate a predominant pattern of behavior: breadth-first search, followed by a depth-first search. This pattern is typical for the duration of the four-hour protocol.

5.2.3 Satisficing solutions

Another important global mechanism observed in the protocols, *satisficing solutions*, has to do with the pattern of application of evaluation criteria. All subjects explored only a handful of alternative solutions initially. Subsequently they selected one of these solutions for detailed development. In all cases only one alternative was examined in detail and the selection made was never subsequently reversed. Although the protocols constitute only a small sample of the overall design process, it should be obvious to anyone with design experience that only a small portion of all possible solutions can be considered, even when design goes on for much longer periods of time.

In design there are simply too many points of departure to generate, let alone examine, all possible solutions. Rapoport (1969) discusses the notion of *criticality* as a function of the freedom available to the designer in making personal choices as opposed to satisfying explicit constraints.

For instance, during the premodern era (prior to the turn of the century) very few technological options existed in achieving large clear spans in buildings. Today the options are almost unlimited: truss, tensile, shell, pneumatic, and spaceframe structures constitute a few classes of alternatives. Similarly, today sophisticated environmental control techniques allow building forms which would have been climatically uninhabitable in the past. As new building technologies become available, the criticality of design constraints diminishes and the extent of freedom in choice of alternative solutions increases. On the other hand, as buildings become more complex users become more demanding, constraints increase, and thus greater criticality results. Often technological innovations are seen as means of relief from this increasing criticality. This notion is significant in understanding how designers search their solution space and use style as a mechanism for balancing this formula.

Presently there is proliferation of architectural styles[29]. Style underscores the need to reduce the number of alternatives to be considered; and reinforces the use of personal constraints as mechanisms, albeit artificial ones, for increasing criticality. Another way of saying the same thing is that most contemporary stylistic 'theories' are aimed at developing systems of constraints which can be imposed on the design problem and reduce the uncomfortably large number of degrees of freedom which have been created by technological advances and breakthroughs. Eclecticism, mannerism, historicism, and postmodernism are some of the more recent stylistic trends that introduce new and alternative systems of constraints on design. The net result of this is that decisions are made within more limited or constrained problem domains, and the architect feels less ill at ease reducing a solution domain containing many viable solutions to a single choice. The average architect indulges in the preachings of the new styles for many different reasons. However, the pragmatic outcome of this is that the architect acquires an a priori palette of forms dictated by the style.

The methodological role of reducing designer's choices to a limited palette is significant in dealing with the differences between well-defined problems and design problems. Simon (1969) makes a distinction between methods suitable for well-defined problems, that is, *optimization*, and the alternative suitable for ill-defined problems, that is, *satisficing*. He argues that in well-defined problem domains there is either a unique or an optimal solution with respect to an objective function that is specified a priori. In design, however, there are no means of finding optimal solutions, let alone objective function(s) with which to optimize. Consequently, in design another metric of evaluation is used, that of satisfying a given set

[29] This era of 'theoretical' proliferation in architecture is best represented by the 'postmodernist' movement symbolized by Jenks's book entitled *The Language of Post-modern Architecture* (1978).

of minimum criteria. This is manifested in present architectural practice
through the development of criteria using stylistic preconceptions.

Piano and Rodgers's Centre Georges Pompidou and Charles Moore's
Plazza D'Italia in New Orleans are two well-known examples where this
relationship between the realm of the possible and the language of the
limited palette are creatively exploited. In the first case the mechanical
systems are turned inside out: establishing a technological style as a
benchmark, thus a criteria of evaluation (figure 5.4). This sets up the
limited hi-tech palette, confining the search space of the designer within
manageable bounds. The choices of the fenestration, interior organization,
and partitions are all determined through the style of the overall design.
Similarly, Moore and associates use the juxtaposition of the classical
styles with contemporary finishes to exploit new frontiers in the realm
of the 'possible' (figure 5.5); and in the same move they restrict their

Figure 5.4. Centre Georges Pompidou, Paris, France, by Architects Piano and
Rodgers.

Figure 5.5. Plazza D'Italia, New Orleans, by Architects Charles Moore and Perez
Associates.

palette to the classical orders. Given that the typical architectural problem formulated in the typical architect's office is underconstrained[30], then the method for determining the acceptability of a solution is governed by stylistic choices and the solution is treated by intuitive designers as a satisficing one, rather than as an optimizing one.

To illustrate further the distinction between satisficing and optimizing solutions consider the following visual analogy to a solution domain: a flat plateau with multiple hills on it (figure 5.6). Let the plateau represent a problem domain and each peak the ultimate state of each alternative solution to the problem. In well-defined problems, the problem-solver has a representational domain, a mathematical notation, for example, which allows him objective codification of the total problem domain. He or she also has a metric, an objective function, which allows the problem-solver to measure the altitude of each peak and select the most appropriate one or the optimal solution.

In the case of the designer, there is neither a universal representation with which to codify the whole problem domain, nor a metric with which to compare potential solution peaks in the problem domain. To complete the analogy with respect to the hillside (figure 5.6), assume that because of limited resources it is not possible to climb all hills and that there is fog in the plateau which makes it impossible to see any of the peaks. The mountain climber has to rely on local data. Initially he or she is forced to examine the bases of each hill. As a function of this (as determined by the size of the circumference of the base of each hill) the climber may decide to climb one of these hills[31]. The only criterion for measuring the success of any given hill is the altitude it yields compared with a certain benchmark, that is, a desired altitude, after its peak is reached[32]. If a peak reached is above the benchmark that was set earlier, then it provides a solution. This is a satisficing solution.

Figure 5.6. The plateau of the search domain with solution peaks.

[30] That is, the number of plausible alternatives are very large because of technological and cultural norms of the times.

[31] The a priori knowledge used in determining how promising a hill is, is part of heuristics search processes.

[32] In design, this benchmark is the conventions and values established by style, theory, and personal conviction.

The basis of the criterion or benchmark for a satisficing design solution is whether or not it meets the program requirements as well as the conventions of the style or the palette of the architect. Many solutions may fulfill this; however, not all turn out to be the 'best' one or the highest peak. The goodness of any design solution is, then, to a large extent, a function of the palette selected to limit the solution space vis-à-vis the designer's stylistic preferences identifying the benchmark he or she is working from.

5.3 Local search methods

Specific goals of the designer often defined through the physical components of the designed object cannot be adequately responded to by the global search strategies alone. Developing a layout in Venn-diagram form, determining the entry sequence, designing a roof structure are all examples of such specific goals. The methods used in response to these subproblems are very different from the global search methods reviewed above. Often local methods contain systematic techniques of alternative generation and well-articulated evaluation functions. These methods are suitable for producing transformations in limited representation domains.

To calibrate the anatomy of these methods consistently and parsimoniously, the PSG defined in section 1.2 will be used. Each PSG represents a pattern of primitive processes used in a small segment of a given protocol. When examined closely the functionality reflected in each pattern resembles that of search methods documented elsewhere in problem-solving literature (Eastman, 1970; Newell, 1970).

Consider figure 5.7 which shows four of the PSGs most frequently encountered in the protocols. Furthermore, consider the process employed in the PSG shown in figure 5.7(a). These are representation (P_r), projection (P_p), and confirmation (P_c) of information. Between these

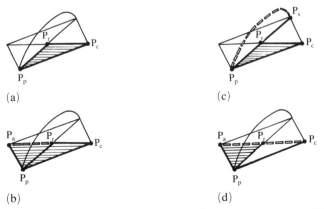

Figure 5.7. Process sequence graphs: (a) generate-and-test, (b) hill-climbing, (c) means–end-analysis, (d) induction.

processes, it is possible to pass control only from P_c to P_p, from P_p to P_r, and from P_r to P_c. This limits the set of possible patterns that can be obtained from these processes to a very small set. Does this specific pattern have a meaning at all? Does it represent a known search method? If so, how does this characterization resemble or differ from other's representations of the method?

Newell in a study that provides the most comprehensive overview in the field, codifies several methods which are akin to the ones illustrated in figure 5.7. He describes five methods in all: generate-and-test, pattern-matching, hill-climbing (figure 4.9), heuristic search (means – end-analysis), and induction. For each method he provides a succinct definition and an operational description to represent their internal mechanisms (see appendix A.2).

Whereas each of Newell's descriptions adequately explains these methods, the *operations* used within each description do not reflect standard primitive functions of the cognitive system, nor is there an overriding concern for parsimony in these definitions. The operations used are: *generate, match, test, apply, test if theorem, test duplicate, insert, select, compare, generate operators, delete, select greatest, best so far,* and *substitute.* Some of these operations are merely specialized versions of others (such as, test if theorem, and test duplicate being specialized versions of test), and others are not mutually exclusive (such as, compare and test). It is conceivable that Newell's purpose is not to describe a parsimonious kernel of operators from which many process descriptions can be constructed. Instead his purpose seems to be to describe and define each method as accurately as possible.

Since our purpose here is to describe the methods of search in design parsimoniously as well as accurately, we must apply a different approach. But first, let us return to the question asked earlier about the PSGs in figure 5.7 and explore their relationships to Newell's methods.

5.3.1 Generate-and-test (GAT)
Newell's codification implies that the primitive processes necessary and sufficient for the GAT method are a *generator* and a *test*. In the case of architectural design the *representation* of generated instances, especially in external memories (EM) [33] and in the form of sketches and writings, must also be an integral part of this method. Thus any combination of the projection – confirmation – representation sequence will approximate the GAT paradigm adequately for design (see figure 5.8). Here the projection process is the equivalent of generating new instances; the confirmation process is the equivalent of the testing of new instances; and the representation process signifies the codification of the results of each of these processes.

[33] In chapter 4 we have already discussed the role and relationship between the external memories and the design process.

By matching the premise of any predicate in EM or LTM with any given association between tokens, the implication of each of these predicates can be evoked for consideration by the confirmation process. Confirmation yields a binary result (+ or −) based on the comparison of each of the implications generated against the desired relationship or goal. For example, in the protocol excerpt illustrated in table 5.1 the designer is trying to find the 'best' relative position for the 'study' in the context of the floor-plan diagram he has developed. After the first trial he recognizes that the best way he can develop the solution is through many repeated trials. This is typical in the GAT process.

What distinguishes the GAT method from exhaustic enumeration is the use of explicit criteria of evaluation. In the example in table 5.1 the suitability of the location of the 'study' hinges upon the success of the circulation scheme that results from it. The creation of superfluous circulation corridors, confounding of private sections of the house with the intrusion of public functions, the lack of proximity between functions that are frequently related in the daily routine of the house are the conditions that violate this requirement. Each test (confirmation) applied corresponds to one of these criteria. Each criterion—economy of circulation, separation of public and private functions, proximity—is in turn used as the premise that generates the next instance. This is

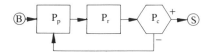

B Begin.
P_p Projection of information: generate a partial solution.
P_c Confirmation of information: test if solution meets goal.
P_r Representation of information: represent solution.
S Stop.

Figure 5.8. Generate-and-test process.

Table 5.1. Protocol excerpt illustrating the generate-and-test process.

Subject 1	$[P_p]$ And would put the core right here. $[P_r][P_c]$ Corridor problem. $[P_p]$ We could define us a core in a different way. $[P_r]$ Put the study over here. $[P_c]$ That's not gonna. $[P_p]$ Put the study over here. $[P_r][P_c]$ That's not a good relationship. $[P_p]$ Put the study over here. $[P_r][P_c]$ That's a good relationship.

This sequence of processes corresponds to the process sequence graph illustrated in figure 5.7(a). The occurrence of legal process transitions in this episode can be represented as:

$$P_p \to P_r \to P_c \to P_p \to P_r \to P_c \to P_p \to P_r \to P_c \to P_p \to P_r \to P_c \, ,$$

where P_p is projection, P_r is representation, and P_c is confirmation.

repeated until an instance is generated which satisfies all criteria. In this way each new instance generated is 'guided' by one (or more) criteria, developing it from a manageable set of instances rather than a much larger exhaustive set of possibilities.

5.3.2 Hill-climbing (HC)

Hill-climbing (HC) is a variation of the GAT method. Each newly generated solution is accepted if and only if it represents an improvement over the best solution developed so far. The difference between this and GAT is in the test applied to evaluate the solutions generated. In GAT the solution is accepted if it satisfies the goal of the designer. In the case of HC, only the solution better than the best solution developed so far is acceptable (figure 5.9). The primitive operations needed in this method, to replicate the portion that corresponds to GAT, are projection, confirmation, representation, as well as acquisition of information to enable the comparison of the most recently generated solution to the best one already generated and represented in EM. The assumption is that, as the designer generates new solutions with the help of the projection process, these solutions have to be compared against the best-so-far solution. The acquisition process retrieves the best-so-far solution from memory and enables its comparison against the current solution. If the new solution is closer to the designer's goal it is stored (representation) in EM (figure 5.9).

Hence, a four-way connection between acquisition, representation, projection, and confirmation of information describes the HC process [figure 5.7(b)]. Sometimes a direct link (a fifth one) between the acquisition and representation processes is needed to allow the codification of each new solution in EM as a part of a running record, regardless of the result of its comparison to the best-so-far solution. This is in agreement with our earlier assumptions about the function of EM in problem-solving.

Take the protocol excerpt illustrated in table 5.2 where the subject is reviewing a floor-plan diagram he has just developed. He discovers a

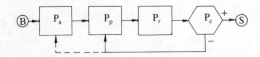

B   Begin.
P_a Acquisition of information: retrieve best-so-far solution.
P_p Projection of information: generate new solution.
P_c Confirmation of information: compare partial solution with best-so-far solution.
P_r Representation of information: record solution.
S   Stop.

Figure 5.9. Hill-climbing process.

deficiency in the diagram. He also recognizes that the problem would be resolved if he were to assume a new constraint, a 'sun deck' to be added to the program. By making this assumption the subject improves the solution particularly as a function of the new criteria added to the list. The goal of the subject in this case is to make the plan layout at hand a successful solution. To accomplish this, he adds a new constraint achieving greater conformance between the plan and the building program. Although this example completely reverses the role of constraints and partial solutions (by forcing constraints to conform to a priori solutions) the method with which this is achieved is an example of HC. That is, incremental improvements made on the constraint set brings it closer to the agreement needed between the constraints and the solution.

Table 5.2. Protocol excerpt illustrating the hill-climbing process.

Subject 1 $[P_a]$ [examining the layout just generated] $[P_p]$ We're saying an axial scheme. $[P_r][P_c]$ Which has no real reason for being. $[P_c]$ It has no ending. $[P_p][P_r]$ [draws in an element at one end, that is, a sun deck] $[P_c][P_p]$ Then it could be greenhouse area or something like that. $[P_p]$ A deck. $[P_r][P_c][P_r]$ a sun deck.

This sequence of processes corresponds to the process sequence graph illustrated in figure 5.7(b). The occurrence of legal process transitions in this episode can be represented as:

$$P_a \rightarrow P_p \rightarrow P_r \Rightarrow P_c \rightarrow P_p \rightarrow P_r \rightarrow P_c \Rightarrow P_p \rightarrow P_r \rightarrow P_c \rightarrow P_r,$$

where P_a is acquisition, P_p is projection, P_c is a consistency check, and P_r is representation.

5.3.3 Heuristic search (means–end-analysis, MEA)

The primary distinction between this method and the others is the need for the active and central involvement of the regulation of control process. As Newell indicates, the MEA applies to the problem state operators selected from a set of given operators. These operators are applied with respect to several parameters of the problem: (a) the result obtained in the previous application of the operator, (b) the comparison between the improvement expected in the problem state and the operations available to bring them about, and (c) the appropriateness of the operators in accomplishing this relative improvement. The critical step is the selection of the operator (or heuristic) that fits these parameters best.

The PSG that represents the MEA method can be described in two distinct parts: (1) *identification*, the analysis of the current state and selection of the appropriate operator, and (2) *application*, the application of the selected method to bring the problem state closer to the desired end. In the first part the heuristic operator is selected from LTM with the aid of the regulation of control process (responsible for the selection of a heuristic operator from a large set), as well as acquisition, representation, and projection of information processes (figure 5.10).

For example, assume that two entirely different partial solutions pertaining to the same aspect of the problem (say, floor-plan organization) are developed in parallel. First, MEA selects a heuristic rule (such as the one entitled 'heuristic rule 1: singular solution', below) to enable the combining of these two partial solutions into a more complete one. Before this can be done, the acquisition process must recognize the existence of the two partial solutions in EM or LTM. Furthermore, the projection process must show that the partial solutions are akin, or related through shared domains (such as, both dealing with floor-plan organization). Then, to account for all aspects of this method, the following primitive processes are needed: regulation of control, confirmation, acquisition, projection, and representation of information.

In the second pass, the heuristic operator selected is applied to the problem. This invariably involves the projection, confirmation, and representation cycles. All heuristic operations call for generation of some new information which is compared with current information and then the recording of the results in memory. Consider the example in table 5.3. At the onset of the excerpt, the designer has already developed an organizational diagram for the plan [figure 5.11(a)]. In the first half of his deliberation he recognizes the conflicts that are caused by this diagram and adopts an approach for solving it: 'divide and conquer'.

Table 5.3. Protocol excerpt illustrating the means–end-analysis process.

Subject 1 $[P_p]$ Entry space leads into the living area. $[P_r]$ Living area is really ... $[P_c][P_p]$. This diagram is in wrong place $[P_p]$ The living area should be in that $[P_r][P_c]$ Normally in that area. $[P_p][P_s]$ Back to orientation

This sequence of processes corresponds to the process sequence graph illustrated in figure 5.7(c). The occurrence of legal process transitions in this episode can be represented as:

$$P_p \rightarrow P_r \rightarrow P_c \Rightarrow P_p \rightarrow P_r \rightarrow P_c \rightarrow P_p \rightarrow P_s \,,$$

where P_p is projection, P_r is representation, P_c is confirmation, and P_s is search.

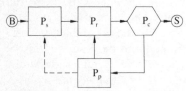

B Begin.
P_s Regulation of control: select heuristic method.
P_r Representatoin of information: record partial solution.
P_c Confirmation of information: does solution meet goal?
P_p Projection of information: apply method.
S Stop.

Figure 5.10. Means–end-analysis process.

He articulates plan *organization* and building *orientation* as the two
independent issues to resolve [figure 5.11(c); *identification* stage] and in
the second half of his deliberations he starts focusing on each problem
separately (*application* stage).

Each time this method is applied, a heuristic operator is selected
from a general pool of heuristics. In the course of analyzing the data
obtained in the four protocols, fifteen distinct heuristics have been
identified. Below are summary descriptions of each. For clarity and
brevity a format consisting of five parts is used in describing each
heuristic rule: (a) a mnemonic title, (b) a short description of the rule
depicting the heuristic, (c) an illustrative example from designers'
protocols, (d) the condition that initiates the rule, and (e) the action to
be performed.

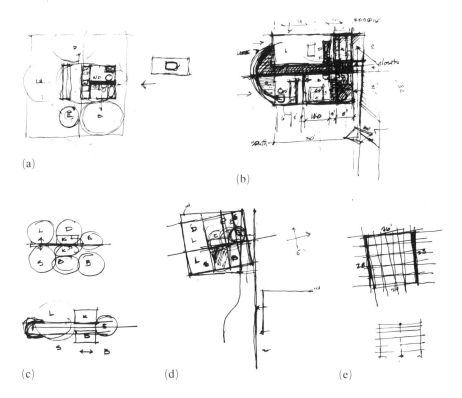

(a)

(b)

(c)   (d)   (e)

Figure 5.11. Sketches by subject 1.

Heuristic rule 1: *singular solution* Often designing involves multiple
representations, each of which deals with a specific aspect of the
solution. Consequently, one of the recurring tasks of the designer is
to bring together solutions developed in alternative representational

domains into one representation, codifying the totality of what is accomplished in each partial solution.

   Example: "Now I'm gonna try to think about how to fit this schematic-schema [a partial solution] onto the site-schema itself [the other partial solution]" [figures 5.11(a) and (c)].
   Condition: Multiple representations have been developed by the designer, each of which represents a partial solution.
   Action: Develop a singular representation that is inclusive of all partial solutions. First match parameters of each partial solution with those of the other; then show both, in one representation, matching their common parameters.

Heuristic rule 2: divide and conquer In design research, the term 'constraint' has been used to refer to many different aspects of design problems. Here it is used in a general sense as it relates to the various components of a problem, such as, design variables, performance requirements, and design criteria. When multiple constraints imply separate solutions that are in conflict with one another, then the problem becomes overconstrained and must be restructured.

   Example: "Let's leave the consideration of blindness out for a second".
   Condition: An overconstrained problem is given with equally important sets of constraints.
   Action: Decompose the problem into parts, each representing a separate set of constraints. Develop solutions for each set of constraints independently of others.

Heuristic rule 3: time sharing between solutions When two partial solutions responding to two separate sets of constraints are to be developed, it is better to develop them in agreement with each other from the onset so that when it becomes necessary to integrate them the task will be easier. An oscillating focus of attention between one partial solution and the next is necessary.

   Example: [At this point the subject is working with the organization of the different rooms of the house] "The living area should be ... in that area; [go] back to [constraint of] orientation" [figure 5.11(a)].
   [At this point the subject shifts his attention to the constraints related to orientation.]
   Condition: The problem can be partitioned into multiple constraint sets that can be dealt with separately.
   Action: Alternate attention on those constraints within or between representations pertinent to the multiple constraint sets. At each shift, carry over the decisions made in one solution domain to the other.

Heuristic rule 4: decision hierarchy When decisions on major design issues are made, these form the basis for future decisions. That is, new decisions have to be based on earlier decisions as if they were constraints of the problem.

Example: "[Decision to have entry on embankment has been made.] Which means we are setting up some parameters in this structure" [figure 5.11(b)].

Condition: Decisions pertaining to some design issues have been made and other related issues are being considered.

Action: The decisions pertaining to the initial issue are considered to be constraints for the other issues.

Heuristic rule 5: conflicting unequal constraints When a partial solution brings multiple constraints with unequal importance into conflict with each other, the conflict can be resolved in favor of the more important constraints.

Example: "But that is [pedestrian – vehicular conflict] an acceptable conflict, I would think" (figures 3.7).

Condition: An overconstrained problem exists with constraints of unequal significance.

Action: Release the insignificant constraints and satisfy the significant ones.

Heuristic rule 6: most constrained first When all of a number of significant constraints are to be satisfied, the search task becomes extensive and a procedure for allocating one's attention to these issues must be found.

Example: "It [mechanical room] should be centrally located. Let's do that first" [figure 5.11(a)].

Condition: Problem has many issues with unequal numbers of constraints applicable to each issue.

Action: Select the most constrained issue to work on first.

Heuristic rule 7: representation selection Often a representation, such as a plan, is suitable for responding to a certain kind of constraint, such as layout organization or horizontal proximities, and is not appropriate for other kinds of constraints, such as passive solar devices or structural spans. As the focus of the designer shifts from one constraint to the next, he or she has to select the representations appropriate for the constraints at hand.

Example: "Maybe I'll think about detailing this [the current partial solution] a little bit [starts a detailed drawing of the solution]" [figure 5.11(b)].

Condition: The current problem representation does not allow the encoding of a solution or partial solution that is desired.

Action: Select a new representation which allows the generation of the desired solution. First identify the aspects of the solution that are necessary: scale, kind of information, spatial location of information. Then find a representation domain that matches this profile.

Heuristic rule 8: *solution testing* A partial solution developed in response to a particular constraint may or may not respond equally, or sufficiently, to other constraints. This must be checked from time to time and especially when a promising solution is obtained. The current solution then should respond to all major criteria of design.

> Example: "Now we come up here [on the main access way] and we have a problem of entering with this wall [because of the privacy of adjoining house]" (figure 5.11).
> Condition: A partial solution is developed.
> Action: Check if partial solution satisfies other important constraints that were not used in its generation. Use GAT method to review systematically all relevant constraints.

Heuristic rule 9: *search in uncertainty* the designer needs a wide range of information. Often this information is not readily available, as in determining user preferences. In such cases the designer will prefer to work with assumptions in lieu of more accurate information which may only be gathered after a time-consuming search.

> Example: "For lack of information I must accept that [the budget is $35,000]".
> Condition: A piece of information is unavailable. To obtain it requires excessive time commitment.
> Action: Make a likely assumption and consider it to be correct until more accurate information is available.

Heuristic rule 10: *simulation of constraint* Some solution ideas are known to work in appropriate circumstances as determined by past experience. Some solution ideas, however, are not acceptable a priori. This may be a result of the nature of the circumstance in which the solution is applied or because it has never been experienced before. Such ideas have to be tested through whatever means are available before they are accepted.

> Example: "You can enter a circle anywhere [drawing and testing the circular entrance]. A blind person would have difficulty entering unless you provide markers" (figure 3.7).
> Condition: A partial solution has to be tested against a constraint and sufficient information is not readily available to carry out the test.
> Action: Simulate a condition in which the test can be performed. Although this may represent an instance and not a generic test, this will be accepted as a datum for future design decisions.

Heuristic rule 11: *hedging the bets* When the testing of a partial solution does not yield a definite result due to insufficient information, then redundant solutions can be consolidated to insure success.

Example: "[Subject 1 is not sure if the circular entry wall he has proposed will work for the blind user, so he decides to make a circular, textured pavement area to mark the entry, which can be perceived through the tactile senses. He is positive this will work.]"
Condition: Whether a partial solution is satisfactory or not cannot be determined.
Action: Find an analogous partial solution for which there are better criteria of evaluation. Consolidate this solution with the previous one to insure that the combined solution will work.

Heuristic rule 12: *sequential processing* When alternative ideas are developed simultaneously, one must be selected for detailed development
Example: "I think this [alternative bridge 1] would work relatively well. This [alternative bridge 2] I've decided to set aside".
Condition: Alternative (partial) solutions are available.
Action: Select one alternative and develop it in detail. The selection may involve tests characteristic of methods such as, HC and GAT.

Heuristic rule 13: *constraint hierarchy* If the functional dependencies between general and detailed issues are recognized at the onset, then the solutions developed to respond to the general constraints can respond to the constraints of the detailed issues as well. In this fashion probable conflicts between these issues, which may arise later, can be avoided and the decisions about the general issues will provide solutions for detailed issues as well.
Example: "If I open this [center wall] up here that automatically takes care of the corridor problem" [figure 5.11(c)].
Condition: Some constraints are inclusive of other constraints.
Action: First satisfy the general constraints that are inclusive of other more specific constraints.

Heuristic rule 14: *least promising first* When alternative solutions are being examined, an obvious strategy for resolving the competition for the designer's attention is to pick the most promising alternative and to examine and develop it further. However, a process of elimination would also be effective. Consequently, when there are only a few alternatives in competition with one another, it is equally effective to examine the unpromising alternative first, rather than the most promising one.
Example: "Or we can enter from Morewood [elevation of which is about 30 ft]. Let me explore this some more".
Condition: A partial solution is developed which has some significant undesirable side effects.
Action: Work on the partial solution to develop it further before discarding it on the outside chance that it may lead to desirable solutions. If not, it will be eliminated, which will result in the pruning of the search tree.

Heuristic rule 15: *first idea* As in many other task domains some designers have a bias in favor of their first ideas. They usually prefer to explore the first solution idea that has occurred to them before others, even though others have been generated and hold promise as successful solutions.

Example: "I found often that the first ideas are the best".

Condition: Many alternative solutions have been developed.

Action: First, work on the first alternative solution developed.

5.3.4 Induction

According to Newell, induction, as a weak method for problem-solving requires (a) a mapping between the given data and the predicted data, and (b) a given form for this mapping which conforms to the data. Both of these conditions are met by the projection-of-information process, by definition.

The if–then structure underlying the projection process allows the use of mappings or chains of mappings between given predicate(s) and desired predicate(s). In chapter 4 we reviewed this form of induction and developed a flow diagram illustrating the mechanics of the projection process. In the next chapter we shall discuss the representational implications of this paradigm further. Here, let us review some illustrative examples from the design protocols.

In the first stage of this process an appropriate source is selected from which the information that is needed can be obtained (figure 5.12). This source can be LTM, a book, drawings of the site, a site visit, or information that other individuals possess. In any case, if the source is accessible the induction process is activated.

If the source is not readily accessible it is abandoned in lieu of other more accessible ones. When the appropriate information source is reached it has to be assimilated in existing information. Existing information consists of the present knowledge of the designer and the current information state of the problem. If new information is

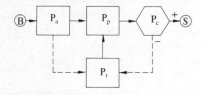

B   Begin.
P_a Acquisition of information: select rules that match predicate.
P_p Projection of information: project new information.
P_c Confirmation of information: does new information match desired goal.
P_r Representation of information: record information.
S   Stop.

Figure 5.12. Induction process.

incompatible with existing information, it is either abandoned or rote acquisition takes place.

New information which is consistent or compatible with existing information will lead to automatic evocation of other sources of information. For example, in the episode in table 5.4 the subject learns about the blindness of the user for the first time. This immediately triggers two sorts of knowledge already stored in LTM, "organization" and "texture", both significant in designing for the blind. Hence the incoming information is not only assimilated by the subject but it automatically leads to the evocation of other information, this time from internal sources.

In another episode (table 5.5) subject 1 is simply struggling with the difficult task of assimilating the incoming information. In viewing the slides he has some difficulty matching this information with his current image of the site. He misidentifies a retaining wall several times until he figures out the correct orientation of the camera in relation to the site. This is a typical example of visual pattern-matching.

The PSGs that fall in this category have projection as their central process. For obvious reasons acquisition, representation, and confirmation, and the links from these to the projection process are also necessary (figure 5.12). As new information is projected, it has to be represented

Table 5.4. Protocol excerpt illustrating the data-manipulation process.

Subject 1   [P_a] [reading the sentence about the blind user] All the users are single and blind. [P_p][P_c] Hmm, that's a new aspect. [P_r] [writes "texture" and "organization"]

This sequence of processes corresponds to the process sequence graph illustrated in figure 5.7(d). The occurrence of legal process transitions in this episode can be represented as:

$$P_a \rightarrow P_p \rightarrow P_c \rightarrow P_r,$$

where P_a is acquisition, P_p is projection, and P_r is representation.

Table 5.5. Protocol excerpt illustrating the pattern-matching process.

Subject 1   [P_a] [examining slide] Which wall is this one?
Experimenter   Wall that supports the garage.
Subject 1   [P_p][P_c][P_r] So, this is one here is (points to a wall in [P_p][P_a] the site plan) is this (wall) turning to stone?
Experimenter   No this wall is not shown on your (site plan)
Subject 1   [P_p][P_c][P_r] Oh, this is the garage.

This sequence of processes corresponds to the process sequence graph in figure 5.7(d). The occurence of legal process transitions in this episode can be represented as:

$$P_a \rightarrow P_p \rightarrow P_c \rightarrow P_r \rightarrow P_p \; ; \; P_a \rightarrow P_p \rightarrow P_c \rightarrow P_r \, ,$$

where P_a is acquisition, P_p is projection, P_r is representation, and P_c is confirmation.

in LTM or EM to maintain an accurate running record. The confirmation process performs the tests necessary for verifying that the induced information matches (or fails to match) the desired information. The acquisition process allows the extraction of information from various sources, especially from LTM.

5.3.5 Accounting for design behavior

As we saw above, the designer's processes represented as PSGs correspond to methods of problem-solving commonly seen in many other task domains and codified by others. Another conclusion that can be drawn from this is that the handful of methods reviewed above account for a very large portion of the data in the protocols. This confirms a conjecture which was proposed earlier about the sufficiency of the five primitive processes in codifying design behavior.

In the two protocols that were completely analyzed (subject 1 and subject 3), the methods outlined above account for 96% and 93% of the data, respectively. The transcription of the protocol into the categories represented by each method reveals that the most popular method in design is generate-and-test, accounting for 56.1% of the data. The next popular method is induction accounting for 31.7% of the data. The least popular methods are hill-climbing and means–end-analysis, representing 8.5% and 3.7% of the data, respectively. Although all methods play significant roles in the overall design process it is clear that the greatest burden falls on the most general and least powerful of the methods: generate-and-test and induction.

Other forms of verification of this result, however, must also be undertaken. One such approach is the replication of these results through independent experiments. This shall be left to other researchers interested in the subject area. Yet, another independent test to validate DIPS will be discussed here. A computer program based on the declarative, IF–THEN structures of DIPS has been used to simulate human behavior in architectural recognition tasks. The results of this work shall be reviewed in chapter 7.

5.4 Synopsis

Newell in his article on heuristic problem-solving defines the power and generality of methods as inversely related variables. As the power of a method increases, he states, it becomes more specialized and its generality of application therefore becomes limited. On the other hand, the most general methods, by virtue of their nonspecificity, apply to many different problem situations. Two of the four search methods, generate-and-test and induction, are the least specific ones in the set. Means–end-analysis and hill-climbing, on the other hand, involve specific tests and specialized operators consequently present a less general and more powerful application domain. This suggests that the intuitive design process, as observed in the protocols we analyzed, rely primarily on general methods. The more powerful methods lacking in generality are reserved for special circumstances and consequently not utilized as much as the other two. Following this train of thought, one can speculate that if designers were able to bring well-defined metrics for measuring the success of their partial solutions to bear on the design process, then processes like hill-climbing would be utilized more frequently. Similarly a richer and more powerful kernel of heuristic operators may increase the frequency of use of means – end-analysis. In any case we are unable to answer these questions here on the basis of the evidence examined up to now. However, the questions present interesting future research topics.

5.5 Suggested readings

1 Eastman C E, 1973, "Automated space planning" *Artificial Intelligence* **4** 41 – 64
2 Lenat D B, 1983a, "Theory formulation by heuristic search. The nature of heuristics II: background and examples, and 1983b, EURISKO: A program that learns new heuristics and domain concepts. The nature of heuristics III: program design and results" *Artificial Intelligence* **21** 31 – 98
3 Moran T P, 1970, "A model of multilingual designer" in *Emerging Methods in Environmental Design and Planning* Ed. G T Moore (MIT Press, Cambridge, MA)

5.6 Exercises

5.1 Collect a protocol from a short design problem.

5.2 Based on this protocol, develop a transcription based on the five primitive processes: acquisition, representation, projection, confirmation, and regulation of control.

5.3 Codify the problem behavior graph (PBG) for the entire protocol.

5.4 Based on the PBG identify and analyze the subject's behavior in terms of the problem-solving strategies discussed in this chapter.

Representation in design

"In the image of the history of the universe, as it is presented to us by science, two opposing forces, or tendencies seem to be operating. On the one hand, we have the tendency represented by the second law of thermodynamics; the tendency that is, for states to become more probable, more chaotic, and for things to run down .... On the other hand, we clearly observe in the record of history a different tendency. This is the tendency for the rise of organization. Organization is anything that is not chaos, anything, in other words, that is improbable."

Kenneth E Boulding *The Image* (1969, page 19)

The concept of organization, or conversely of chaos, is central to the issue of representation. Representations are based on implicit or explicit organizations found in the realities that they stand for. Even though in previous chapters we focused on representation as a participant and partner of the design process, there is a great deal more to be said for representations as organizers of things and processes alike[34]. For example, a building plan organizes information pertaining to the circulation, structure, and visual pattern intended in a design idea better than most other representations. A perspective abstracts the visual manifestation of the designed object in a way that a plan cannot accomplish. Although there is some question about the universality of each of these statements, it is generally true that any given representation will best lend itself to a particular task. The selection of a representation is tantamount to the selection of a method for solving a problem[35].

This principle, by and large, is an axiom of design. Since design involves the manipulation of symbols that stand for realities, design is an excellent example of abstract problem-solving. Plans, sections, elevations, perspectives, axonometric and isometric drawings, models, and a host of other graphic representations are the abstract tools of the designer. Through these tools the designer can generate alternative solutions and test them before implementing them in real life and running the risk of costly errors. Representations afford the designer the luxury of testing ideas with little cost.

The only cost involved is that representations through their contents limit the number of relevant considerations that can be tackled; thus the method of the designer is constrained. This issue becomes even more involved because in representing real objects the contents of

[34] For a discussion of representations and their properties see appendix A.3.

[35] Hunt (1975) expresses an idea similar to the one already discussed in section 4.3.2, for the realm of building intelligent computer programs.

representations themselves assume new dimensions. Each representation constitutes an entirely new stimulus and a reality for the designer. During the course of the design process, representations fulfill the role of real objects. The designer evaluates the success of ideas, manipulates their form, or generates new forms as a result of his interactions with representations. In part, these representations are encoded directly in the designer's LTM. Thus, they produce second-order realities or represented abstractions[36]. The designer often finds himself or herself relying on these second-order realities while making design decisions.

The purpose of this chapter is to pry into the LTM, and to study these second-order abstractions. More specifically we shall try to answer the questions: 'how are representations *stored* in the mind?', 'how are they subsequently recalled?', and 'what are the forms used in encoding information in LTM?'

6.1 Representations of design in memory
From an information-processing point of view there are two basic modes that account for all representations proposed for the designer. These are the *verbal-conceptual* and *visual* modes. Verbal-conceptual refers to all schemata that make up a representation and that have single specific visual equivalents. For instance, consider the symbol 'chair'. We can associate a large number of visual images with a 'chair'. Conversely, if we consider a specific view of a specific chair it would provide a single visual entity which incidentally may have many verbal-conceptual schemata that are associated with it (for example, 'a seat', 'a chair', 'a place to rest', etc) but only one visual equivalent. This second schema is a visual one whereas the first is a verbal-conceptual one.

The distinction between visual and verbal-conceptual schemata and their processing in the mind seems to be one of convenience rather than a reflection of distinct information-processing mechanisms. It is conceivable and quite likely that the same cognitive mechanisms deal with both modes. However, the nature of the information, its rate of processing, its recall from memory, and its use in problem-solving tasks are different. In this chapter we shall not attempt to explore the question of the presence or absence of these modalities. Instead, two empirical studies undertaken to explore the functionalities that correspond to these modalities will be reviewed. Let us first review three representational paradigms that are consistent with this distinction: *productions, conceptual inference structures,* and *chunks.*

6.1.1 Productions
Productions are control structures resembling the simple $A \rightarrow B$ type associations in form (Newell, 1973). The A part, or the left-hand side

---

[36] In many contexts the term abstraction is not an uncommon substitute for the word 'representation'.

of the association, stands for the *condition*. The *B* part, or the right-hand side of the association, stands for the *action*. The arrow, or the association, simply means that when the condition is met, the action must be taken. For example, let us represent the hammering action, codified by the TOTE unit discussed in chapter 4, to illustrate a production:

head of nail is not flush → strike nail with hammer.

The condition in this production, that the head of the nail is flush, is one of the possible results of the *test* of the TOTE unit. The other possible result of the same test, that the head of the nail is flush, suggests another distinct production:

head of nail is flush → stop.

These two productions together form a complete *test–operate* cycle equivalent to the TOTE unit in figure 4.5(a). When a number of productions such as these are assembled to mimic more complex patterns of behavior, then this assembly is called a *production system*. Production systems, in addition to being assemblies of productions, also contain sets of rules regulating the transfer of control between each production.

For example, control can be applied on the basis of an 'activate the first matching condition' rule. This means that the action of the first condition that matches a production in a list of productions is activated, or *fired* immediately. Alternatively, the firing sequence can be altered by requiring that the search for the next condition on the list continues from the point where the last production fired, or by eliminating all productions that fired previously, or by traversing the list from the opposite direction, and so on. What is important to recognize is the fact that control in a production system can be as complex or as simple as desired and can be regulated by a simple rule or in turn by a whole new production system.

Productions and production systems are one of the most robust and generic of all control structures developed in information-processing research. Not only do they present an intuitive and powerful theoretical framework, but they have also been used numerous times to simulate problem-solving successfully. Production systems, because of their modular structure, lend themselves to parsimony in the design of control structures and have been also demonstrated to accommodate the double memory functions of humans: LTM and STM (Newell and Simon, 1972). In addition, the modular structure permits simulation of learning through accumulation of facts.

As a psychological construct, the production system itself, with its list of productions and rules for regulation of control, corresponds to functions of the LTM. This is consistent with the operational parameters of LTM (large overall capacity, small structural units, or parts suitable for one production at a time) and approximates closely the temporal nature and limited span of STM. In summary, the properties of parsimony, flexibility, and open-endedness coupled with its general agreement with psychological attributes of information processing make production systems an ideal device for modelling the behavior of designers and representing inference making.

6.1.2 Conceptual inference structures

Formal inference making is defined by the rules of deductive and inductive reasoning in logic. Given a set of relationships:

$$A \rightarrow B, \qquad B \rightarrow C,$$

and the rule of transitivity:

if $X \rightarrow Y$, and $Y \rightarrow Z$,
then $X \rightarrow Z$,

we can infer the truth of a new relationship:

$$A \rightarrow C.$$

Conceptual inference making is a term coined by Shank (1975) and his colleagues to refer to a much broader set of inferences that do not necessarily obey logical rules of inference, yet are considered valid for all intents and purposes. Such inferences, although not formal, are no less significant in their utility. They are routinely used in everyday human tasks, such as natural language, problem-solving, and syllogistic reasoning.

Shank (1975) has modelled natural language understanding as a form of conceptual inference making. The kinds of inferences they deal with can be illustrated in the following excerpt about a cartoon character out of the children's television program, *Sesame Street*:

1 If I stuff this balloon with this pin,
2 then (if) this balloon pops,
3 then (if) that would scare my sister,
4 then (if) she would drop the vase she is carrying,
5 then (if) that would make my mother angry,
6 then (if) she would send me to bed without my supper,
7 then (if) I would not be able to eat the chocolate cake she is baking,
8 then ... oh well, who wants to pop a nice balloon like this anyway.

This excerpt illustrates a segment from a nearly endless chain of inferences, all attached to each other informally and tentatively. One can easily extend the chain in either direction or build connections to it at any point. A mechanism which enables such chaining is proposed by Shank and his colleagues. This mechanism is also analogous to the basic $A \rightarrow B$ type association, where A corresponds to the IF-clause or the *premise* and B corresponds to the THEN-clause or the *implication* of the IF–THEN structure.

When a conceptual inference is made, this is equivalent to matching the implication of a *predicate* (an IF–THEN structure) whose truth is known; and the premise of another predicate whose implication is to be asserted. For example, given the IF–THEN structure:

if a balloon is punctured (P_1),
then the balloon will pop (I_1)

and that event E ('the balloon has been popped with the pin'), then, the truth of a new implication, I_2 ('*then* the balloon has been punctured'), can be asserted. If we take each statement of the *Sesame Street* character to be the premise of the following statement, the pairs of statements: IF P_n, THEN I_{n+1}; where n ($n = 1, 2, ...$) is the number of given statements, would approximate the set of all IF–THEN associations necessary and sufficient to generate this excerpt.

Conceptual inferences, in contrast to logical inferences, have many characteristics that make them suitable for everyday use and difficult to contain within finite knowledge bases. Reiger (1975, page 185) identifies four such characteristics:

"1 It [conceptual inference] is spontaneous and automatic.
2 It is subconscious for the most part. It is not normally subject to direct introspection or conscious control.
3 It is performed by what we visualize to be parallel, associative 'firmware' in the brain.
4 It has little goal direction until certain criteria are met."

Let us consider each of these observations, starting with the last one. The lack of goal directedness is probably the most salient aspect of conceptual inferences. The chain of inferences by the cartoon character is clearly an excursion with no prior understanding of the goal. In fact, the final outcome turns out to be rather disappointing for our character. Whereas the whole episode, as in most cartoon situations, is somewhat exaggerated, it clearly illustrates a salient property of conceptual inferences. Almost like the expanding rings around the point of impact of a rock on the surface of water, the initial predicate 'popping the balloon' spontaneously propagates all other predicates that follow.

The next point made by Reiger is that this is in agreement with the associative 'firmware' of the brain. With IF–THEN structures forming a lattice, or network, in LTM, any conscious probing of a node in the network creates the spontaneous chain reaction originating from a node and traveling in various directions. The example of the *Sesame Street* character illustrates inferences only in one direction. The effectiveness of propagations in a multitude of directions obviously depends on the density of the links the original node has and its centrality in the lattice of associations. The activation of a multitude of inference chains is the key element enabling the spontaneity or parallel behavior common in human reasoning. This is clearly in agreement with the remaining arguments by Reiger: the subconscious nature and spontaneity of conceptual inferences.

One of the side effects of spontaneity is inconsistency. Unlike logical inferences, where inductive and deductive principles help maintain the integrity of the reasoning process, conceptual inferences are prone to errors. As the cartoon character boldly infers one statement after the other, she finds herself contradicting her premise, 'popping of the balloon'. Because of the possibility of not being able to eat the chocolate cake, a natural outcome of the initial premise, she finds herself also at odds with the hidden premise of the sequence of inferences: 'to have a good time'. Obviously it is not a profitable trade-off to be deprived of chocolate cake just to be able to pop a balloon.

The ability to accommodate contradictory and imprecise relationships make conceptual inferences a suitable tool for use with ill-defined and informal problems. This is one of the reasons that makes conceptual inferences an ideal tool for the designer, where tentative, incomplete, and even contradictory relationships must be accommodated and used to develop permanent, complete, and consistent solutions.

6.1.3 Chunks

The appropriateness of the simple associative form '$A \rightarrow B$' is debatable in the case of memory organizations that accommodate spatial information and their manipulations. Instead, in task domains with a predominantly spatial problem spaces (chess, pattern recognition, quantification, and recall of graphic elements), *chunks* are the most robust information structures which have been shown to account for memory functions.

Although the recent origins of this notion come from Miller's work on STM memory span, other convincing accounts can also be found in studies comparing experts and novices in chess. The startling finding that 'expertness' in chess is a result of superior memory structures or chunks rather than processing power came initially as a result of deGroot's (1965) studies. Later Chase and Simon (1973) defined and extended the notion of the chunk as an organizer of hierarchical multiassociative links in memory. What they demonstrated in chess has been shown to apply in other task domains as well (Akın, 1980; Reitman, 1976).

Memory organizes tokens into clusters or chunks that have one or more common relationships 'binding' them together. The first three digits in a phone number, three white pawns in a defense relationship, Peter, Paul, and Mary, are all examples of information organized as chunks. The associative links, sometimes spatial and at other times symbolic, are always stronger between units of information belonging to the same chunk than between information belonging to different chunks.

For example, the digit 3, a white pawn, and Peter do not necessarily constitute a chunk[37].

Chunks are justifiable because of the limitations of the human cognitive system. More specifically, a fundamental cause of what limits the number of items that can be stored in STM all at once, is the span of STM. As we encode events and patterns observed in the environment, STM takes the input and transmits it to LTM. For this information to remain in LTM it must be rehearsed or activated, at a minimum, for a certain period of time (no less than five seconds). It is this rehearsal as well as the transmission function of the STM that makes it the likely candidate that is responsible for packaging information into chunks. Needless to say, there must be reciprocal structures present in LTM to receive and retain these chunks that are prepackaged in STM. The same constraints also effect the recall or 'depackaging' of chunks. In this case the process is reversed.

A primary strength of this theory is that it accounts for the limitations of STM span, the capacity of the 'conduit' connection between STM and LTM as well as the extremely large quantities of information that human beings can move into and out of LTM. The packaging or chunking of information allows larger numbers of units, or 'bits' of information to be processed at one time.

Chunks also support the hierarchic and multirelational organizations of information. By nesting chunks within other chunks, one can achieve multilayered hierarchies. This is critical in spatial representations, such as in the game of chess, where the entire gameboard can be broken into many chunk-clusters and chunks, before all relevant groupings of the pieces are exhausted. Similarly, designers recalling drawings of floor plans use multiple and alternative groupings between lines drawn, often assigning a building element or a wall segment to more than one chunk simultaneously. It is this redundancy of association inherent in spatial relationships that makes chunks a suitable memory organization for modeling visual knowledge.

6.1.4 Logistics of memory organization
Production systems, conceptual inferences, and chunks each define distinct views of memory organization all consistent within themselves and relevant to certain functional aspects of cognitive management of information. Production systems model the control mechanisms necessary to simulate goal-directed behavior. Conceptual inferences allow low-level spontaneous information-processing capabilities. Chunks organize the input and output of information and its maintenance in memory.

---

[37] Unless, of course, special circumstances are presented; for example, one has experienced a memorable chess game, where the critical, third move was made by the player named Peter using the white pawn.

The relevance of these structures to DIPS is obvious. Each mechanism corresponds to one or two of the primitive processes defined in chapter 4. Chunks provide the memory organizations underlying the processes of information acquisition and representation. Conceptual inferences provide the processes underlying both projection and confirmation of information. Production systems provide the basis for regulating the transmission of control between these processes within the framework of an overall design strategy.

The problem emerges when one attempts to fuse these three structures into one coherent memory system. Although there is a degree of overlap between the domain of each, there are certain aspects of database organization that are inconsistent from one structure to the next. Chunks suggest a hierarchic organization of schemata. Conceptual inferences operate in a lattice-like network. Production systems presuppose structures that resemble ordered lists.

The inconsistencies are nontrivial; yet our intent is to use all three models of memory, not as isomorphs of the actual memory organization in humans, but as a description of functionalities present in humans. That is, no a priori structural organization is attributed here to the memory systems under study. The only things attributed are their operational capabilities that suggest production systems, conceptual inferences, and chunks. In this chapter, the validity of chunks and conceptual inferences in memory and recall tasks with architectural drawings shall be reviewed. In the next chapter, the validity of production systems and conceptual inference structures will be explored in the context of a computer simulation.

6.2 Representation of architectural drawings

The act of encoding information implies organization. This is generally true for architectural design tasks. There is virtually no evidence, however, about the way in which architectural objects are encoded in memory. How do we structure information to allow ourselves to recall or make inferences about the floor plan of a building? What organizational properties relevant to the object govern the structure of the traces of information in our memory? In this section the findings of two experiments conducted to answer these questions will be discussed.

The first experiment deals with the question of chunks and interchunk structures used in encoding and recalling information about floor plans. The second experiment deals with the inferences made about architectural objects. The results of both experiments contribute to the insights about representation in architecture.

6.2.1 Experiment 1: chunking

The experimental method dealing with chunking was derived from a study by Chase and Simon (1973). This study examined the recall of chess positions used by chess players, of varying skill levels. The method consists of (a) allowing a player to examine visually a given position from a chess game, that is, chess pieces on a chessboard, and (b) subsequently requiring the player to reconstruct the positions of all of the chess pieces observed, from memory. The first stage is called the *learning* phase and the second stage is called the *recall* phase.

Chase and Simon were able to show through this experiment that the duration and nature of the learning phase as well as the skill level of each player determined the extent to which they could correctly reconstruct chess positions. By examining the sequences of and latencies between correctly recalled chess pieces, they were also able to show how each player organized these chess positions into easily recalled 'chunks'. Each chunk represented a number of chess pieces in particular relationships to one another, stored as a single entity in memory.

It has also been found by deGroot (1965) that master chess players do not search solution spaces more extensively than less skilled players. Yet they are able to perceive readily the critical relationships on the board during the course of a game. Subsequently, studies conducted by deGroot, and Chase and Simon showed that expert chess players had bigger chunks than less skilled players. These two findings together imply that bigger chunks, or better representations in the LTM, allow expert chess players to be 'masters' at their game. Schemata used in representing objects and their organization in memory then seem to hold promise for the discovery of the 'secrets' of the skilled problem-solver particularly in the domain of design.

6.2.2 Experimental design

Studies of learning indicate that new information, whether it is about the positions of chess pieces, three-dimensional shapes, or a set of lines, can be stored in the LTM within 4-10 seconds. Furthermore, only five to nine such units or chunks of information can be held in STM while this learning takes place (Miller, 1956). These estimates clearly indicate that if we were to take a quick glance at a complex drawing such as the one in figure 6.1 and process this information, line by line, we should remember hardly anything about the drawing afterwards. On the other hand, it would be obvious to any one who tries the experiment (that is take a 3-4 second glance then look away and try to recall the contents of the drawing) will find that a great deal of information will indeed remain in memory as a result of such a brief glance. Findings of the experiments we shall review here indicate that architects can accurately recall at least 50% of all lines contained in these drawings after only short exposures to the drawings. The question then is 'how is this possible?' or 'how does the limited capacity of the human memory account for such levels of recall?'

Part of the answer is in the mnemonic memory aids discussed in chapter 2. Human memory is full of prepackaged information which aid the labelling or naming of new information to assist future recall. The logic of this process is that such labelling of information is accomplished much faster than encoding it afresh. This is especially true with visual information. Architects with years of experience in looking at drawings carry around many chunks or prestored composite units of information about shape, functional relations, and architectural elements. Subsequently, they can retrieve from LTM those chunks that match parts of the stimulus. In the experiment we shall review here, the primary question has been the structure and contents of the chunks used by architects[38] while learning and recalling drawings of floor plans.

Let me now introduce some of the parameters of the experiment. Floor plans of three moderately complex buildings were selected as stimuli. To avoid the effects of preexperimental exposure to stimuli, all three are little known buildings. One which will be used here to illustrate the findings, a plan of a church designed by Jose Louis Sert, is shown in figure 6.1. Three types of *learning* tasks were used: *trace*, *copy*, and *interpret*. Each task is needed for the application of Chase and Simon's technique for codifying visual chunks used in recall. Furthermore, each provides a different kind of learning experience, allowing the investigation of the role of learning in understanding visual representations.

In the trace task, subjects trace from the given building plan onto tracing paper overlaid on the plan. This constitutes a 'cursory' exposure to the drawing with special emphasis on the sequence and pattern of

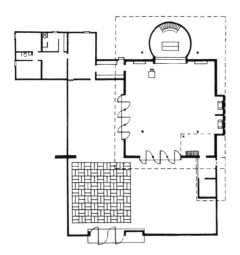

Figure 6.1. Plan of a church designed by Jose Louis Sert.

[38] From now on they shall be referred to as subject 5, subject 6, and subject 7.

lines as they are drawn, one by one. Typically subjects draw structural walls, windows, and doors together; and cluster horizontal and vertical lines separately for efficiency in drawing. In the copy task, subjects copied from the given building plan onto an opaque sheet of paper. In this case the conventions used by the subjects are similar to those of the trace task, except the information drawn has to be temporarily stored in STM as the subject glances away from the original drawing so as to draw the next few lines on the work sheet. This forces the subjects to organize lines that are drawn each time into clusters to maximize memory efficiency. In the interpret task, subjects were required to examine an unlabelled building plan and determine the type of building represented and the functions of the individual spaces of which the building is composed. Here an understanding of the functional make-up of the building as it is manifested in the drawings is mandated.

Immediately after each of the learning tasks, the subjects were asked to recall by drawing from memory the plan they had just interpreted, traced, or copied. All sessions were recorded on videotape. The sequence in which subjects drew each line was extracted from these recordings. The latencies separating each line drawn was also estimated from the recordings to the nearest $\frac{1}{16}$ th of a second[39].

6.2.3 Chunks in architectural drawings

The chunks, or groups of lines, used in drawing each plan during recall were determined by examining the magnitude of latencies that occurred between the moment a line was completed and the next one was begun. The data interpreted in this form consist of a linear sequence of latencies representing the time taken to draw each line and the latencies between each line. These latencies, according to deGroot, and Chase and Simon, correspond to the time needed to recall information from LTM (that is, retrieval of a complete chunk) or from STM (that is, retrieval of a single line from within a chunk already in STM); and the lines drawn represent the components that make up the chunks recalled. Since we know that the retrieval of information from LTM takes longer than from STM, this method of analysis predicts long latencies separating lines that belong to separate chunks. Thus by defining the minimum latency which corresponds to an interchunk pause, it is possible to identify a threshold that separates lines belonging to different chunks in the data.

The chunks discovered in this manner consist of elements like 'wall segments forming corners', 'wall segments containing a set of openings of the same type', functionally consistent elements like 'steps', 'furniture', 'coatracks', 'exterior walls', 'structural walls' (see figures 6.2 and 6.3). The chunks and the sequence in which they were recalled by subject 5

---

[39] This was a function of the video equipment which recorded a frame every $\frac{1}{16}$ th of a second.

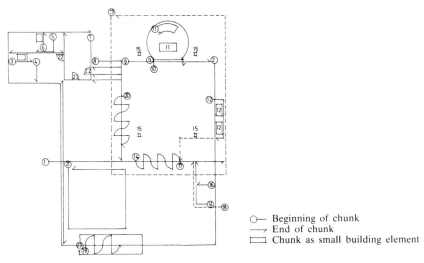

Figure 6.2. Chunks of church plan as recalled by subject 5.

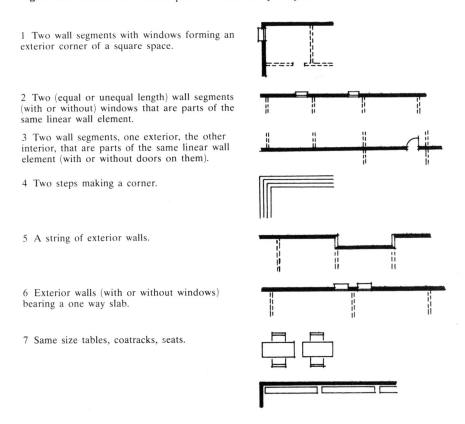

1 Two wall segments with windows forming an exterior corner of a square space.

2 Two (equal or unequal length) wall segments (with or without) windows that are parts of the same linear wall element.

3 Two wall segments, one exterior, the other interior, that are parts of the same linear wall element (with or without doors on them).

4 Two steps making a corner.

5 A string of exterior walls.

6 Exterior walls (with or without windows) bearing a one way slab.

7 Same size tables, coatracks, seats.

Figure 6.3. Generic chunks abstracted from subject 5's protocol.

are indicated in figure 6.2. Each chunk is shown as a continuous broken line with a circle indicating the point where it begins and an arrow indicating its end. The integer inside the circle shows the position of that chunk in the overall sequence of recall. Some examples of generic chunks are shown in figure 6.3.

Two observations stem from this analysis. First, the level of resolution that is embodied by the codified chunks is very low. That is, chunks seem to correspond to the lowest level design elements represented in the drawings (steps, corners, walls, furnishings) or specific aspects of a given floor plan (structure, access) rather than to larger components, such as rooms or groups of rooms. Although this sounds counterintuitive at first, it is consistent with taxonomies developed for automated representations of three-dimensional objects. For example, Guzman (1968), using a vocabulary of line segments representing edges, line intersections, and various corner conditions, was able unambiguously to encode complex three-dimensional line drawings. Similarly at a basic level of processing, we can assume that the architect makes use of visual primitives, such as the architectural chunks illustrated in figure 6.3.

The second observation has immediate consequences for our analysis. Since we know from experience that buildings are considered in parts larger than the low-level chunks shown here, we can postulate the existence of memory structures larger than chunks. These structures— rooms and clusters of rooms—can be regarded as organizers of interchunk relationships, thus accounting for the processing of larger building parts by the subjects as if they were chunks. That is, when four corners are assembled in an orthogonal layout to define a room, the corners may constitute the chunks and the room constitutes a higher-level organization. Rooms in turn can be joined to make wings of buildings creating higher level organizations, and so on. This is one way in which chunks can be instrumental in representing larger scale architectural elements.

6.2.4 Structure of architectural elements

To uncover the ground rules of these higher order organizations based on the present chunks we must ask: 'What spatial properties can be used to form higher level chunks?' In fact, the same question must be asked in turn about the line segments which constitute the lower level chunks. In the absence of readily available answers in this area a separate experiment was designed to obtain an answer. A new set of subjects were asked to play a form of the twenty-question game with the experimenter[40]. Subjects were required to identify the type of a building,

[40] Subjects participating in this experiment, subject 8 and subject 9 were of compatible skill level, and stimuli used were selected from the works of Jose Louis Sert whose church plan was used in the chunking experiment. For a detailed description of this experiment see section 6.3.

represented by a floor plan they were not allowed to see. Their inferences were based only on answers they got for their questions about the floor plan which was in the possession of the experimenter. This forced subjects to ask questions directly about the relationships between lines and other parts of the information contained in the floor plan.

The relationships between parts of the floor plan fell under two general categories: 'graphic' and 'architectural'. The *graphic* relationships were things that pertained to the medium: *adjacency, size,* and *orientation.* Although architecturally important, all of these relationships are also meaningful independent of any reference to architectural content. The *architectural* relationships, on the other hand, are relevant only in the context of the architectural intent of the drawings: *function, circulation,* and *structure.* Without a specific architectural reference, lines drawn on paper have no function, circulation, and structure-related meaning.

These six dimensions (adjacency, size, orientation, function, circulation, structure) were sufficient in representing all categories of information requested by subjects in the twenty-question task. Thus they were assumed to be adequate as a set of organizational relationships for structuring information in memory.

Next a test was devised to determine whether this set of relationships (as defined to exist between successively recalled line segments) were in fact sufficient and necessary for representing floor plans. Each line encoded in the recall task of the chunking experiment was transcribed in two forms: (1) *probability of recall,* whether the line is correctly recalled; and (2) *time of recall,* the speed with which it is recalled. The probability and the recall times associated with each line segment were correlated against the six structural relationships that were postulated to exist between a line segment and those drawn immediately before and after.

Several kinds of statistical tests were conducted to measure these correlations and whether they were accounted for by the probabilities related to chance only. Z-scores obtained by comparing the actual probabilities against those dictated by chance showed that all six structural dimensions (adjacency, size, orientation, function, circulation, and structure) did in fact significantly account for the grouping of line segments into chunks. The greater the number of dimensions along which two line segments were related, the greater the likelihood that they were members of the same chunk. More specifically, four of the six dimensions—adjacency, orientation, structure, and function—helped predict the variance in the recall of each line segment given the previous line recalled. This result was obtained by analysis of variance (ANOVA).

Furthermore, ANOVA was used to show that adjacency and orientation were predictors of variance in the recall times. This is perhaps a result of the time saved through motor efficiencies stemming from the relative ease of drawing line segments that are adjacent and similarly oriented. An alternative explanation can be provided if we assume that the variances in reaction times are directly attributable to time of recall from memory. This suggests that, in representing visual objects, LTM requires the encoding of each line along multiple dimensions of graphic organization: size, orientation, and adjacency. This supports the existence of visual analogs in LTM for storing images in addition to verbal-conceptual ones (Collins and Quillian, 1969). That is, the recall times for those lines related to previous ones along the structural dimensions are relatively faster when this relationship is encoded iconographically rather than in the form of verbal-conceptual representations that are inefficient in encoding graphic relations. In the latter case, calculation of the values of adjacency, orientation, and size (or alternatively retrieving them from precompiled[41] verbal-conceptual data) should prove to be more time consuming.

6.2.5 Interchunk structures

Next, the manner in which individual chunks are interrelated to form organizations larger than chunks was studied. First, the accuracy of recall of each floor plan by each subject was examined. The accuracy of recall was directly correlated to the type of learning task which immediately preceded recall. The trace task facilitated recall least, whereas the interpret task facilitated recall most[42]. In other words, the accuracy of encoding or decoding in LTM seems to be a function of the learning task. This supports the importance of the functionality of representations. What was recalled in the trace task was a set of lines which did not necessarily have semantic associations between them and in the interpret task the lines seemed to correspond to the various semantic relationships represented in the floor plans.

The hypothesis that explains this result is that recall is more efficient in the case of the interpret task because the organization of information in LTM is implemented differently as a function of this task. To test this hypothesis, principles of information organization exhibited in the recall data were examined. Each floor plan was divided up into unit elements called *domains* as a function of the chunks identified earlier. Each domain by definition corresponds to the smallest area in the floor plan that is outlined by a continuous ring of line segments and one that completely contains all line segments included within at least one chunk.

---

[41] The term 'compiled' refers to the appropriateness of the state of information for the purposes for which the information will be used. For example, if the purpose is to plot an exponential curve, the generalized form of the information would be the exponential equation and the specific form of the information would be all data points on the curve. Hence the compiled form is easy to use but requires excessive storage space whereas the general form requires virtually no storage space yet needs a lot of computation or compilation before it can be used.

[42] The significance of these results have been verified statistically (Akın, 1978b).

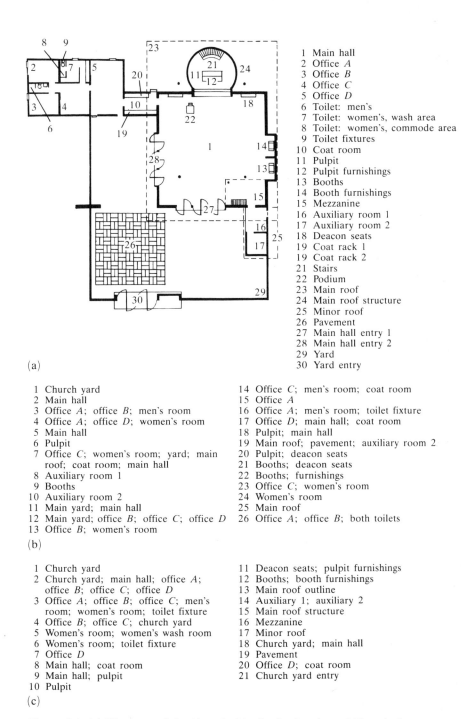

(a)

1 Main hall
2 Office *A*
3 Office *B*
4 Office *C*
5 Office *D*
6 Toilet: men's
7 Toilet: women's, wash area
8 Toilet: women's, commode area
9 Toilet fixtures
10 Coat room
11 Pulpit
12 Pulpit furnishings
13 Booths
14 Booth furnishings
15 Mezzanine
16 Auxiliary room 1
17 Auxiliary room 2
18 Deacon seats
19 Coat rack 1
19 Coat rack 2
21 Stairs
22 Podium
23 Main roof
24 Main roof structure
25 Minor roof
26 Pavement
27 Main hall entry 1
28 Main hall entry 2
29 Yard
30 Yard entry

1 Church yard
2 Main hall
3 Office *A*; office *B*; men's room
4 Office *A*; office *D*; women's room
5 Main hall
6 Pulpit
7 Office *C*; women's room; yard; main roof; coat room; main hall
8 Auxiliary room 1
9 Booths
10 Auxiliary room 2
11 Main yard; main hall
12 Main yard; office *B*; office *C*; office *D*
13 Office *B*; women's room

14 Office *C*; men's room; coat room
15 Office *A*
16 Office *A*; men's room; toilet fixture
17 Office *D*; main hall; coat room
18 Pulpit; main hall
19 Main roof; pavement; auxiliary room 2
20 Pulpit; deacon seats
21 Booths; deacon seats
22 Booths; furnishings
23 Office *C*; women's room
24 Women's room
25 Main roof
26 Office *A*; office *B*; both toilets

(b)

1 Church yard
2 Church yard; main hall; office *A*; office *B*; office *C*; office *D*
3 Office *A*; office *B*; office *C*; men's room; women's room; toilet fixture
4 Office *B*; office *C*; church yard
5 Women's room; women's wash room
6 Women's room; toilet fixture
7 Office *D*
8 Main hall; coat room
9 Main hall; pulpit
10 Pulpit

11 Deacon seats; pulpit furnishings
12 Booths; booth furnishings
13 Main roof outline
14 Auxiliary 1; auxiliary 2
15 Main roof structure
16 Mezzanine
17 Minor roof
18 Church yard; main hall
19 Pavement
20 Office *D*; coat room
21 Church yard entry

(c)

Figure 6.4. (a) The uses of the 'domains' in Sert's church, and 'domains' identified from (b) the trace task, and (c) the interpret task of subject 5.

Figure 6.4 shows the total set of domains, obtained in this fashion for
the trace [figure 6.4(b)] and interpret tasks [figure 6.4(c)].

What can we say about the organization of these domains in memory?
One logical organization seems to be the physical part–whole relationship
that exists between these domains. In terms of area, all domains with
the exception of the largest domain—the total floor plan—are subsets of
at least one other domain. If a memory system organized hierarchically
in terms of parts and wholes was used to encode the information
contained in figure 6.4, the representation of the domains would
probably 'look' something like the graphs shown in figures 6.5 and 6.6.

In these graphs each domain is placed at a level that is immediately
below the lowest of the levels which contains a domain of which the
first domain is a direct subset. For example, if domain A is a subset of
domains B, C, and D; domain B is a subset of C and D; and both C
and D are direct subsets of the largest domain, Z; then Z occupies the
highest level, say level 1; D and C occupy level 2; B occupies level 3;

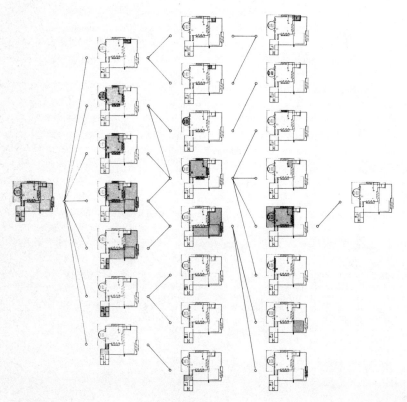

Figure 6.5. 'Domain'-dependent organization of chunks after the interpret task
(subject 5).

and A occupies level 4. This is consistent with the assumption of a proper hierarchic ordering. That is, if all domains were proper subsets of one and only one other domain then a perfect tree structure would result. In all other cases lattice-like structures with multiple parent nodes will result.

The graph resulting from the interpret task, shown in figure 6.5, is not a perfect tree structure; however, it is only four extraneous links away from it. Furthermore, no links cross over intermediary levels, the

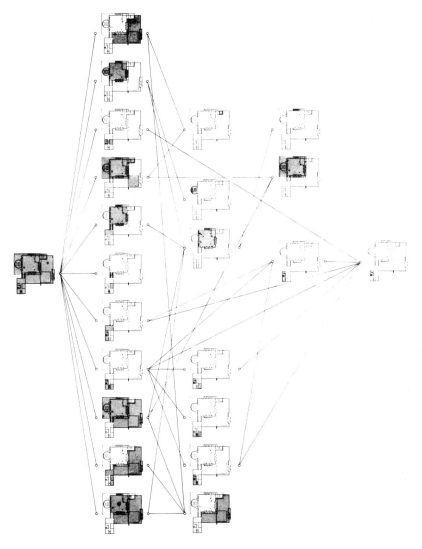

Figure 6.6. 'Domain'-dependent organization of chunks after the trace task (subject 5).

number of domains in each level is constant, and the sequence of recall is generally ordered in a top-down fashion (figure 6.7). On the other hand, the graph resulting from the trace task (figure 6.6) is as removed from a perfect tree structure as would be any randomly generated lattice structure. More than half of all of the links violate the principles of singular parent nodes and across-level boundaries. It is clear that the task of tracing over drawings induces memory organizations radically different from hierarchic tree structures and relatively poor recall performance. The interpret task, in contrast, induces a significantly more accurate recall performance and almost perfect tree organization, as suggested by the organization of nodes in figure 6.5 and the sequence of recall shown in figure 6.7.

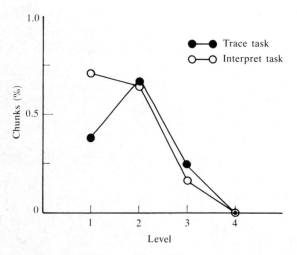

Figure 6.7. Frequency of recall of chunks during the first half of the protocols from the levels of the tree structures in figures 6.5 and 6.6.

6.3 Representation of inferential knowledge

Although the representation of visual entities is a significant part of design, architectural meaning is a product of verbal-conceptual information, as well. When the designer examines a required proximity matrix of different rooms of a building he or she may conclude that different clusters of rooms have to go together to make up the different wings of the building. Or, after examining the problem brief, he or she may decide on a particular structural grid for the building. Although visual information is utilized extensively, we can characterize the knowledge producing these conclusions as conceptual constructs. Let us now review rewriting rules, an example of such a construct illustrating the thought process underlying the manipulation of conceptual information, particularly in the case of architectural problems.

Rewriting rules, a term selected for brevity and from a precedent in cognitive psychology and artificial intelligence literature, is descriptive of the more general IF–THEN structures we reviewed earlier. That is, in contrast to procedural information, as in the case of production systems, they simply define equivalency of descriptions or attributes of schemata. For example, if we know that A is equivalent to B and B to C, then we can write B in place of A, and C in place of B or A. Similarly, if we know that 'Michael designed a building' and that the building he designed is 'exceptionally good' then we can say 'Michael is a good designer'. That is, we can rewrite the two earlier statements in a new form. The information we convey is purely descriptive and does not directly call for any action.

In this section we shall review an empirical study which focuses on this process of rewriting in the context of architecture. As in the section dealing with visual representations, the experimental task used to study rewriting rules is not a design task, but a task called building-puzzle that requires interpretation of architectural drawings. The reasons behind this decision are:

1 The design task is too complex to allow tight experimental design for the study of rewriting rules;

2 The building-puzzle task, although involving only a subset of the design process, incorporates a sufficiently interesting subset of design behavior, namely information acquisition.

6.3.1 Experiment 2: building puzzle

The task used in this experiment, building-puzzle, was derived from the picture-puzzle task devised by Ohlander et al (1976). The task requires the 'understanding' of a building from a set of drawings. This understanding was formed through answers obtained to questions asked by the subjects about the drawings. Subjects were not allowed visually to examine the drawings throughout the experiment. The experimenter was responsible for answering the subject's questions about each drawing. The level of understanding required of each subject was (a) to identify the name of the category the building belongs in, such as residence, school, hospital, and (b) to describe the use and physical properties of the parts of the building, such as rooms, halls, adjoining areas, and functions.

The stimulus used in the building-puzzle experiment was a residence designed by Jose Louis Sert. The experimenter had in his possession a section and a plan of the building (figure 6.8, see over). The average session lasted about one and a half hours. Table 6.1 illustrates the typical exchange between the subjects and the experimenter. At the end of the sessions the subjects had considerable information about the building and its parts. Two architects from the faculty of the Department of Architecture, Carnegie-Mellon University, participated in this experiment[43].

----

[43] They are subject 8 and subject 9 (referred to in section 6.2.4).

Table 6.1. Sample protocol of subject 8 from the building-puzzle task (*S* subject, *E* experimenter).

S OK. Let's get the maximum dimensions in *X*, *Y*, and *Z*. That is what's the length and the height.

E I don't have a scale. I'm going to scale everything off this person. These are inches .... Why don't I construct a scale here.

S OK.

E You want the maximum dimensions of the drawing?

S I want *X*, *Y*, and *Z*.

E Ah. *X* is 126–128, *Z* is around 16.

S 16?

E Of course you realize that it varies. I'm just sort of taking the average. And the *Y* dimension is 64.

S Is *Y* the height?

E No. *Z* is the height.

S OK. Fine. Is it all ... are the exterior walls all ... are the exterior surfaces all plane?

E Yes. Except for the top. If you have a top view, you might have some nonplanar surfaces.

S And except in the *X* and *Y* are they all right angles?

E *X* and *Y* ... they are almost 99%, yes.

S Is the ... I assume that this is a building.

E I guess so.

S In the normal. People occupy them.

E I guess so.

S Not necessarily occupy there are spaces that people go in and out of.

E Yes I guess so but this sort of infringing on my limit to understand so ...

S Is the main door on the long or the short side?

E Main door. Well, I can see some doors but I don't know which one is really the main door.

S Is it important what the materials are?

E Well no, I guess that's too long and we may not have time to go into that.

S Let's move up and get the roof shape down a little bit. Being long and rectangular like this, I assume that there's probably a ridge. Is there a ridge?

E I don't know what that is.

S A ridge means that there is a beam, a longitudinal beam that supports two planes of the roof. I don't know what a ridge is but that is what I think is a reasonable definition of a ridge. So that there are two planes intersecting one another somewhere in covering this surface.

E I really don't know what ... I really don't have a picture of a ridge yet.

S OK. Is there, is the, I assume that the bottom plane, that is the minimum *Z* is approximately perpendicular to gravity. Maybe different heights I haven't discovered.

E Yes.

S OK. The top of this shape then ... is it made of more than one plane?

E Yes, well in this one drawing which is the section, there are different planes that are parallel to.

S You're talking about the outside.

E Yes, at the top—the very top there are different planes, disconnected planes.

S Let me ask you about that section. Is the section a long section or a short section?

E It's a long section.

S OK. How many planes are there?

E How many planes?

S On the roof.

E On the roof. OK, I can identify ... are you talking about any old plane or just a flat plane?

S Any old plane.

E About four disconnected planes ... that section goes through.

S On the top. I'm at the top. OK, I guess its important to .... If there's that many it's likely that there's some reflection of those plane levels with the floor plan so let me come back and pick up something about the topology of the plan.

E If at any time you have any hypotheses or conclusions about what's gathered or inferences made, if you verbalize that will be very valuable.

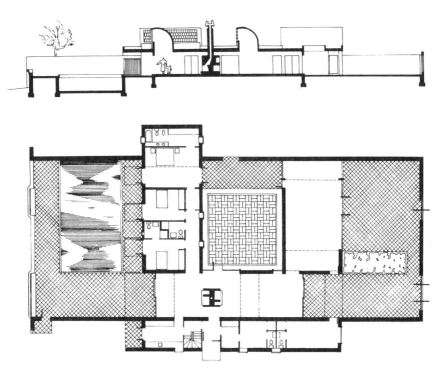

Figure 6.8. Plan of a residence designed by Jose Louis Sert.

6.3.2 Rewriting rules

The exchange between the experimenter and the subjects was recorded on audiotape. To identify the rewriting rules used by subjects the following method was used: (1) all of the *information* that was made available to the subjects by the experimenter was identified in the protocols, (2) then all the *conclusions* reached by the subjects about the stimulus were identified; since the subjects were explicitly asked to report their knowledge about the building at the end of each protocol most of the data in this category comes from those portions of the protocols, (3) then all those instances where the *information* gathered by the subject matched his conclusions were encoded. The information obtained in step '3' was defined as rewriting rules.

Consider the following examples. A subject reviews the information obtained about a portion of the building which is a 7 ft high room[44] with no visible access relationships to any other area. He concludes that this area is not inhabited. Thus, we infer that he uses a rewriting rule, such as: "If there is no access to an area, then that area must be uninhabited". Similarly, at some later point in the protocol he states: "In the normal buildings ought to be occupied by people". This can

[44] Which, in reality, is a swimming pool.

also be represented as a rewriting rule: 'if the object is a building, then it must be occupied by people'. Although alternative interpretations of this rule are possible, ambiguities in transcription of the data were minimized by prompting the subjects to report their assumptions and conclusions during the course of the experiments.

At this point it should be noted that rewriting rules represent generalities that are imprecise and even incorrect. For example, in the case of the above examples all areas without regular stair access need not be considered uninhabited. Elevators under special circumstances may be totally adequate substitutes for stairs. Or not all buildings, such as those that are abandoned or reserved for mechanical use alone, are occupied. Yet the possibility of such ambiguities do not render rewriting rules useless. On the contrary, they are more suitable for simulating human behavior precisely because of this property. Humans seem to draw their problem-solving expertise from their ability to deal with imprecise information. Thus, the imprecise nature of rewriting rules allow them to be used as general tools for problem-solving with a wide range of applicability. Before we get preoccupied with discussing the role of rewriting rules, however, let us first study their structural properties.

The syntax developed earlier for IF–THEN structures is perfectly adequate as a general purpose representation, suitable also for the rewriting rules observed in this experiment. Based on this syntax a rewriting rule consists of two major parts; a premise and an implication where each part in turn consists of tokens and their attributes. In formal BNF notation[45] (Bachus, 1960) this can be expressed as:

⟨rewriting rule⟩ :: = IF ⟨predicate⟩ THEN ⟨predicate⟩
⟨predicate⟩ :: = ⟨token⟩⟨connector⟩⟨token⟩ | ⟨predicate⟩⟨predicate⟩
⟨token⟩ :: = NULL | BUILDING | WINDOW
   (see table 6.1 for a complete list)
⟨connector⟩ :: = ⟨relation⟩ | ⟨qualifier⟩ | ⟨connector⟩⟨connector⟩
⟨relation⟩ :: = IS | HAS | REPRESENTS
⟨qualifier⟩ :: = NOT | I ASSUME | AN INSTANCE OF |
            IN THE NORMAL | WITH RESPECT TO |
            APPROXIMATELY | AND | OR | OUGHT TO |
            PART OF | THAT | MORE | ATTRIBUTE OF |
            IN BETWEEN | FULL OF | SOME.

[45] In this notation the entries in capital letters stand for the *primitives* (natural language words) that make up the rules. Entries inside angle-brackets represent higher order constructs of the formal language and its grammar. Vertical bars stand for OR and the symbol :: = stands for equivalency, that is, the right-hand side can be substituted for the symbol on the left-hand side.

The list of all tokens found in one of the protocols from the building-puzzle task are provided in table 6.2. Types of tokens observed are categorized into three groups: spatial, architectural, and functional. Each predicate defines a relationship between these tokens or declares their attributes. This is accomplished by the *relation* constructs. A relation is made up of a simple relation (IS, HAS, or REPRESENTS) and a *qualifier*. The three simple relations with the aid of sixteen qualifiers are sufficient to express all of the relationships found in the subjects' protocols. The function of the qualifiers is to specify further the intended nuances within each simple relation category. For example, when the relation 'has' is coupled with the qualifier 'part of' it implies a

Table 6.2. Tokens used in the building-puzzle protocols.

Representational	*Architectural*
dimensions	environment
length	street
width	building
height	side of
coordinates (x, y, z)	(right, left, front) side of
drawing	enclosed
single-line drawing	top
outline of	axis
bottom half of	portion of
left side of	enclosed, inside
right side of	outside
top, upper half of	minimum z-plane, perpendicular to
rectangular decomposition	gravity
axis	plan-view
edge, linear, line segment	horizontal section
angles	long side
right angles	short side
Functional	outline
function (of building)	roof reflection
zoo	enclosed part
major	outdoor part
many	section
activity space	long
circulation, access	short
people going in and out	rooms, spaces, areas, locations
connection (via doors)	hierarchy of
direct access	major
from outside	accessible
from other spaces	toilet facility
recreation	commode
inhabited, occupied	lavatory
support	shower
beam	corridor
	walls, partitions
	uninterrupted, continuous

whole-to-part relationship between two tokens. Similarly, when 'has' is coupled with 'is part of' it implies a part-to-whole relationship.

The qualifiers are much more diverse in scope than the relations, and they determine whether the predicate formed is a premise or an implication as well as whether it is in negative form (IS NOT), in stochastic form (IS APPROXIMATELY), or in normative form (IS IN THE NORMAL). An examination of the protocol segment in table 6.1 will further illustrate each category.

6.3.3 Rewriting rules and inductive reasoning in design

Rewriting rules have properties that render them useful in the context of tasks, such as understanding architectural drawings or even designing. One such property is modularity. Each rule represents a fragment of knowledge that is valid in a limited context, that which is defined by the premise of the rule. Hence, the same premise can be applicable in a wide range of problem contexts. For example, the rule, 'IF passive solar heating is needed in room x, THEN room x ought to have a south facing wall', is useful in designing passive-solar-heated rooms in general. On the other hand, because of this property of modularity, individual rules can easily lead to erroneous conclusions. For example, if the solar heat to be used in a room is to be obtained from a wall surface belonging to another space with better solar orientation, then the rule given above is clearly insufficient. To resolve this problem, some means of airflow must be established between the two rooms. The correct solution can be reached if and only if the designer uses another rule related to heat transfer such as 'IF heat transfer between two rooms is needed, THEN provide a duct or heat-conducting medium connecting the rooms', in conjunction with the previous rule. Alternatively, a rule may not work in contexts other than the ones implicitly considered. For example, the above principles would apply only in the northern hemisphere. The potentially erroneous use can be resolved by applying the rule in conjunction with another rule modifying the first one and adapting it to the specific context; such as, 'IF in the southern hemisphere, THEN the directional conventions must be reversed'.

To accomplish this kind of collaboration between independent rewriting rules the designer must be able to identify all rules applicable to the problem state at hand, isolate the implications which can be used in connection with the production of a solution, isolate the implications which are in conflict with one another, and use this knowledge to identify new goals. Erman and Lesser's (1975) work in speech recognition provides an example of such an application. Because of modularity in the knowledge-base they used, they were able to bring a large set of rules to bear on the speech-understanding problem. In this way, they were able to minimize redundancy in the knowledge base. Also the modular structure allows ease of modification enabling the simulation of learning and contextual adaptation of the knowledge base[46].

6.3.4 Learning and rewriting rules

Learning new rules, or the generation of new rules from the old, is also accommodated by the rewriting rule paradigm. If we consider the space of all rewriting rules as a pool of premises $(P_1, P_2, ..., P_l)$ and implications $(I_1, I_2, ..., I_m)$, then the rules themselves $(R_1, R_2, ..., R_n)$ could be presented as causal associations between these premises and implications;

$$R_r : P_p \to I_i, \qquad \text{where } 1 < r < n; \quad 1 < p < l; \quad 1 < i < m.$$

It should be obvious that not all premises can be logically associated to all implications. Even if this were possible, all associations, in reality, may not be present. This is equivalent to saying that the designer may not know all logical implications of all premises that he is aware of. For example, consider the sequence of rewriting rules used by the cartoon character of *Sesame Street* as she considers popping a balloon (section 6.1.2). Initially she does not know that the ultimate implication of the premise 'popping the balloon' would be 'not being able to eat the chocolate cake'. Not until she chains a particular set of rewriting rules, by making the implication of one the premise of the next, does she discover this new association. The chaining of rewriting rules $(R_1, R_2, ..., R_n)$ in this fashion can be represented as:

$$R_1 : P_1 \to I_1,$$
$$R_2 : P_2 \to I_2,$$
$$R_3 : P_3 \to I_3,$$
$$R_n : P_l \to I_m.$$

Where

$$I_1 :: = P_2, \qquad I_2 :: = P_3, \qquad ... \qquad I_{m-1} :: = P_l.$$

Thus, if the association $P_1 \to I_m$ did not exist in the rewriting rule space up to the time when the chaining occurred, then the chaining may be sufficient evidence to recognize it as a new rule. Hence, it can be added to the knowledge base as an entirely new rule. Such a rule is also an example of a precompiled rewriting rule. A precompiled rule is one that has been obtained through internal inferences rather than through direct observation of external events. In the case of our *Sesame Street* character the precompiled rule would read 'IF I pop this balloon, THEN I will not be able to eat any chocolate cake tonight'. Next time she

---

[46] The modular representation of knowledge sources have been used extensively in research of automated understanding of speech and images, undertaken by Reddy and his colleagues at the Computer Science Department of Carnegie-Mellon University (Reddy and Newell, 1974).

encounters an identical circumstance she will apply the precompiled rule, thus avoiding lengthy deliberations.

It should be noted that this represents one form of learning akin to 'discovery'. Another form of learning is also necessary if we consider the generality of rewriting rules. For instance, in the above example the precompiled rule lacks generality and is not applicable unless the identical circumstances of the little girl, the balloon, her baby sister, the mother, and the chocolate cake exist all at once. On the other hand, learning through an extended period of time based on many inferences about 'mischiefs' and 'punishments' will enable the cartoon character to compile a new rewriting rule, such as 'IF I do some mischief, such as popping a balloon, THEN I am likely to be punished, (AND one form of punishment is not eating chocolate cake)'. This kind of learning is certainly less 'error-inducing' than the earlier one.

A third form of learning is the common 'learning from experience' type. In this case, observation (or assumption) of causal relationships in the external world will imply rules that formalize those relationships. If B is observed every time A is observed, then the rule would be 'IF A THEN B'. Or if we see many residents moving out of inner-city neighborhoods we may assert that 'IF an inner-city neighborhood, THEN residents will move out'. However naive this may sound, it is a prerequisite for the other more complex forms of learning, discussed above.

The syntax and properties of rewriting rules are also suitable for automatic simulations of human behavior. In fact, the similarities between this syntax and other information-processing models of human reasoning is not accidental (Lenat, 1976; Newell, 1973; Shank, 1975). In the next chapter, I shall describe and discuss a computer system that simulates the rewriting rule paradigm for the building-puzzle task using a representation domain that is modelled after the findings of this chapter.

6.4 Suggested readings

1 Boulding K, 1969 *The Image* (University of Michigan Press, Ann Arbor, MI)
2 Chase W G, Simon H A, 1973, "The mind's eye in chess" in *Visual Information Processing* Ed. W G Chase (Academic Press, New York) pp 215–282
3 Eastman C, 1978, "Representation of design problems and maintenance of their structure" in *Artificial Intelligence and Pattern Recognition in Computer Aided Design* Ed. J C Latombe (North-Holland, New York) pp 335–366

6.5 Exercises

6.1 Recall a familiar room and its contents, other than the one you are now in. Record on paper all that you have recalled. Use these notes and your introspections to record the parts and subparts of the room and the sequence in which you have recalled them. Draw a tree graph representing these parts and subparts. What kind of recall strategy have you used in accessing the information about the room and its parts? How can recall be made more efficient, in the context of the graph you have drawn? Illustrate.

6.2 Enumerate all representations of the room cited above that would allow you to
(a) estimate the volume of your room;
(b) estimate the volume of air in your room;
(c) estimate the amount of paint needed to change the color of all wall surfaces in your room.

6.3 Determine which representations are most suitable for each and all of the three purposes cited in exercise 6.2.

6.4 Write a chain of rewriting rules that would allow you to assert, 'the client is always right', given that your premise is, 'form follows function'.

Inductive reasoning in architecture

"Proposals to construct man-like machines are nothing new. The following particularly charming excerpt from the *Scotsman* newspaper of 100 years ago recently came to my attention: 'A STEAM MAN – The "Newark Advertiser" (New Jersey) describes the very extraordinary invention of a machine which, moved by steam, will perform some of the most important functions of humanity—stand upright, walk or run, as he is bid, in any direction, and at almost any rate of speed, drawing after him a load whose weight would tax the strength of three stout draught horses. In order to prevent the "giant" from frightening horses by its powerful appearance the inventor intends to clothe it and give it as nearly as possible a likeness to the rest of the humanity. The boilers and such parts as are necessarily heated will be encased in felt or woollen garments. Pantaloons, coat and vest, of the latest styles, are provided. Whenever the fires need coaling, which is evey two or three hours, the driver stops the machine, descends from his seat, unbuttons "Damel's" vest, opens a door, shovels in the fuel, buttons up the vest, and drives on."

D Michie *On Machine Intelligence* (1974, page 4)

The simulation of human functions by tools and machines is not a new preoccupation. Surprisingly, the similarities between the simulation reported in *The Scotsman* of a century ago, the Steam Man, and the information-processing research of today are many. First of all, both deal with the manifestation of humanlike behavior through artificial means. They both measure the success of this task through the similarities produced in behavior rather than physionomic similarities. And they both take the human system as the model of the machine.

IPT, on the other hand, deals with cognitive skills as its central concern and its purpose is to achieve an understanding of the human system. Consequently, its motive and methods are fundamentally different from the pragmatic motives and methods of the Steam Man. The major purpose of computer simulation is to test the validity of process models in the context of IPT. That is, by showing that the computer systems produce behaviors closely resembling those of humans, the validity of these models can be demonstrated.

The purpose of this chapter is akin to this general objective. Here we shall explore the process of reasoning with architectural information, using the computer as the medium of simulation. The particular aspect of DIPS which will be tested is its inductive reasoning capacity. Hence, this chapter has three goals: (1) to implement the design information-processing model, DIPS, in the computer to demonstrate its reasoning capability, (2) to demonstrate that the model has reasoning capabilities compatible with those seen in human protocols, and (3) to show that this capability can be extended to other tasks.

7.1 Inductive reasoning with computers

The most complete computer implementation of conceptual reasoning to date comes from the research of Shank (1975) and his associates. Their system, called MARGIE, can take an input statement of the kind 'John gave Mary a beating with a stick', and, based on its knowledge about semantics, generate a set of responses of the kind: 'a stick touched Mary', 'Mary became hurt', and 'John wanted Mary to become hurt'.

MARGIE performs this task in three stages. First, it translates the input sentence into an internal representation. Then it makes some inferences consistent with this input. Finally, it transforms these internal inferences back to the natural language format. Shank and his associates call the kind of reasoning that MARGIE performs *conceptual inference making*. They contrast this against logical inference making in ways already reviewed in section 6.1.2.

Conceptual inference making has been modelled in many different contexts but most often and skilfully in the area of natural language-understanding systems. Reddy and his associates at Carnegie-Mellon University have developed sophisticated speech-understanding systems that are knowledge intensive. They use a form of reasoning which discriminates natural language utterances in real time (Reddy and Newell, 1974). Diverse sources of knowledge structured in modular form assist in developing hypotheses about the identity of speech sounds. The power of their system comes from the diversity and cooperation of these knowledge sources as well as from the superiority of their search algorithms.

Natural language understanding is not the only application of knowledge-intensive reasoning with computers. Lenat (1976) has applied reasoning to the area of mathematical discovery and heuristics. His system, called AM, starts out with the basic axioms of mathematics and builds upon this knowledge using its reasoning capabilities. Lenat was able to show through this that AM could in fact discover mathematical concepts that are entirely new to the system, such as multiplication and division, as well as concepts somewhat new to the scientific community at large. Lenat's finding, although fundamentally unrelated to reasoning, bears similarities to Reddy's work, through the form and content of its knowledge base.

In the area of architectural applications, knowledge-intensive systems are rare. Latombe (1977) in his dissertation work has developed an information-processing model of the designer. His work primarily dwells on developing superior prescriptive algorithmic methods for design subtasks and then orchestrating these pieces into a total design system. Although powerful because of this approach, his model is confined to analytic methods and therefore lacks the generality we need to model the human designer.

The best implementation of reasoning with architectural stimuli to date is the drawing–understanding system built by Herot (1974). This system

works on sketches produced by designers. Based on the lines drawn on
a tablet, the system builds internal representations of objects consistent
with the 'intentions' of designers. The system works in collaboration with
various sketch-interpreting systems, such as HUNCH (Taggart, 1975)
and STRAIN (Herot, 1974). Herot's system uses the line-coordinate
information developed by these interpretation systems and the a priori
knowledge about the building type the designer intends to sketch. As a
first step in this process, the system selects an internal representation
that is most appropriate for the building type the designer is working on.
To enable this, the system is equipped with prior knowledge about building
types, their parts and attributes, stored in a hierarchical fashion.
Basically, the system conducts an iterative top-down search in this
knowledge space to reduce the difference between it and the information
it is given in the form of a sketch.

Herot's system, although powerful in many respects, has shortcomings
in terms of the general purpose understanding task. For one thing, it
does not seek knowledge from external sources to perform its task. Its
communication channel works in only one direction, that is, from the
user to the system. Second, it is dependent on other systems for its
input and it can only operate in the visual mode. Third, it can only
deal with a 'better defined' problem, that is, must have prior knowledge
about the type of building. Fourth, it cannot deal with representations
other than floor plans. Fifth, its knowledge base cannot be easily
expanded. However, it is the first of its kind integrating an architectural
knowledge base with a graphic input system.

In this chapter, I shall review a computer system I have developed
called architectural inference maker (AIM). AIM was designed to
simulate the inference-making process in architecture and overcome
some of the difficulties cited above. Before examining AIM in more
detail, let us try to develop a description of the task domain of
architectural 'inference making' which it models.

7.2 Codifying human reasoning
The inference task used here is the building-puzzle already discussed in
section 6.3. Since there is incomplete information about how humans
perform this task in the first place, our initial objective is to define the
human understanding process for this task domain. Subsequently, this
will be used as a benchmark for developing AIM.

This benchmark will be used as the basis for evaluating AIM. That
is, the success with which AIM carries out its task will be measured
against the performance of a human carrying out the same task. In
calibrating the performance of automated systems, Turing (1950)
proposed a similar test, named after him. He argued that, if an
independent observer is unable to discriminate between the behaviors
exhibited by the computer system and the human, both performing the

same task, then the intelligence of the computer system must be considered to be equal to that of the human for the task in question. In essence, the Turing test provides the impetus for casting AIM in the image of its human counterpart from the onset.

7.2.1 Experimental design

To enable better calibration of human performance in the context of the building-puzzle task, an experiment was conducted. Four practicing architects served as subjects (they shall be called subject 10, subject 11, subject 12, and subject 13). Each session lasted about forty minutes and was completely recorded on tape. The drawings used in the experiments were a site-plan, plan, and sections of one of the single-person residences designed in the experiment discussed in chapters 3 and 5. A portion of the conversation between subject 10 and the experimenter is provided in table 7.1 (see over). During the protocol excerpt included in table 7.1, only the site-plan (figure 7.1) was used.

Let us now review this protocol excerpt. The first question asked by subject 10 is about the size of the site (lines 3 and 5). He explains his intent in asking this question in a statement in line 6 of the protocol. Because of the small size of the site, he decides to eliminate a set of building types like a baseball diamond or office building and to concentrate on things like residential buildings. Next he asks about the amount of parking, hillyness of the site, coverage on site, number of stories, and the structural span of the building (lines 7 – 11). In the following exchange (lines 13 – 17) the subject explains that each of these issues is potentially useful in determining the identity of the building. The number of parking places being nonexistent, the number of storeys being just a few, the site coverage being small, and the spans being less than 20 ft all imply a residential use on the site. At this point subject 10 is either satisfied with his accomplishments or simply runs

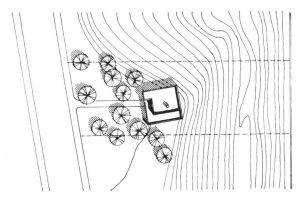

Figure 7.1. Stimulus used in building-puzzle experiment with subject 10.

out of questions and stops. After the experimenter asks him to continue with the task some more, he continues to explore the building.

Table 7.1. Protocol excerpt from building-puzzle task of subject 10 (*S* subject, *E* experimenter).

S Am I going to look at the drawing 1 immediately?

E No you won't look at the drawings at all.

S Oh, I see I thought I was going to 2 be looking at abstract drawings

E Until, the end of the whole thing. Just try to understand it based on the answers I give you.

S Fine. What's the site area?   3

E What do you mean?

S Site, size.   4

E Oh size, OK.

S Acreage or whatever.   5

E OK, site is, OK, let's find a scale ... it's about ... uh ... let me just figure this out. About 60 by 150.

S So we know it isn't a baseball   6 diamond. 60 × 150. How much parking?

E I don't see any parking at all.

S No parking. Uh, what's the site 7 character? Hilly, flat.

E One portion of it, like 60 by 60, roughly, it's not a square shape ... at all but somewhat that type of an area is almost flat, and the rest is quite steep.

S How much of the site does the   8 building occupy?

E I'd say, ... about one twelfth, roughly. You see I'm trying to get at how you arrive at conclusions. So if at all you have some hunches about what this thing is, even if they're not very accurate I would appreciate it if you would say it, whenever I say OK, the site is one twelfth, does that mean anything, can you infer something from that?

S Well only from the standpoint that 9 its ... the next question is well how many stories is this building?

E How many stories, I see, so in itself it doesn't mean anything without ... it's about two stories.

S Now the one twelfth coverage   10 doesn't mean anything. Two stories.

E Well it may not be two full stories, but there are two levels at least.

S Structural spans?   11

E I am just again trying to get at what you're ... why are you asking?

S Well I want to know if it's a big 12 clear span, then it's assembly type space, and ....

E Well the largest span is about 16 feet.

S The largest span is 16 ft, sounds 13 like a residence

E OK, why did you say that?

S The span   14

E Any of the previous information contributing to that.

S Well this was the no parking, on- 15 site parking ... was a tickler. The site size is approximately residential.

E I see.

S It might be a city residential lot, 16 but that's not necessarily so, it could have been a branch bank or something. But it still could be a branch bank, for that matter.

E What other type of building could it be if you were to speculate at this point, if you had to guess what this building was without asking any further questions, what would you.

S I would say ... uh, probably a   17 residence. Because of the site coverage.

E OK, go on.

7.2.2 Knowledge used in the task domain
Even from this short excerpt it is clear that the ability to make inferences in the building-puzzle task relies on vast amounts of prior knowledge. As demonstrated in Lenat's work on mathematical discovery (1976) and Reddy's work on speech understanding (Reddy and Newell, 1974), the ability to understand knowledge-rich domains (architectural drawings included) hinges on the effective use of knowledge in making inferences. Therefore, the thrust of the analysis here is directed towards codifying the knowledge used in the understanding process. The three categories of knowledge used in modelling DIPS (figure 4.2)— representational, inferential, and heuristic—will also be used here to codify the building-puzzle task.

7.2.2.1 *Representational knowledge*
This is the knowledge that is specific to the representation of the problem at hand. In the case of the protocol excerpt in table 7.1, this information is illustrated in the form of factual statements: the site is "about 60 by 150" feet; "I don't see any parking". A collection of such facts form a context that is akin to the collection of notes and drawings on the designer's sketchpad. This allows the subject to formulate assumptions and goals about the task as well as to keep a running record of findings. This knowledge seems to be codified in a structured way and as a function of the parts of the object under examination. Often this structure is a hierarchic one.

7.2.2.2 *Transformational knowledge*
This category of knowledge allows the problem-solver to transform a given information state into another. Through this transformation process he or she can move from one representation to the next, and ultimately towards a representation that provides a solution to the problem at hand. In the case of the building-puzzle task this solution is a detailed description of the object to be understood. For example, the subject knows that the site has no parking facilities. He transforms this information into several probable implications: 'the function on the site requires no vehicular access', 'users do not drive', 'the user cannot drive or is disabled', 'the site is in an urban context and is accessed only by foot', or 'the user does not choose to own a car'. Further expansion of these assumptions vis-à-vis new transformations enables the subject to decide which are (or are likely to be) the correct inferences.

7.2.2.3 *Procedural knowledge*
This category allows the problem-solver to organize his or her activities in a goal-directed manner. At least in the context of the building-puzzle task this comes in the form of heuristics. Heuristics allow the subject to reduce the size of the space to be searched, or the operations to be executed to

find a solution, without jeopardizing the chances of reaching a successful solution. A heuristic rule typically has three parts: (a) specification of the context within which it is applicable, (b) sequence of operations that must be performed to apply the heuristics, and (c) the results that are likely to follow if the heuristics are applied properly.

The general heuristic method used in the building-puzzle tasks is generate-and-test (GAT). Subjects first develop a hypothesis about a property of the object being investigated (the generate part) and then they seek specific information to verify or refute their hypothesis (the test part). Although other methods also provide a plausible paradigm, the GAT strategy is the most parsimonious one that characterizes the totality of all subjects' behaviors. Through the repeated application of this strategy, subjects accumulate information about the object to be understood, bringing their information states progressively closer to an acceptable solution state.

7.3 An architecture for machine reasoning: AIM

AIM is a system designed to perform the building-puzzle task. Its objective is to discover the identity of an object by sampling information about its general properties. In conformity to the three types of knowledge summarized above, AIM is designed around three major components: working memory space, rewriting rule space, and heuristic rule space.

7.3.1 The working memory space

The working memory space (WMS) of AIM has two basic parts: (a) action stack (AS): a temporally ordered record of actions of the system, and (b) object representation space (ORS): a node–link graph which records all information obtained about the object being examined. AS simulates a chronological memory facility and records all interactions in their temporal sequence. ORS is a time-independent record of all the knowledge acquired and the transformation of information performed to acquire this knowledge. The contents of AS are very similar to the chronological nature of the protocol itself and allow AIM to remember its past actions and as a result plan its future actions. ORS provides a clear and concise summary of AIM's current understanding of the object at any given moment and thus corresponds more closely to a human working memory.

7.3.1.1 Action stack (AS)

This is a simple list structure that operates as a single push-down stack[47]. When AIM applies a heuristic that consists of several steps,

[47] A push-down stack is a structure for storing information in memory systems. Its operation resembles a set of physical files stacked up on top of a desk where the file at the very top is processed first and each file on the stack retains its temporal recency to all the other files when scanned top-down. In building memory systems many different ways of processing stacks exist; such as, first-in last-out, first-in first-out, etc.

AS also serves as a goal stack. It contains a chronological list of all operations. The only time when the temporal sequence of this list is modified is when AIM runs out of things to do and revives an operation that was planned earlier but never implemented. In such cases this operation is simply moved up to the top of the stack. Each entry on the AS has three parts represented as three successive list entries (figure 7.2). The first entry in the list is a symbol indicating the type of operation or heuristic step. The second entry is a keyword signifying the 'status' of the operation, that is, whether it is completed, not completed, or postponed. The final entry is a list structure in itself which allows the storing of parameters computed by the current operation or heuristics. This entry is not used in all cases but is useful when a parameter has to be conveyed to an action to be performed later and which constitutes another step in the heuristic processes being applied.

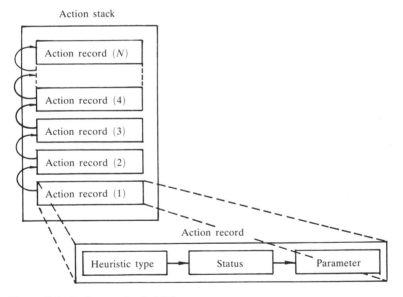

Figure 7.2. Action stack of AIM.

7.3.1.2 *Object representation space* (*ORS*)

AIM's understanding of the drawing at any given time is represented internally as a node–link graph (figure 7.3). Each node contains a name signifying a schema or token, such as 'site', 'building', 'rooms', etc, and each link represents a relation that is observed between these names or schemata, such as 'has', 'is', 'is-a-type', 'has-a-part'[48]. The syntax of the strings formed by these nodes and links are identical to

[48] The complete list of symbols used corresponds to the relations constructs codified in section 6.3.2.

the syntax of the predicates that are used in representing AIM's long-term transformational knowledge, which will be discussed in the next section.

Each token in ORS represents a specific object as opposed to a general one, such as, *the* chair, versus *any* chair[49]. Each token is represented as a name (for example, chair) coupled with an identity number. This allows the coexistence of many instances, or tokens, of the same symbol class in the ORS. Also multiple nodes can be related to the same token via many predicates. Hence, the individual node–link strings stored in the ORS form lattice-like structures. This allows the use of the same token to form parts of many different strings, or predicates (figure 7.3). For example, figure 7.3 indicates that 'parking 1' 'is large' and also 'has users 1'. It also states that both 'parking 1' and 'building 1' have the same user group, 'users 1'. In this way, tokens in ORS are related unambiguously to each other as dictated by the current state of AIM's 'understanding' of the drawing.

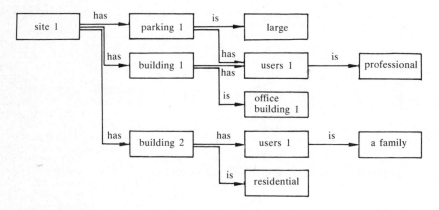

Figure 7.3. Object representation space of AIM.

7.3.2 Rewriting rule space (RRS)

To reason or to make conceptual inferences, AIM has to transform information it has about the object it is studying into other forms. This is accomplished by AIM's long-term knowledge of the object world represented in the form of rewriting rules (or IF–THEN structures). The first part, the IF-part, is a predicate that describes the necessary context within which the rule can be applied. The second part, the THEN-part, is a predicate that describes a relation that is likely to hold if the context described in the first part is applicable.

To avoid redundancy, each rewriting rule is represented as the association of two predicates. This permits modularity in the representation

---

[49] A more complete definition is provided in chapter 2.

of the RRS. Hence, each predicate can be used as an IF-clause and be connected to many other predicates which are appropriate THEN-clauses, and vice versa. That is, a predicate can be used as an IF-clause as well as a THEN-clause.

Predicates consist of sets of symbols (defined in section 3.3.1) associated by relationships. A frequently used relationship is the part–whole relationship. For example, schemata, such as, 'site', 'building', 'rooms', are often related to one another through 'part–whole' relationships. That is, rooms are parts of buildings and buildings are parts of sites.

Table 7.2. Rewriting rule space of AIM.

Predicate	Pointers to	Pointers from
(1001 1)		
TASK HASTYPE PICTURE-PUZZLE	((1002 1))	((1002 1) (1003 1))
(1001 2)		
TASK HASTYPE TUNNEL-VISION	((1002 2))	((1002 2) (1005 1))
(1002 1)		
OBJECT HASA MODE-OF-INPUT IS-A VERBAL	((1001 1))	((1001 1))
(1002 2)		
OBJECT HASA MODE-OF-INPUT IS-A VISUAL	((1001 2))	((1001 2))
(1003 1)		
SYSTEM HASA PICTURE-PUZZLE-KNOWLEDGE IS-AMOUNT SUFFICIENT	((1001 1))	(NIL))
(1005 1)		
SYSTEM HASA TUNNEL--VISION-KNOWLEDGE IS-AMOUNT INSUFFICIENT	((1001 2))	(NIL))
(2001 1)		
OBJECT HASA REPRESENTN IS-A SECTIONS	(NIL)	((2123 1))
(2001 2)		
OBJECT HASA REPRESENTN IS-A SITE-PLANS	(NIL)	((2121 1))
(2001 3)		
OBJECT HASA REPRESENTN IS-A SECTIONS-AND-SITE-PLAN	(NIL)	((2122 1))
(2011 1)		
SITE HASSLOPE SHALLOW	(NIL)	(NIL))
(2011 2)		
SITE HASSLOPE MILD	(NIL)	(NIL))
(2011 3)		
SITE HASSLOPE STEEP	(NIL)	((2031 1))
(2021 1)		
BUILDING HASCOVERAGE LITTLE	((2023 1))	(NIL))
(2021 2)		
BUILDING HASCOVERAGE MEDIUM	(NIL)	(NIL))
(2021 3)		
BUILDING HASCOVERAGE LOT	(NIL)	((2031 1))

When these relationships are explicitly stored in the RRS then a
part–whole hierarchy is established between the symbols. This
information is explicitly used by AIM in focusing its attention during
search.

Table 7.2 contains a list of a number of predicates and their pointers
used during an implementation of AIM. Although this is typical, during
each run, AIM can use a new or different set of predicates. The
heuristics it uses do not rely on the contents of the RRS; however its
performance does to a great extent[50].

7.3.3 Heuristic rule space (HRS)

Functionally, this component of AIM consists of individual operations
executing the GAT method. All operations are implemented through
thirty-two procedural rules programmed in LISP. During a run, each
rule is activated when the keyword that stands for that rule is found on
the AS, in 'active' state. Once a rule is activated, the keyword that
causes its activation is put into 'passive' state to avoid its reactivation.
Heuristic rules also 'push' new keywords onto the AS to nominate other
rules for activation in the future. In this way, a series of operations can
be carried out in succession to perform composite operations.

The complete set of composite operations can be summarized under
nine categories: shifting of AIM's focus of attention, searching for new
information, hypothesizing unknown properties of the object, output
of information to user, input of information from user, parsing user
input, saving information acquired, inferring new information from
existing information, and stopping. These composite operations and the
individual procedural rules constituting each were extracted from the
protocols of subjects performing the building-puzzle task. All heuristic
rules observed were included in the design of AIM regardless of the
frequency of their use by the subjects. Let us now review these in
detail.

7.3.3.1 *Shifting the focus of attention*

The general-purpose control structure used in shifting AIM's focus of
attention can best be characterized as a 'blackboard' type mechanism
(Reddy and Newell, 1974). Many individual modules that are charged
with specific operations write their findings on the blackboard and a
central focus-of-attention mechanism, in turn, reassigns the attention of
the system to the various modules available to it as a function of the
contents of the blackboard. A first come first served principle is used
to make this selection in all cases except where the urgency of one
operation overrides the others. The modules of operation used in
shifting AIM's focus of attention are represented as a production system:

---

[50] An auxiliary system to AIM for creating and editing RRS files is available.
This allows for easy input and modification of the contents of RRS by the user.

PR1: Primary target-setting If a schema in the hierarchy of the present contents of RRS has not been identified as the *target* of AIM's investigation, then SEARCH for the schema, highest in the levels of RRS's hierarchy, to focus AIM's attention on[51].

PR2: Stopping If the system has insufficient knowledge about the task being performed and fails to identify a target, then STOP.

PR3: Target-setting If the first schema identified as the target has been successfully explored[52], then SEARCH for a new target schema in the RRS.

PR4: Breaking-set If the same schema is selected as the target more than once with similar results, then SEARCH for a different target in the RRS.

PR5: Recency in focus of attention There are three possible states for actions that AIM can take: 'active', 'passive', and 'asleep'. If one or more actions are marked as 'active', or alternatively marked as 'asleep', on the AS, then SELECT the most recent one as AIM's new focus of attention.

7.3.3.2 *Search*

The main search strategy AIM uses to search its own RRS is means – end-analysis. Before proposing a hypothesis, AIM searches its knowledge space (RRS) for the shortest chain of rewriting rules relating a schema to another one the system wants to find out about, that is, the target. Each question AIM asks is based on the rules discovered by creating paths between two predicates. This serves as a test to prune the knowledge network and to formulate plausible hypotheses. This network is implicitly defined by the tree-like structure of the RRS (table 7.2). This allows AIM to function as an EPAM [53] recognition

---

[51] The term 'target' means that part or subset of the object, upon which AIM temporarily focuses its attention to conduct its search. For example, in the building-identification task the levels that have been targeted are 'site' and 'building'. All capitalized words refer to the composite operations represented by the set of productions enumerated in each subsection. When such a word is used it indicates a point where control is passed to another composite operation category. Keywords composed of the letters 'PR' and integers are abbreviated identifications for each production used. See chapter 5 for a review of production systems.

[52] This involves the use of all other productions and constitutes a test of AIM's central task. PR8 provides an explicit test for this condition. Also see section 7.3.3.9.

[53] EPAM network is a paradigm for recognition. Given an unknown entity it applies a series of queries to it. Queries are assigned to nodes in a tree-like, hierarchical space. Each query moves the entire inquiry closer to the branches and leaves of the 'tree'. The leaves of the tree contain the possible identities for the unknown entity. When EPAM reaches any particular leaf as a consequence of satisfying all the queries on the branches leading to that leaf it announces the identity found and concludes its task.

network (Feigenbaum, 1961) as well as a general-purpose search mechanism. This is largely because AIM's SEARCH rules are independent of the inference chains implicitly defined by the RRS.

PR6: Primary-target-search If no target is identified (or specified by the user), then DEFINE the target as the first schema found in the first and highest level predicate stored in the RRS.

PR7: Target-search If a new target is needed, then SELECT the first schema in the predicate stored in the next level of the RRS which does not apply to the current target.

PR8: Satisfaction of task objectives If all possible levels of hierarchy represented in the RRS have been adequately described by AIM's findings, with respect to a measure of adequacy defined a priori, then propose to STOP. This measure has been defined as hypothesizing at least half of all possible relationships presented in RRS.

PR9: Finding-inference-paths If a schema is identified as the target and predicates are found that lie on the path[54] between already known predicates and predicates containing information about that particular schema, then HYPOTHESIZE these predicates.

PR10: Finding-exploration-paths If no predicates on the 'inference path' are found, then HYPOTHESIZE about the highest level predicate not yet explored.

7.3.3.3 *Hypothesize*

In hypothesizing certain inferences, AIM starts by identifying a schema on which to focus its attention. Then AIM selects one of the predicates found by SEARCH. This selection is based on an aggregate measure of the expected speed with which a solution can be reached. The factors included in this aggregate measure are (a) the 'bushyness' of the links assigned to the predicates in the RRS, (b) the distance of the predicate from the targeted schema, (c) the distance of the predicate from AIM's current knowledge about the object as indicated in the ORS. Some additional productions that enable AIM to hypothesize about general as well as specific schemata or predicates are included below.

PR11: Targeted hypotheses If a schema is identified as a target, then find predicates that contain it in the RRS and propose predicates pointing to it as candidate HYPOTHESES.

PR12: Predicated hypotheses If a predicate is identified as a target, then find predicates that point to this predicate in the RRS and propose them as candidate HYPOTHESES.

PR13: Rating hypotheses If one or more candidate hypotheses exist, then rate each one with respect to a set of a priori criteria related to their expected usefulness in the task, such as, number of then-clauses they point to, number of alternative parameters they have, and distance, in terms of number of predicates spanned, from the target schema.

[54] A set of predicates chained through IF–THEN links.

PR14: Selecting hypotheses for testing If one or more hypotheses have been rated, then select the top three that are rated highest and TEST them.
PR15: Lack of testable hypotheses If no hypotheses are generated or rated high enough to warrant testing, then SEARCH for a new target schema, worthy of consideration.

7.3.3.4 *Output*

Output of AIM consists of questions posed to the users about the object under study. These questions provide it with the tests needed to conduct its search. To accommodate a range of user interactions, a variety of input types are acceptable to AIM, namely, true – false, multiple-choice, and free-format answers.
PR16: Asking a specific question If a specific predicate is hypothesized, then ask the user if the predicate is true for the object being studied.
PR17: Asking a general question If alternative values of the same predicate are simultaneously hypothesized, then ask the general question about the predicate.
PR18: 'Oops' If the predicate hypothesized has already been asked as a question, then move on to the next task.

7.3.3.5 *Input*

The productions in this section simply allow AIM to interpret the user's reply based on simple semantic principles.
PR19: Negating answers If the user replies in the negative, then ASK the general case of the same question. Because of multiple-choice cases where more than two alternative answers are possible, AIM has to consult the user in this fashion.
PR20: Affirmative answer If the user replies in the affirmative, then SAVE the predicate used in formulating the question.
PR21: Retiring a hypothesis If the user abstains from answering the question just asked, then put the hypothesis that generated the question to 'sleep', that is, reserve it for future attention.
PR22: Novel answer If the user chooses to provide a complete predicate, or part of a predicate, as an answer, then PARSE it.
PR23: Multiple-choice answer If the user indicates the truth of a relation between one or more schemata in response to a multiple-choice question, then SAVE the schemata in the context of the predicate used in formulating the question.

7.3.3.6 *Parsing*

The syntax of AIM's internal language is simple but general and does not support context-sensitive rules. Because of this simplicity, the parsing of the input consists of comparing the input with the schemata and syntax of the predicates present in RRS. The generality of the syntax allows the use of a wide range of information as part of AIM's knowledge. However, once the RRS has been defined, the interaction mode with AIM becomes specific. Semantic parsing is limited to the 'consistency' tests applied during the SAVING operations. These tests are confirmed if the information contained in the predicate can be unambiguously represented in the ORS.

PR24: Syntax verification If a user-provided predicate has not been checked for correctness of syntax, then check (a) each schema and relation used in the predicate against those used in the RRS, and (b) each pair of schema relations found in the predicate against all those used in the RRS.

PR25: Token identification If a user-provided predicate is syntactically correct, then match the token(s) used in the question against those used in the predicate of the answer. If internal knowledge is insufficient, then ASK the user to identify the tokens.

PR26: Failure to parse If any of the tests applied in the parsing heuristics fail, then reject the predicate and ASK the user to restate his or her answer.

PR27: Successful parsing If the predicate passes the tests in PR25, then SAVE the predicate in RRS.

7.3.3.7 *Saving*
The consistency of information given to AIM is checked against the knowledge AIM already has with respect to 'alternative' values present in the RRS. For example, if the color of an object in question is allegedly red *and* blue at the same time and these two colors are included as *alternative* values in a predicate in the RRS, then this constitutes an inconsistency. More elaborate semantic translations are not available to AIM.

PR28: Saving If a user-provided predicate is not already present in WMS, then insert the predicate in WMS.

PR29: Consistency check If the user-provided predicate is in conflict with another predicate in the WMS, then if one of the conflicting predicates is an inference, delete the predicate which is inferred. However, if both or neither are inferred then HYPOTHESIZE the predicate.

7.3.3.8 *Inferring*
Operationally, productions for inference are the simplest ones. This is because the structure of AIM's permanent knowledge space, or the RRS, is based on the inference relations that are assumed to exist between predicates. When a certain predicate is confirmed, AIM infers the truth of all predicates pointed by this predicate.

PR30: Inferring If a predicate has just been saved, then identify all predicates in RRS that the first predicate points to, or implies, and SAVE them as valid inferences.

7.3.3.9 *Stopping*
At the present, AIM considers its investigation to be complete when at least one half of all predicates pertaining to the target have been tested

by AIM. When all schema categories have been satisfactorily investigated, then AIM stops. This ratio is an arbitrary one. However, the user has the option to override this and cause AIM to continue a run.

PR31: Stopping request If STOPPING is requested (see PR2), then consult user to see if a new target-scheme is to be examined.

PR32: Stopping If no new target schema is given by user when all others are investigated, then STOP.

7.3.4 Runs of AIM

Three alternative RRS for three alternative tasks were implemented during the course of AIM's development. The first one (table 7.3) was derived from knowledge used by subjects performing the building-puzzle task. The second RRS contained knowledge adequate to identify uniquely any one of thirteen academic buildings on the Carnegie-Mellon University campus. The third RRS was designed to fulfill the task of identifying any one of eighteen musical wind instruments. Each RRS was used in multiple runs of AIM where tokens included in the RRS were successfully identified by AIM[55]. The text of one typical run is included in table 7.4 below. Before examining the particulars of this run of AIM, let us explore how the size and contents of the RRS relate to the class of tasks represented here.

In all three cases the RRS were formed a priori and refined after many runs of AIM. Refinements were made in two ways: (a) deleting unused predicates and inference links, and (b) adding new links where indirect links, vis-à-vis many rules chained continuously by inference, were frequently used. In this way each RRS became progressively more

Table 7.3. Summary of questions and inferences by subject and AIM.

System	Questions	Inferences
Subject 1	task procedure site area parking on site site topograph coverage of building number of stories structural spans	is a residence site is small could be a branch bank coverage of building is small
AIM-run 1	task procedure number of stories building area context of site parking on site number of occupants	is a residence is for private use number of occupants is few area of building is little

---

[55] In each case the users of AIM served in the role analogous to that of the experimenter of the building-puzzle task.

parsimonious for each task domain. The size of the RRS was reduced by 20% on the average throughout this process. The overall size of the ultimately developed RRS varied with the range of tokens identifiable in each task domain.

The total number of links (L) between predicates of the RRS and the total number of tokens (T) identifiable in each task domain are plotted in figure 7.4. Estimates of knowledge sources used in areas of specialty, such as chess and mathematics, indicate that the number of task-specific facts experts use are on the order of 50 000 (Gilmartin and Simon, 1973). Although our observations in figure 7.4 are based on a small sample, a linear projection can, nevertheless, be obtained. The numbers of tokens that can be identified with 5 000 and 50 000 links based on the linear projection are 812 and 8120, respectively. This implies that in simulating an expert's knowledge base containing 50 000 relations in a system like AIM, the recognition capacity of the system would be about 8120 distinct types, that is building types for architects, stress conditions for civil engineers, diseases for medical doctors, and so on. Since there are no other known estimates of the average number of recognizable building types by an architect, the above estimate is one that needs to be tested against the observations and intuitions of others.

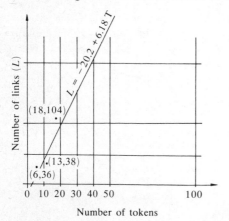

Figure 7.4. Total number of links in the rewriting rule space, in relation to the total number of tokens recognizable by AIM.

7.4 Evaluation of AIM

Two basic objectives underlie the design and implementation of AIM. The first one is to develop an operational model of inductive reasoning applicable to the task of understanding architectural drawings. The second one is to produce an experimental tool that simulates the relationship between a priori knowledge about a class of objects and the understanding process. In this section, I shall discuss the degree to which these objectives are met by AIM. The central question to be answered then is: 'how well does AIM perform the task of understanding?' Since I assumed at the onset that the benchmark for the understanding task is human performance, we can state the same question in a different way: 'how close does AIM come to humans in performing the building-puzzle task?'

First let us examine the excerpt of a typical run of AIM. The first two questions and inferences of AIM (lines 1 – 7 in table 7.4) are about the task at hand. This is similar to the first few questions asked by a subject performing the building-puzzle task (lines 1 – 2 in table 7.1). Since AIM has no learning capabilities this initial exchange looks very similar in different runs of AIM.

The target-schema[56] hierarchy used by AIM in this run is defined a priori to be top-down, that is, site and building, respectively. Hence, to discover the context of the site, the first question AIM asks is about the number of floors in the building (line 8 in table 7.4). The presence of only a few floors leads AIM to the inference that the context is 'rural' (line 11 in table 7.4). This is a premature assumption. It also reflects the behavior of conceptual inference mechanisms which is like a stream of consciousness. Later we shall observe how AIM deals with this difficulty.

Next AIM inquires about the total area of the building (line 12 in table 7.4). This hypothesis like the previous one is aimed at discovering the context using the relevant rewriting rules in AIM's memory. From the relatively small 'coverage' of the building on the site, AIM infers that the building is residential in nature (lines 13 – 14 in table 7.4).

Before moving to the building, as its next target-schema, AIM asks a last question about the context (line 16 in table 7.4). Although AIM had made an inference about the context earlier, it proceeds with the more direct line of questioning because of greater confidence attributed to external sources as opposed to internal inferences. To its credit this line of questioning allows AIM to revise the erroneous inference made about the context earlier (line 11 in table 7.4) and to relabel the content as 'urban' (lines 17 – 18 in table 7.4).

Next AIM asks directly about the identity of the building. Since this is a question which is disallowed in the building-puzzle task by definition, the experimenter refuses to answer. AIM's SEARCH heuristics traces this unsuccessful hypothesis back to the rewriting rules that triggered it. This kind of self-diagnosis is built into the SEARCH production system and leads AIM to new hypotheses with regard to the amount of parking

---

[56] The target-schema is a schema that AIM identifies as the subject of its inquiry at any one time. All questions it asks are structured to find out about this schema. When sufficient information is gathered about a particular target-schema a new one is selected. The new target-schema is selected in top-down order from the list of schemas known to AIM vis-à-vis the contents of its RRS.

Table 7.4. A sample run of AIM (AIM uppercase; user lowercase).

Line number	Output
1	(★★★ PLEASE ANSWER ★★★) ((WHAT IS THE MODE-OF-INPUT OF OBJECT) (VERBAL ⟨OR > VISUAL)) (★★★ IF YOU WANT TO TYPE IN A PREDICATE AND NEED HELP; TYPE H ★★★) > verbal
2	(I INFER THAT THE TYPE OF TASK-1 IS PICTURE-PUZZLE)
3	(I HYPOTHESIZED EARLIER ABOUT WHAT THE (TYPE OF TASK IS)) (★★★ PLEASE ANSWER ★★★)
4	((WHAT IS THE TYPE OF TASK) (PICTURE-PUZZLE ⟨OR⟩ TUNNEL-VISION)) (★★★ IF YOU WANT TO TYPE IN A PREDICATE AND NEED HELP; TYPE H ★★★) > picture-puzzle
5	(I INFER THAT THE AMOUNT OF PICTURE-PUZZLE-KNOWLEDGE
6	(OF SYSTEM-1) IS SUFFICIENT)
7	(I ALREADY KNOW WHAT THE (TYPE OF TASK IS)) (★★★ PLEASE ANSWER ★★★)
8	((IS GTR-FOUR THE AMOUNT OF LEVELS OF BUILDING)) (★★★ IF YOU WANT TO TYPE IN A PREDICATE AND NEED HELP; TYPE H ★★★) > n
	(★★★ PLEASE ANSWER ★★★)
9	((WHAT IS THE AMOUNT OF LEVELS OF BUILDING)
10	(LESS-THREE ⟨OR⟩ GTR-FOUR)) (★★★ IF YOU WANT TO TYPE IN A PREDICATE AND NEED HELP; TYPE H ★★★) > less-three
11	(I INFER THAT THE CONTEXT (OF SITE-1) IS A RURAL) (★★★ PLEASE ANSWER ★★★)
12	((IS LESS-ONE-K-SF THE AREA OF BUILDING)) (★★★ IF YOU WANT TO TYPE IN A PREDICATE AND NEED HELP; TYPE H ★★★) ⟩y
13	(I INFER THAT THE USE OF BUILDING-1 IS RESIDENTIAL)
14	(I INFER THAT THE AREA OF BUILDING-1 IS LITTLE)
15	(I HYPOTHESIZED EARLIER ABOUT WHAT THE (CONTEXT (OF SITE) IS A)) (★★★ PLEASE ANSWER ★★★)
16	((WHAT IS THE CONTEXT OF SITE) (URBAN ⟨OR⟩ RURAL)) (★★★ IF YOU WANT TO TYPE IN A PREDICATE AND NEED HELP; TYPE H ★★★) ⟩urban
17	(NEW KNOWLEDGE CONFLICTS WITH PRIOR INFERENCE)
18	(I ASSUME MY INFERENCE WAS WRONG)
19	(I INFER THAT THE EXTENT OF PARKING (OF SITE-1) IS LITTLE)
20	(I HYPOTHESIZED EARLIER ABOUT WHAT THE (USE OF BUILDING IS)) (★★★ PLEASE ANSWER ★★★)

21	((WHAT IS THE USE OF BUILDING) (RESIDENTIAL COMMERCIAL ⟨OR⟩
	  BUSINESS))
	(★★★ IF YOU WANT TO TYPE IN A PREDICATE AND NEED HELP; TYPE H
	  ★★★)
	⟩I cant answer

22	(I HYPOTHESIZED EARLIER ABOUT WHAT THE (EXTENT OF PARKING (OF SITE) IS))

Table 7.4. (continued)

Line number	Output
23	(∗∗∗ PLEASE ANSWER ∗∗∗) ((WHAT IS THE EXTENT OF PARKING OF SITE) (LITTLE MEDIUM ⟨OR⟩ LOT)) (∗∗∗ IF YOU WANT TO TYPE IN A PREDICATE AND NEED HELP; TYPE H ∗∗∗) ⟩little
24	(I INFER THAT THE USE OF BUILDING-1 IS PRIVATE-BLDG) (∗∗∗ PLEASE ANSWER ∗∗∗)
25	((IS GTR-TWENTY THE AMOUNT OF OCCUPANCY OF BUILDING)) (∗∗∗ IF YOU WANT TO TYPE IN A PREDICATE AND NEED HELP; TYPE H ∗∗∗) ⟩n (∗∗∗ PLEASE ANSWER ∗∗∗)
26	((WHAT IS THE AMOUNT OF OCCUPANCY OF BUILDING)
27	(LESS-EIGHT BETWEEN-EIGHT-TWENTY ⟨OR⟩ GTR-TWENTY)) (∗∗∗ IF YOU WANT TO TYPE IN A PREDICATE AND NEED HELP; TYPE H ∗∗∗) ⟩less-eight
28	(I INFER THAT THE AMOUNT OF OCCUPANCY (OF BUILDING-1) IS LOW) (∗∗∗ PLEASE ANSWER ∗∗∗)
29	((IS LOW THE AMOUNT OF OCCUPANCY OF BUILDING)) (∗∗∗ IF YOU WANT TO TYPE IN A PREDICATE AND NEED HELP; TYPE H ∗∗∗) ⟩y (∗∗∗ PLEASE ANSWER ∗∗∗)
30	((IS LESS-ONE-K-SF THE AREA OF BUILDING)) (∗∗∗ IF YOU WANT TO TYPE IN A PREDICATE AND NEED HELP; TYPE H ∗∗∗) ⟩y
31	(I DONT KNOW WHAT ELSE I SHOULD DO)
32	(WHAT ELSE WOULD YOU LIKE ME TO FIND OUT ABOUT)
33	(REPLY WITH N (FOR NONE) OR NAME OF A CONCEPT) ⟩n
34	(I KNOW THAT:)
35	(AMOUNT OF OCCUPANCY (OF BUILDING-1) IS LOW)
36	(AMOUNT OF OCCUPANCY (OF BUILDING-1) IS LESS-EIGHT)
37	(EXTENT OF PARKING (OF SITE-1) IS LITTLE)
38	(CONTEXT (OF SITE-1) IS A URBAN)
39	(AREA OF BUILDING-1 IS LESS-ONE-K-SF)
40	(AMOUNT OF LEVELS (OF BUILDING-1) IS LESS-THREE)
41	(TYPE OF TASK-1 IS PICTURE-PUZZLE)
42	(MODE-OF-INPUT (OF OBJECT-1) IS A VERBAL)
43	(I ASSUME THAT:)
44	(AMOUNT OF OCCUPANCY (OF BUILDING-1) IS LOW)
45	(USE OF BUILDING-1 IS PRIVATE-BLDG)
46	(EXTENT OF PARKING (OF SITE-1) IS LITTLE)
47	(AREA OF BUILDING-1 IS LITTLE)
48	(USE OF BUILDING-1 IS RESIDENTIAL)
49	(AMOUNT OF PICTURE-PUZZLE-KNOWLEDGE (OF SYSTEM-1) IS SUFFICIENT)
50	(TYPE OF TASK-1 IS PICTURE-PUZZLE)

on site and the number of occupants in the building (lines 22–25 in table 7.4). These questions reaffirm AIM's earlier hypothesis about the nature of the building, that it is residential in nature (line 13 in table 7.4).

The issues AIM asks about—floor area, number of levels, number of occupants, and amount of parking—are all selected from the RRS because of their likelihood of leading to information about the identity of the target-schema. After a few more questions, AIM runs out of unused rewriting rules in its memory that are relevant to the object being investigated. So it suggests stopping (line 31 in table 7.4). A command from the experimenter not to stop would cause AIM to seek new target-schemata to investigate (line 32 in table 7.4), causing new and lower levels of schema hierarchy to be formed in addition to the two it presently has: site and building. Then, AIM would have continued to ask new questions appropriate to these new target-schemata as long as rewriting rules pertaining to these were present in the RRS.

7.5 Human versus machine reasoning

If AIM exhibits behavior that we can call 'ability to learn about an object and discover its identity', then at a minimum we must convince ourselves that its behavior is sufficiently representative of that of the human subject performing the same task. To measure *the degree of similarity* some concrete criteria of evaluation must be established. From the protocols of the four subjects performing the building-puzzle task we can specify several behaviors that form a basis for defining evaluative criteria, such as reasoning, use of prior knowledge, and question asking.

A primary category of comparison which can be used as a measure is AIM's ability to reason. All subjects' questions use a variety of attributes, such as size, structural spans, occupancy, parking, and so on. Based on their prior knowledge about these attributes they are able to make inferences about the stimulus. Subjects display an ability to reason. AIM's success in simulating subjects' behavior can be measured by comparing the number of correctly identified stimulus properties through inference. Two other measures—number of incorrectly identified properties and the presence of conflict between the correctly and/or incorrectly identified properties—complement this comparison.

Another category of relevant measures is the number of knowledge sources brought to bear on the task. Effective reasoning often depends on bringing to bear on the task at hand a wide range of knowledge sources, resolving conflicts and considering alternatives that exist. The quality of thought is often measured by its depth. Then, the bigger the ratio of knowledge sources used to the total number of knowledge sources available, the better is AIM's performance.

A third category of measures is the number of questions asked that produce relevant inferences. This introduces the issue of efficiency;

that is, 'does AIM perform its task as efficiently as its human counterpart?' Efficiency in fact provides the structure necessary to operationalize all measures listed above. Efficiency can be defined as a function of the resources used in accomplishing a unit task. When making inferences about an object such as in the building-puzzle task, these resources are the knowledge sources that are available to the problem-solver, such as the answers obtained from the experimenter, time expended, and the clarity of the inferences made. In more operational terms we can express these criteria of efficiency in four categories:

1 number of incorrectly identified[57] (or conflicting) attributes of the stimulus divided by the number of correctly identified ones;
2 number of questions asked divided by the number of correctly identified attributes of the stimulus;
3 total time spent divided by the number of correctly identified attributes of the stimulus;
4 number of knowledge sources considered (or applied) divided by the number of correctly identified attributes of the stimulus.

The *fewer* the number of incorrect attributes, the number of questions, the number of knowledge sources applied, and the *shorter* the duration of time spent per correctly identified stimulus attribute the *more efficient* the system. Table 7.5 shows the scores for these measures for subject 10 in the sample protocol in table 7.1 and three separate runs of AIM.

It is clear from this evidence that the performance of AIM, within the scope of the three RRS created for the applications in this study, is as effective as, if not more effective than, its human counterpart. In other

Table 7.5. Performance of AIM compared with human subject.

System	Criterion[a]			
	1	2	3	4
Subject 10	8.33	2.67	4.0	65
Aim				
run 1	0.0	5.25	3.0	40
run 2	0.25	4.5	3.0	90
run 3	0.2	4.2	2.4	40
mean	0.15	4.65	2.8	56.6

[a] Criteria key:
1 number of incorrect inferences per correct inference; 2 number of questions asked per correct inference; 3 number of knowledge sources used per correct inference; 4 Total time expired (CPU-time in case of AIM) per correct inference (in seconds).

[57] By 'identification', I mean reaching a predicate through the inference mechanism.

words, it arrived at similar conclusions after asking nearly as many questions as the subject. Furthermore, the inferences made and the questions asked in the run of AIM illustrated in table 7.4, where the stimulus is identical to the one used by subject 10, are in general agreement with the subject's behavior. The only significant inefficiency of AIM seems to be in terms of criteria 2 which measures the number of questions asked. AIM is much more 'verbose' than subject 10. This is largely a result of the rather primitive abilities AIM has when it comes to natural language. Often AIM has to ask extra questions to make sure its interpretation of the references made in the user's input are correct. Also, AIM used fewer knowledge sources in making its inferences. This is a function of the limited knowledge it possesses about the problem domain (maximum number of predicates reaching thirty-eight in one case) which is the case in most manual knowledge acquisition systems.

There is a match between better than 50% of the questions asked and the inferences made by AIM and subject's protocols. This is desirable because a perfect match, close to 100%, would be theoretically impossible to justify. It is the contention of almost all researchers in the area that IPS are reductionist models of real systems and their predictive abilities are imperfect (Newell and Simon, 1972). This is attributed to the expectation that differential behaviors under different circumstances result from the complexity of interactions between parameters of the system and its interface with the environment, even though these parameters may be constant.

7.6 AIM as an experimental tool

In addition to the fact that AIM provides a model for human reasoning, it makes it possible to develop experimentally reliable knowledge bases for a variety of stimulus domains suitable to the building-puzzle task. One of the difficulties in the manual encoding of knowledge arises from a need to demonstrate that each knowledge source is potentially useful in the context of the task. Most such sources are discovered through the examination of the introspections and behaviors of experts. The databases used by Buchanan et al (1969) in their automated diagnosis system and Akin and Reddy's study on image understanding systems (1977) are efforts to build large databases incorporating expert knowledge. The problem with these approaches lies in the difficulty of determining the credibility and efficiency of each knowledge source before allocating resources to encoding them.

With a computer program like AIM, it is possible to test with relatively little cost the usefulness of new knowledge sources in making inferences. This is largely possible through AIM's completely modifiable knowledge base. By simply typing in a new set of rewriting rules that define attributes of any given object, or concept class (for example, musical instruments, cars, rooms of a house), it is possible to examine the sensitivity of AIM's behavior to the contents and format of the new knowledge. This allows for the fine tuning of a knowledge base that may be inefficient at first, as well as identifying new sources of knowledge applicable in a given stimulus domain.

Although many artificial intelligence systems deal with the question of knowledge acquisition and knowledge engineering, there are few tools for convenient testing of the contents of knowledge sources against system performance. AIM provides a useful tool in this respect.

7.7 Summary
The foregoing discussion of AIM's performance gives the impression that AIM is equal to its human counterpart. This is clearly not the case. If the Turing test (defined in section 7.2) were applied to AIM, I have no doubt in my mind that it would fail. There are many reasons for this. Some have to do with problems of interface and others with the 'reasoning' skills AIM currently has:

1 The input–output language used by AIM is at best Pidgin English and its manner of interaction with the user is predictable.

2 AIM does not make 'less-likely' inferences, such as the one made by subject 10, in table 7.5, about the 'branch-bank'.

3 AIM does not make sufficient use of negative inferences or predicates.

4 AIM does not deal with time-related information.

5 AIM does not make as effective use of the semantic connotations of knowledge as humans can.

6 AIM does not process visual data.

7 AIM does not automatically learn from its own experiences.

8 AIM does not detect implicit semantic conflicts (although it can find explicit ones) that may be present between two or more predicates it knows.

9 AIM does not tune the knowledge it accumulates to the priorities of the user.

On the other hand, there are some things that AIM can do which are nontrivial in terms of information processing:

1 AIM applies its processing knowledge in a variety of stimulus domains as long as there is domain-dependent knowledge represented in its RRS.

2 AIM allows users to respond in a variety of verbal formats.

3 AIM makes 'likely' inferences in a stimulus domain more efficiently than its human counterpart.

4 AIM converts negative predicates, with the aid of the user, into the positive form and then utilizes them in its process.

5 AIM uses knowledge about its own temporal experiences in controlling its focus of attention.

6 AIM detects conflicts that arise from syntactic and explicit semantic inconsistencies present between predicates in its memory.

7 AIM deals with general concepts and their instances successfully.

8 AIM sets and satisfies a hierarchic set of goals in meeting the overall goals of the building-puzzle task.

It is difficult at this point to come up with an indisputable balance of the pros and cons of AIM. This is difficult because many avenues of development of AIM have not been explored at this point and the relative importance of each attribute cited above, whether an advantage or a disadvantage, will depend on different applications of AIM. Hence the balance sheet that is feasible to draw at this point should consist of the things that AIM allows and will allow the user to accomplish now and in the foreseeable future[58].

7.8 Suggested readings

1 Akın Ö, 1978a, "Architectural inference making" in *Third International Conference and Exhibition on Computer Engineering and Building Design, CAD-78* (IPC Science and Technology Press, Guildford, Surrey) pp 506–521

2 Freeman P A, Newell A, 1971, "A model for functional reasoning in design" *Proceedings of the Second International Joint Computer Conference on Artificial Intelligence* British Computer Society, 13 Mansfield Street, London W1M OBP pp 621–640

3 Herot C F, 1974, "Context in sketch recognition", Department of Architecture, Massachusetts Institute of Technology, Cambridge, MA

4 Reddy R, Newell A, 1974, "Knowledge and its representation in a speech understanding system" in *Knowledge and Cognition* Ed. L W Gregg (John Wiley, New York) pp 253–286

5 Shank R C, 1975 *Conceptual Inference Making* (American Elsevier, New York).

7.9 Exercises

7.1 Design a manual or automated system that can be used to make chains of inferences, starting from an initial predicate and using rewriting rules prestored in the database of the system. Observe the relationship between the conclusion, or final rules, reached and the initial predicate, each time a chain of inferences are formed. Can a general principle be drawn from your experience?

7.2 Test the system you have designed using the inferences constructed for exercise 6.3 of chapter 6. Does the system work as well? What are the problems you have encountered in interfacing the two?

[58] Presently AIM is implemented in Stanford LISP 1.6 and available on the PDP-10 Computer Science system at Carnegie-Mellon University. However, its design and documentation do not permit easy transportation to other sites. Those interested in obtaining the existing documentation or developing similar systems should contact the author.

8

Summary: modelling the design process

All studies on design to date, with the partial exception of Krauss and Myer's study (1970), model a specific component of the design process. This is done to achieve better experimental control and manageability of data during investigations. Works by Eastman (1969), Henrion (1974), Herot (1974), Fox (1973), and Baer et al (1979) are examples of this strategy. Such efforts assist in the constructing of a comprehensive picture of design by carefully describing its individual parts. This is like mosaic work. To see the whole picture and detect gaps, redundancies, and inconsistencies in the whole, one must step back from time to time and observe the whole. This has been the main objective of this text. Here I have tried to paint a broad-brush picture of the total scene and to develop an understanding of how the parts make up the whole.

By virtue of this approach in the model proposed here I have described a wide range of issues concerning the *process of design* and the *knowledge* necessary for design. I have delineated and described, as potential *areas of research*, those parts of the whole which are critical in understanding the whole. I have also identified the parts which have already been defined well enough to comprise tools or *aids for the design process*. And last, the model has enabled the codification of design knowledge explicitly and in clear relation to the total design process. This chapter is a summary of the observations already discussed as they apply to the calibration and verification of DIPS.

8.1 Calibration of the model

DIPS is the framework of a design model (chapter 4). It is a descriptive rather than a prescriptive model. Also DIPS provides parts, their format, and relations, without specifying the contents or substance of these parts, just like a chest of drawers which specifies the format and relations of the household items it accommodates without predetermining content. The content of DIPS is the knowledge necessary and sufficient for design. Three such categories of knowledge are described in this work: (a) knowledge for search, (b) knowledge for representation, and (c) knowledge for reasoning.

8.1.1 Search

Two kinds of search knowledge are found in protocols of designers: methods and rules (chapter 5). By methods I mean 'plan-like' procedures as suggested by Miller et al (1960) that characterize designers' behaviors over long time periods. Many of these methods are known from previous work: data manipulation, generate-and-test, means – end-analysis, hill-climbing, depth-first search, breadth-first search, and back-tracking.

The rules, on the other hand, fall in the category of heuristic search and are mostly tools for ad hoc decision situations. Whenever a special circumstance is encountered, such as an overconstrained problem or a contradiction of constraints, the rules advise the designer to take specific courses of action that are known by experience to suit the circumstance. Although the heuristics identified in this study are diverse and inclusive, they are by no means the total set used by designers. Because of the method of analysis some of the heuristics which are important for design may have gone undetected. The heuristics which are discovered, however, provide a core that adequately responds to the tasks studied.

8.1.2 Representation

A significant part of design synthesis is assisted through physical intuition. This plays an important role when the problem can be represented in the graphic domain (externally) or imagery domain (internally). When external representation is possible, our everyday knowledge about the nature and behavior of physical objects become readily useful in the search for a solution. This is the case even for more analytical problem domains such as physics (Simon and Simon, 1978), chemistry (Novac, 1976), and geometry (deKleer, 1977). For example, in solving a pulley problem it is often useful to draw a diagram showing the geometric layout of pulleys, ropes, and loads. Through such diagrams, intuitive rules derived from the behavior of everyday objects can be applied to the specific problems at hand.

Since architectural problems deal intimately with everyday objects and their physical representations it is only natural that physical intuition plays an important role in design. In fact, many of the heuristics discussed in this work have to do with the selection of appropriate representations. A significant portion of the analysis dealing with structures used in representing, learning, and recalling architectural drawings is *chunks* (chapter 6). Chunks constitute the organizational principle behind visual information.

The composition of chunks used by architects is based on edges (or walls), corners, and functional clusters, such as doors and furniture. The reliance on edges and corners as the description of architectural drawings is consistent with the formal definition of perceptual systems in cognitive psychology and artificial intelligence. Another finding pertaining to chunks is that learning architectural drawings is a direct function of the nature of the learning experience. Architects passively 'tracing' drawings were not able to form robust[59] representations of the drawings compared with architects 'interpreting' these drawings. A third finding is that architects who interpreted drawings seemed to use higher

---

[59] By robust I mean representations that facilitate accurate access and recall of information.

level structural organizations in their recall of the drawings. Initially, chunks belonging to the overall outline of the plan were recalled. Then the chunks from the clusters of rooms, rooms themselves, and furniture in these rooms were recalled. Finally, chunks related to surface patterns and small objects were recalled.

This study also underscores, in a general way, the importance of nonlinear organizations of spatial information. Because of the multi-dimensionality of the visual representation domain (each element or edge is adjacent to or a part of many other elements), alternative chunk decompositions are likely for a given stimulus. A room may be a part of many groupings of rooms of the same building simultaneously. This is why the external graphical domain is so useful in evoking associations in the mind during design, and hierarchical and lattice-like organizations provide good representations of spatial knowledge. Foz (1973) in his study of the development of the architectural *parti*,[60] has pointed out to the power of external representations during the course of designing. The implementation of AIM (chapter 7) designed to make inferences about objects and their identity also relies on the hierarchy of physical parts, in shifting its focus of attention in a top-down hierarchical form.

8.1.3 Reasoning
An analysis of the architectural reasoning process has resulted in a model of knowledge representation consisting of modular information units called rewriting rules (chapter 7). Rewriting rules resemble other syntactic formats used in computer programming and cognitive modelling, such as conditional statements and production systems. This allows the modularization of knowledge into disaggregate parts which, in turn, allow (a) their application in many different contexts, (b) the modification of an initial kernel of such rules, and (c) the modelling of human learning.

Rewriting rules are inherently weak. They are likely to induce errors, they are probabilistic, they are activated spontaneously, and they are usually not goal directed. For them to represent a powerful reasoning system analogous to the human mind, Shank (1975) suggests that they have to be accessed in parallel and Reddy and Newell (1974) suggest that they have to be used cooperatively. The computer-simulation system, AIM, uses all three knowledge structures outlined above, including tools for search, representation, and reasoning to perform the building-puzzle (chapter 6) task in ways similar to human subjects.

8.1.4 Research objectives
In chapter 1, four purposes for this work were identified: (a) to describe how design takes place, (b) to develop new areas of research, (c) to facilitate an interface between the designer and new design aids,

[60] An Ecoles des Beaux Arts term referring to preliminary design, particularly, as intended by the floor-plan organization.

and (d) to promote teaching-by-instruction in design. Let us now review the extent to which these goals have been met.

8.1.5 Understanding the design process

Methodological precedents for studies of this kind have been set by early studies in the area of artificial intelligence (Baylor, 1971; Farley, 1974; Moran, 1970). The methodology has two critical stages: (a) developing a problem-solving paradigm and (b) simulating and testing the paradigm in the computer. This study is no exception. DIPS corresponds to the first and AIM corresponds to the second phase of this methodology. The two phases together define the structural makeup of the design process and allow us to discuss its internal mechanisms. What then does this study add to our understanding of design?

This work introduces a perspective for the study of the design process. This perspective is characterized by two interrelated ideas: design behavior and the knowledge base that drives this behavior. Methodologically, this relationship operates in the reverse direction. Pertinent categories of design knowledge are inferred from careful examinations of designers' behaviors. The three categories of design knowledge that have been identified as a result of such analysis, reported in the earlier chapters, are *problem-solving*, *physical intuition*, and *inductive reasoning*.

Heuristics seem to have a central role when it comes to problem-solving in design (chapters 5 and 7). This is a consequence of the ill-defined nature of design problems. Because of the impossibility of describing the total solution domain of a given design problem, search is best conducted with locally powerful search techniques such as heuristics. This is primarily why design solutions tend to be locally optimized or *satisficing* solutions rather than globally *optimized* solutions. When a satisficing solution is needed, heuristics provide an ideal tool for identifying and refining solutions within a delimited portion of the problem space. Furthermore, the adaptability of heuristics to rule-based problem-solving makes DIPS suitable for simulating the learning process. As new experiences become available, new rules can easily be added to the knowledge base of DIPS without adversely affecting its basic control structure.

This should not imply that the only strategies used in design are those that are locally applied. Often, constraint-planning techniques are used to organize the overall design process. The subjects studied here without exception exercised a top-down strategy where the more general problem constraints, such as site, orientation, access, and cost, are considered and resolved before more specific constraints, such as organization, structure, and amenities. These two sets exemplify the top two levels of a many-leveled hierarchy of constraints used by the subjects.

Parallel to this hierarchy there is a second hierarchy that helps the decomposition of design problems. This is the partitioning of the architectural object into smaller parts or 'chunking' (chapter 6). Although data about the focus of attention of subjects suggest that the decomposition from these two hierarchies are used additively, the precise nature of their interaction is a potentially fruitful area of research, which has not been addressed here.

When visual chunking is used to learn about or to recall drawings, a top-down hierarchy seems to account best for subjects' behaviors. First, the overall outlines and dimensions of drawings are recalled. Details of drawings, such as windows, doors, furniture, are retrieved from memory last. The process of 'learning' a drawing seems to control the manner in which such hierarchical representations are constructed in the mind.

The logic underlying representations are critical for understanding design. For example, different drawings provide representational media which vary in their degree of appropriateness for certain operations rather than for others. Often subjects use special heuristics to change the representational medium as a function of the stage their solution is in. Another invariant found in the data analyzed here is that subjects use all three orthographic views plus many other supplementary representations in studying the problem.

The actual driving force pushing the design process forward, however, seems to be totally unrelated to heuristics or skill of representation. The workhorse of design is the inductive reasoning process. All manipulation of data or transformation of architectural concepts during design can be explained as an induction process. Subjects transpose given symbol systems into others as a function of their knowledge. It is assumed that this knowledge is developed through discovery of new associations between concepts as design progresses. The richness of these associations is a function of experience. Experience seems to dictate the power of induction for the designer.

As a general rule, subjects make progress in their designs when inductive transformations are forthcoming, as opposed to those instances when associations are not as available. In cases where the flow of transformations is stalled, heuristic techniques are used to move design forward, such as use of analogies, making educated guesses, weighing the pros and cons of conflicting ideas. When this fails, then graphic stimuli are used to evoke new ideas and inferences.

8.1.6 New research areas

Psychology of architectural design is a new and little developed research area by many standards. A primary purpose of this study has been to structure this area for future research. DIPS provides this structure. It identifies a set of heuristic skills which can be individually examined in the context of well-defined design exercises. It also proposes two representations, one for physical intuition and the other for architectural reasoning, that can be tested and further calibrated in well-defined experimental contexts using tasks of recall, recognition, and reasoning with architectural information. A number of potential research topics have already been identified in the body of the text. Let me provide a short list of some of the salient questions:

1 What is the relationship between spatial hierarchies and procedural hierarchies in decomposing design problems?

2 What is the relationship between higher level problem-structuring strategies and lower level problem-solving strategies?

3 What is the size of the architect's permanent knowledge and how is this related to external memories during the course of a design task?

4 How does learning affect design performance?

5 How do partial solutions get integrated into a final unique solution?

6 How does the set of criteria used in solving design problems vary from one problem to the next, from one designer to the next, from one session to the next?

8.1.7 Developing and interfacing design aids

Currently, a good number of design aids have been developed in two major areas of research. Traditionally, the methods that utilize manual techniques have been called design methods and those that utilize automated techniques have been called computer-aided design. However, rarely have any of these become widely used tools in the profession. The main reason for this is the presence of difficulties in the interfacing of two entirely dissimilar systems: the design aid and the human designer (Akın, 1978b).

The interface problem can be helped by better understanding the design process. Such an understanding allows us to describe accurately the input and output of information to and from the designer whose functionalities are meant to be augmented by the design aid. For example, let us consider a design aid that enumerates all possible two-dimensional arrangements of a set of spaces with predefined adjacency requirements (Flemming, 1978; Mitchell et al, 1976; Steadman, 1983). Ideally, the user would input to the 'aid' all the spaces and their desired relations and obtain from it all possible organizations in graphical form. This interface will be considered an appropriate one if the user does not have to translate the input information into a special syntax and the output information is easily understandable. Typing in coordinate information to describe each space or having to sort through many intuitively undesirable alternatives, that is, alternatives containing inaccessible spaces or ill-dimensioned rooms, are unsuitable interface practices.

Some of the facilities defined in this work, such as heuristics, physical hierarchies, and rewriting rules, provide useful constructs for developing 'good' design aids with accurate anticipation of input–output requirements of the user. This brings us at least one step closer to understanding what is needed in developing analytical design aids compatible with the human design process. By the same token, existing design aids can be made more friendly in terms of the design process and the input–output of design information. AIM, for example, is a design aid that can be used to develop new knowledge bases, to examine architectural reasoning, and, eventually, to automate the design criticism task.

8.1.8 Teaching of design

The foundation of architectural education is 'experiential'. That is, it takes place in the design studio. Students design a specified building and instructors give criticism about their progress and design ideas. All generalizable knowledge gained in this process is derived inductively from specific examples encountered in practice. This is basically an inefficient process because of the lack of specificity in instruction. To improve architectural education, teachers should be in a position to teach design skills directly as well as experientially (Akın, 1982a; 1984).

Most design methods reviewed here: generate-and-test, means–end-analysis, hill-climbing, are well-defined processes in format and can be taught by direct instruction. Although these methods are commonly known even during the early stages of design education, students are generally unaware of the actions, goals, and preconditions that define each. Education of the architect consists of a series of personal experiences with little room for shared ideas and generalized knowledge. Many such principles are embedded in the heuristics we reviewed in the earlier chapters. More efficient use of these heuristics would be possible with the help of specific instruction about their anatomy and purpose. Similarly, strategies in dealing with hierarchical representations, problem constraints, and search for relevant sources of knowledge can be formalized for instruction. All of this suggests that the study of uncertainty, conflict resolution, and resource allocation could become formal parts of design education.

9

Epilogue: a position on design

A motivation that underlies all phases of the research in this study is to observe the totality of the design activity from the viewpoint of IPT. This is a significant point of departure in architectural research because it combats many traditional as well as contemporary beliefs which are equally counterproductive.

The traditional view of design research asserts that:
1 Creative processes are intuitive and inconsistent. It is not possible explicitly to describe design behavior. Even if this were possible, sufficient regularity would not be found in these behaviors to allow generalization or formalization.
2 Knowledge used in architectural design is broad enough not to permit perfect codification. Since all past experience can potentially be drawn upon during design, it is assumed that the knowledge base of architectural design is virtually endless.
3 The problem-solving tools used in architecture are radically different from those useful in solving other problems. Synthetic processes are products of 'mysterious' mental feats which cannot be rationally described.
4 The sole means of learning how to design is experiential. Since it is not possible to characterize and formalize procedures used in design, it cannot be taught by explicit instruction.

On the other hand, after the recent applications of techniques of operations research and systems theory to design, researchers have asserted that:
1 Creative processes can be accounted for through purely rational processes. After all, all processes, no matter how complex, can be partitioned into rational subprocesses and these can be solved using rational methods. Intuitive methods have no place in the design process.
2 Design processes must be undertaken in a systematic and exhaustive fashion. To perfect the design process we must take into account all constraints that act upon a given design decision, and all alternative solution paths must be pursued.
3 Design is optimization of search in a large problem space. The problem-solving tools of design are the same as those used in scientific prediction and discovery.
4 Design can be taught by pure instruction, using a 'cookbook' approach. This is feasible because of the clear-cut nature of the design process.

Both of these views are equally dangerous for design and design research. On the one hand, we have the inhibiting dogma of the past. On the other hand, we have the premature confidence developed in pioneering applications of scientific methods that underestimate the task of the designer. Information-processing models of design behavior are principally in opposition to both of these views. They propose to account scientifically for the design process as well as to make explicit the description of its task context, and yet they do not claim to be purely analytical nor anti-intuitive in their methods. More specifically, such models of design imply that both sets of views of design summarized above are inaccurate. Let me now propose some alternative views for each of these issues.

9.1 Description of the design process

The information-processing model of design provides explicit descriptions of systems that account for the behavior exhibited by the problem-solver (s), across tasks, subjects, and time. This is inclusive of the intuitive as well as the rational aspects of behavior.

DIPS provides a basis for transcribing and characterizing the behavior observed in the protocols of designers. An aspect of this model, which represents the architectural reasoning, is simulated in the computer. These results clearly contradict the argument that explicit descriptions of the design process are not possible. Simulation of reasoning behavior in AIM demonstrates that at least parts of the process, however intuitive they may seem at first, can be formalized and represented in the computer. I further suggest that it is possible to formalize intuitive aspects of design as well. Formalization of less than well-structured processes paves the way to understanding, predicting, and modelling the whole design process.

For example, it is not far-fetched to imagine systems that can integrate functionalities of representation, search, and reasoning processes during the production of designs. Recent work in the areas of design and artificial intelligence shows that there are no major obstacles to this. Many of the search processes attributed to design in this work have been successfully modelled for other task domains: means – end-analysis (Newell and Simon, 1972), heuristic search (Lenat, 1976), hill-climbing (Simon, 1973), and generate-and-test (Eastman, 1968). What still remains to be done is to develop the detailed blueprint of the designer's workbench with all of these capabilities, formally represent it, and implement it in the computer. This is certainly not a trivial task but it is becoming progressively more feasible as research efforts are channeled in this direction.

A word of caution, however, is necessary. Unlike the modellers of the 1960s, we have the benefit of their largely unsuccessful experiences. These efforts were directed to formalizing intuitive methods through purely rational paradigm (Alexander, 1964; Jones, 1970). Undoubtedly, the 'discovery' of algorithmic tools and computers have played a major role in this naive optimism. Caution is necessary against prophets of rational methods that cast all design-related phenomena into the mould of a single paradigm, whether this is linear programming or optimization techniques. The last two decades have shown this to be an over-simplification. Also, new avenues of research now allow us to be scientific about the rational as well as about the intuitive.

9.2 Finite nature of architectural knowledge

Information-processing models of design can be made to include all knowledge brought to bear on the task domain by humans. This knowledge is potentially infinite but is manageably finite in given task contexts.

A codification of all issues focused upon in the protocols shows that a manageable number of issues, (an average of 192 issues in all) are considered during the first four hours of design (chapter 5). The new sets of issues considered by the designer diminish exponentially with time (figure 9.1). This implies that the knowledge used in any continuous design session is relatively small and can be formally represented. In an independent study, Henrion (1974) obtained similar results. This finding has far-reaching implications in terms of design education and automated systems for design.

The primary implication is the one already mentioned. The number of issues considered in design are finite and manageably small, lending themselves to formal modelling. In other words, the knowledge base necessary for simulating three to four hours of design behavior in the concept-development stage is certainly feasible with today's technology. Lenat's inference-making system which has a total of 300 heuristic rules to work with is commensurate with the magnitude to which I am referring. Other database systems (Eastman, 1976) are sufficiently developed to allow manipulation of hundreds of thousands of entries without difficulty. A search space of a couple of hundred nodes observed in the case of the design tasks studied here is clearly within the order of magnitude of these systems. With supercomputers on the horizon it is conceivable that automation of design is becoming an increasingly viable task, of course, with respect to its functional aspects.

The second implication has to do with the search and decisionmaking tools necessary in this context. Computer applications in complex task

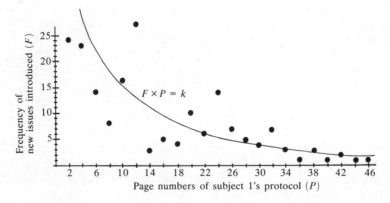

Figure 9.1. Number of new design issues introduced as a function of time spent designing.

environments, such as chess, image understanding, and so on, show that brute force methods taking on the combinatorics of all possible search paths find themselves in insurmountable problems of storage or computation capacity. Consequently, modelling of the design process cannot rely on hardcore analytical tools[61] alone and succeed. Heuristic search methods, which are standard tools in complex problem-solving tasks, must be used creatively to circumvent the toils of exhaustive methods (Lenat, 1983a; 1983b).

9.3 Tools of problem-solving in design

Information-processing models of design are based on operations which can be explicitly specified and are also more often than not useful in other task domains.

All operations of design proposed in chapters 3 and 4 and calibrated later in chapters 5, 6, and 7 are the same as or analogous to operations in many other problem contexts. Except for some specialized heuristic rules, no additional[62] operations are necessary to account for the designers' behaviors. This is indication that these tools are part of a general kernel of cognitive tools which transcend task domains let alone different problems or different designers within architecture. Several aspects of information processing seem to approach a level of ubiquity for the data examined in this work. Let me mention once more the three categories of knowledge discussed earlier: *representation, reasoning,* and *search*.

The primary issue in design representation seems to be the ability to sketch, mark, write, draw, with greatest ease. All subjects studied were keen on selecting a few tools for representing their thoughts graphically. They seemed to prefer a certain subset of tools: freehand versus hard edge, transparent sheets versus opaque sheets, pencil versus color pens, during the different phases of their work. Similarly, the kinds of sketches used progressed from more abstract to more representative drawings as their design ideas developed. Also, graphic conventions dominated what they sketched throughout. Plans, plan-diagrams, and site-plans were the favorite drawings used. Sections and elevations were of less importance, or at least next in order of priority. There was also repetition or duplication in these drawings. That is, each drawing was drawn more than once and each new drawing was marginally different from previous drawings. Furthermore, each drawing was typically abstracted as a 'diagram' or three-dimensional graphical symbol consisting of a few salient parts of the whole. Each drawing started by laying out these symbols as their standard reference points. It seems then that a tool for design representations must provide a wide range of

---

[61] Such as, optimization and linear programming.

[62] By additional I mean over and above those that make up the state of the art in information-processing literature.

representational forms, the facility for different conventions of drafting and documentation, the ability to redraw any part of the documentation with variations, the ability to reproduce documents with ease, and the ability to generate multilayered representations allowing the designer to peel off or lay on layers of element sets.

Reasoning requires the ability to maintain and manipulate a highly associative memory. Several important characteristics of this memory derive from the operational basis of reasoning. First, knowledge used in design is extremely large. Second, the process of reasoning is extremely fast. Designers seem to find their way in this vast sea of facts and associations rather quickly. Third, multiple semantic associations about these facts prestored in memory contribute to the reasoning process. Apparently, all knowledge sources even remotely related to one another have something to contribute to the end result. Fourth, designers constantly revise contents and associations of their knowledge bank and add new sources as they use these facilities. Several inference-making systems, including AIM (chapter 7), have simulated this process. It is clear that, in the short run, such capabilities can become useful design tools if applied to well-understood design tasks (preliminary sizing of beams, preliminary estimates of cost and square-footage).

Search involves knowledge which seems to be most universal and transferable to and from other task domains. This is supported by the fact that all search methods, that is, means–end-analysis, generate-and-test, top-down, and breadth-first search, as well as heuristics, are common to other problem domains as well. To show the generality of heuristic rules, one has to show how they apply to different circumstances. Lenat's work on mathematical inference is a prime example of the use of heuristics as a general problem-solving tool. In chapter 7 we observed that rules developed from human reasoning behavior were adequate for AIM to make inferences about different sets of objects, such as buildings and musical instruments. This is further evidence that general purpose heuristics can be developed to simulate specific context-dependent behavior.

9.4 Teaching design
Information-processing models of design imply that design skills can be assimilated by humans through learning by instruction as well as by doing.

No direct evidence is provided here to support learning design instructionally as opposed to experientially. On the other hand, all above assertions indirectly lead to the hypothesis that, since we can formalize design behavior, we can teach it through instruction, in much the same way we can do with other algorithmic tasks, (problem-solving mathematics, physics, and chemistry). This is sufficient to make a case against the rival hypothesis that argues for 'purely' experiential methods of teaching. Essentially this latter argument is also derived indirectly from the belief that the nature of the design activity is inexplicit and belies formalization.

Let us first examine what we mean by learning. Learning in a broad sense entails acquisition of knowledge in such a way that it can be applied in a relevant context. Hence, learning to swim, for example, implies the acquisition of the motor skills that are necessary to propel oneself on the surface of the water; learning to play chess implies the acquisition of necessary knowledge to make appropriate chess moves with the goal of capturing opponents' pieces. Similarly, learning to design entails acquisition of the skills and knowledge to develop appropriate design solutions.

A critical notion in learning is the generality of the information being acquired. This is necessary so that the skill or the knowledge acquired can be transferred to situations which may be somewhat different from the situation in which learning has taken place. As we learn, we constantly strive to generalize what we know so that specific context-dependent information can become secondary and generic sources of knowledge assume primary importance. For example, each chess game presents a novel situation to the player. However, the skilled player has generalized knowledge that can be applied to many circumstances, even those that have never been encountered before[63].

The fundamental question is how to acquire generalized knowledge or knowledge that can be applied to many specific instances of the general form. This is where the distinction between two methods of teaching, *experiential* and *by instruction*, become important. Should teachers simply place students in many specific contexts and help them generalize from their experiences, or should they instruct them directly about generalized knowledge? There does not seem to be a straightforward answer to this question. As stated earlier the two methods best go hand in hand to insure a rich domain for learning and to accommodate special cases of individual students. Evidence from developmental psychology has been used in successful arguments for both methods since Katona's (1940) early work on memory and concept acquisition.

Learning by experience seems to be best helped by *repetition* of experiences and *induction of knowledge* through novel expectations. *Repetition* obviously helps learning by providing a set of experiences from which generalized principles can be induced. If the set of experiences cover a very wide range, then the task of generalizing will be difficult. If, on the other hand, the set of experiences cover a very narrow range, then generalization is easier, but its transferability to other contexts will be limited. That is, it will not be applicable to a

[63] The opposite of this is impossible to conceive. This would imply that, to learn to play chess, one would have to be exposed to all possible positions on the board and learn how to behave in each case. This would make learning of even the easiest of games, for example, tick-tack-toe, a nontrivial task.

sufficiently large set of new circumstances. Therefore the selection of design problems must represent experiences that clearly overlap and nontrivially differ from each other in some respects. For example, designing a community center in an urban setting provides some experiential knowledge. Redesigning for the same program in a different physical and social context would help the designer to identify generalizable issues, that is, those that are invariant from one problem to the next.

Learning is readily *induced* by new expectations. Anything we observe in the environment becomes new or worthy of taking note or learning about when it is outside our expectations. Hence, to facilitate learning by experience, appropriate expectations about the end result of design must be formed. This is possible in well-defined problem domains. For example, in solving the 15-puzzle problem (chapter 3) the goal state provides the metric that allows the evaluation of each new move made. Thus an idea about the validity of each move is formed as a function of the problem-solver's expectations. This is not so in design. Unless it is deliberately given as a part of the problem, no obvious expectations about the goal of the design exist in the mind of the student, especially one who is a beginner. Hence, illustrating, specifying, or describing the solution domain in design is a significant aid for design learning. In this way, each design action can be assessed in relation to a clear design goal and not to its relative improvement over earlier solution ideas.

Definition of design goals usually comes about through examples of what the designed product should be like or archetypes of such examples. In either case, whether an archetype or an instance of a building is used, the model defines the domain of discourse in the problem context, the salient parts and properties of the object being designed, and the criteria of evaluation. Hence the model provides the information source necessary in decomposing the problem into its *salient parts* as well as in evaluating design ideas using the *salient properties* of the model (Foz, 1973).

The representation of the goal of design through archetypes can also illuminate how complex design problems can be decomposed into simpler parts and how design decisions are related to each other. In chapters 5 and 6 evidence about the hierarchical makeup of physical decompositions of buildings and the hierarchical relationship between design processes are discussed. It is shown how methods of search are nested in one another, that is, macromethods (means–end-analysis) containing micromethods (generate-and-test). While one process is undertaken, a new one is started and completed so that the findings of the second can be used as data within the body of the first. Similarly, issues of global significance for design decisions, (cost, organization, so on) are also included in lower level decisions (such as selection of windows and solar panels). Consequently the substance and structure of instruction in design education should model an overall hierarchical framework of this kind to reinforce the cognitive tools necessary in understanding complex objects.

9.5 Final thoughts

After having studied this problem area and the architectural design
activity under different circumstances during the past eight years, I find
that I have formed certain convictions which do not necessarily derive
from any one specific finding but from the overall experience of having
done this work.

(1) Creative behavior is a complex manifestation of the interactions
between many concrete mental operations. The only reason why we
could not characterize its underlying mechanisms with precision in the
past is because we did not examine them long enough with the right
tools. Now we have the right tools, that is, IPT, and its understanding
is only a matter of sufficient time and interest.

(2) Knowledge brought to bear on a complex task domain like design is
not infinite or impractical to codify. By clarifying the scope of this
knowledge we can help ourselves define the purpose and value of
architecture. We can also equip ourselves better to teach these.

(3) The mental processes used in design have many commonalities with
processes used in other problem domains. By employing the taxonomy
of IPT we can bridge the gap between design and other problem domains.
This can only improve the understanding of all problem domains,
including design.

(4) More and better descriptions of problem domains, evaluation
functions, and human problem-solving techniques for design must be
developed. A set of such models, if provided, will become invaluable
aids to education and professional practice of architecture. The
computer provides the best opportunity for realizing this goal.

(5) I trust that this book has provided experiences for the reader which
are similar in many ways to the ones I have had in researching the
area. I have tried to share my experiences through narration, example,
and exercises included at the end of each chapter. The firsthand
experience to be gained by doing these exercises is an effective way of
understanding the material in this book.

An appropriate test for the success with which the purpose of this
work has been accomplished is to reflect on the conjectures listed
above. If at this point the reader is left with similar or complementary
impressions, then the task of this book is complete. In any case, it is
important for the reader to examine the attitudes he or she has
developed and the knowledge gained. Better yet, the reader might ask
himself or herself research questions that can be formed as a result of
this work. We must bear in mind that the scientific examination of
design has merely started and it can progress no further without the
input of all those who take an interest in design and science.

Protocol analysis is a technique first used by Newell (1968) in studying information-processing mechanisms. A protocol is the recorded behavior of the problem-solver. It is usually in the form of sketches, notes, video or audio recordings. For example, the design episode examined in chapter 3 is a protocol. The subsequent analysis of the episode is an example of protocol analysis.

According to some researchers, the use of protocol analysis in experimental work is a controversial issue. Often these critics claim that:

1 since subjects are asked to verbalize their behaviors during protocol experiments, there is room for erroneous introspection;

2 because of the extent of the analysis required to interpret the data and the quantity of the data itself, only small numbers of subjects can be used in each experiment—this is contrary to good experimental practice;

3 the thought process, being much faster than motor behavior, cannot be fully reflected through the motor responses of subjects;

4 there are usually gaps or periods of silence found in most protocols, which obviously do not correspond to lack of cognitive activity.

The first two objections cited above stem from misinterpretations of the protocol-analysis process. Verbalizations during the act of problem-solving are no different from observations made during well-accepted methods of experimental psychology. For example, in reaction-time experiments, subjects' reactions to stimuli are timed and subsequently analyzed to explain cognitive phenomenon. In this sense, verbalizations are no different from reaction times. Most, if not all, verbalizations are not a posteriori introspections but are statements from which the current knowledge state of the designer can be studied. The small size of the samples used is greatly offset by the thousands of observations found in the protocol of each subject. Conclusions reached at the end are generalizations about the behaviors of each problem-solver rather than the consistency observed between many individuals. This is also compatible with the goals of good experimental design.

On the other hand, the problem of 'missing data' reflected in the latter two objections cited above is a serious concern, especially in the case of design. A lot of visual and implicit processing cannot be expressed in words with ease. Sometimes subjects fail to report such experiences fully. Furthermore, the ability to report what one is doing and the degree to which this distorts the normal course of behavior may be a significant factor for some subjects. Hence, careful consideration must be given to accurate interpolation of 'missing data' in the analysis of design protocols.

Despite the drawbacks, protocol analysis usually yields much richer and more comprehensive data than more conventional techniques such as reaction-time and eye-tracking studies. Thus they are useful in studies of this kind where complex and little understood processes are under investigation and the breadth of issues to be studied are just as important as those to be studied in depth. It is not possible to describe complex processes through a handful of variables, as is the case in better-controlled experimental studies. Furthermore, since we know relatively little about the process of design, it is not possible to predict which measures are going to be better indicators of the designer's behavior.

A.2.1 Generate-and-test

This is the weak method par excellence. All that must be given is a way to generate possible candidates for solution plus a way to test whether they are indeed solutions.

A generator is a process that takes information specifying a set and produces elements of that set one by one. It should be viewed as autonomously 'pushing' elements through the system. Hence there is a flow of elements from generate to the process called test. Test is a process that determines whether some condition or predicate is true of its input and behaves differentially as a result. Two different outputs are possible: satisfied $(+)$ and unsatisfied $(-)$ (Newell, 1970, page 377).

We are given the following expression in symbolic logic: $E:(P \vee Q)[(P \vee Z) \vee (RP)]$. A variety of problems arise from asking whether E is a member of various specified sets of logic expressions. Such problems can usually be thrown into the form of a generate and test, at which point the difficulty of finding the solution is directly proportional to the size of the set.

If we know more about the structure of the set, better methods are available. For instance, consider the following two definitions of sets: $S_1 : x(x \vee y)$, where x and y are any logic expressions, for example,

$$p(p \vee q), \qquad q(q \vee q), \qquad (p \vee p)[(p \vee p)p] , \ldots ;$$

$S_2 : a$, where a may be replaced (independently at each occurrence) according to the following schemes:

$$a \leftarrow q, \qquad a \leftarrow (p \vee a), \qquad a \leftarrow 2a$$

for example,

$$q, \qquad p \vee q, \qquad qq, \qquad p(\vee p \vee q), \qquad (p \vee q)(p \vee q) , \ldots .$$

In S_1, x and y are variables in the standard fashion, where each occurrence of the variable is to be replaced by its value. In S_2 we have defined a replacement system, where each separate occurrence of the symbol a may be replaced by any of the given expressions. These may include a, and hence lead to further replacements. A legal logic expression exists only when no as occur.

It is trivial to determine that e is a member of the set of expressions defined by S_1, and not so trivial to determine that it is not a member of the set defined by S_2. The difference is that for S_1, we could simply match the expressions against the form and determine directly the values of the variables required to do the job. In the case of S_2 we had essentially to generate-and-test (Newell, 1970, page 380).

A.2.2 Hill-climbing

The most elementary procedure for finding an optimum is akin to generate-and-test, with the addition that the candidate element is compared with a stored element—the best so far—and replaces it if higher. The element often involves other information in addition to the position in the space being searched, for example, a function value. With just a little stronger assumption in the problem statement, the problem can be converted into an analog of climbing a hill. There must be available a set of operators that find new elements on the hill, given an existing element. That is, new candidate elements are generated by taking a step from the present position (one is tempted to say a 'nearby' step, but it is the operators themselves that define the concept of nearness). Thus the highest element so far plays a dual role, both as the base for generation of new elements and as the criterion for whether they should be kept (Newell, 1970, page 382).

A.2.3 Heuristic search (means-end)

The best-known method in heuristic programming is the one whereby the problem is cast as a search through an exponentially expanding space of possibilities—as a search which must be controlled and focused by the application of heuristics. All of the game-playing and theorem-proving programs make use of this method, as well as many of the management science applications.

A most elementary variant of the method assumes a space of elements, the problem space, which contains one element representing the initial position, and another representing the final or designed position. Also available is a fixed set of operators, which when applied to elements in space produce new elements. (Operators need not always be applicable.) The problem is to produce the final desired position, starting at the initial one (Newell, 1970, page 386).

A.2.4 Induction

The first essential feature of the method is revealed in the problem statement, which requires the problem to be cast as one of finding a function or mapping of the given data into the associated (or predicted) data.

The second essential feature of the method is the use of a form or kernel for the function. This can be matched (in the sense of the match method) against the exemplars (Newell, 1970, page 391).

It is not often possible to express the entire space of functions as a single form (whence a single match would do the job). Consequently a sequential generation of the kernels feeds the match process. Sometimes clues in the exemplars are used to order the generation; more often, generation is from the simplest functions to the more complex.

This method is clearly a version of 'hypothesis-and-test'. However, the latter term is used much more generally than to designate the class of induction problems handled by this method. Furthermore, there is nothing in hypothesis-and-test which implies the use of match; it may be only generate-and-test. Consequently, we choose to call the method simply the induction method, after the type of task it is used for (Newell, 1970, page 392).

A.3.1 Properties of representations

Random House Dictionary of the English Language provides among others, two descriptions for the verb 'represent': (a) "to express or designate by some term, character, symbol or the like" and (b) "to present or picture to the mind". Representation then is the product of representing. The first definition is the popularly known meaning of the two. That is, a representation is a symbol that expresses or stands for something else, very often a reality or another representation. The second definition implies that representations are external to the mind and serve as the medium through which the mind accepts information. This meaning of the term signifies the importance of second-order realities that occur during representation; abstracted once as external representations and then once again as LTM representations. If we go beyond the dictionary meaning of 'representation' and consider instances of representations, several properties significant to their form, use, and contents can be observed: (a) multiplicity, (b) consistency, (c) functionality, (d) abstraction, and (e) organization. Let us now consider each of these.

A.3.2 Multiplicity

There can be multiple representations of the same reality. This is because realities have many different properties or attributes and each representation abstracts only a finite subset. This does not necessarily mean that all realities have inherent contradictions. It simply means that representations select only a part (usually a small part) of the meanings that realities have or assume under different circumstances. For example, a door can be seen as a connector between two spaces or conversely as a separator between two spaces. Although we are accustomed to thinking of it as both, it is easily represented in either one of these two alternative forms. A floor-plan diagram used for calculation of the area of each room would assume doors as separators between rooms. On the other hand, a diagram showing circulation patterns must allow flow of traffic through these doorways, using them as connectors (figure A.3.1).

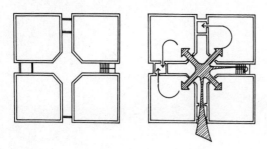

Figure A.3.1. Hypothetical plan.

A.3.3 Consistency

Another property of representations is that they are made up of parts that are consistent over a range of circumstances. For example, a flow diagram such as the PSG illustrated in chapter 4 is a representation commonly used in process descriptions. It consists of nodes and directed links. Each node stands for an information state and each link stands for an action, or vice versa. To violate this consistency would mean that the diagram would have some nodes that stand for states and others for actions. This renders the representation practically useless and violates the sole purpose of a flow diagram: it would be impossible to determine which actions result in which states and which states are suitable for which actions.

Consistency, or inconsistency for that matter, may arise from many different aspects of information contained in representations. Potentially, a representation may convey information through its *form*, its *contents*, or its relation to the *context* within which it is used. All three sources of information are usually defined as a priori parts of the conventions that surround any particular representation. The form of the PSG, for example, is defined as a set of nodes and links each having a consistent role: an action or a state. This is constant over many instances or uses, with the proviso that new roles can be assigned to the form. Thus the contents of each PSG vary from one instance to the next. Whether in a PSG, the nodes stand for rooms and links for circulation, or the nodes for transistors and the links for circuits, its contents are clear because of the consistency of its form.

The context of a representation is the totality of external information that is necessary to interpret correctly the meanings of symbols that constitute it. For example, take the drawing made by Adolph Loos for the Chicago Tribune competition (figure A.3.2, see over). If we change the context of this building, that is forget for a moment that it is a metaphor, then it is an inconsistent representation. A known convention such as the shape of a column is now something else: a building. What would normally be interpreted as the shaft, the base, and the capital of the column are now office tower, entrance, and penthouse floors of a building, respectively. Without the knowledge that this object was designed as a metaphor, it loses its relevance.

The format of a representation is the set of rules that implicitly define the way in which conflicting contents can be derived from different representations of the same 'object'. For example, a section consists of all visible surfaces when an object is sliced by a hypothetical plane. All poché[64] areas represent cut masses, all thin lines represent edges in elevation, beyond the slicing plane. These rules are sufficient to allow one to draw the section of a simple three-dimensional representation of

[64] To poché is to fill in the parts of architectural drawings representing solids.

an object [figure A.3.3(a) and (b)]. If some parts of the section are produced in violation of these rules then the format of the section will become inconsistent and the information obtained from this representation will be in conflict with information contained in the object [figure A.3.3(c)]. This is analogous to the notion of syntax which defines the rules of composition in natural language.

The content of a representation is the information that is presented through its format. The content of a representation is inconsistent if some parts of the content contradict the truth of others. For example, let us assume that no inconsistencies are present in the context and

Figure A.3.2. Entry by Adolph Loos to the Chicago Tribune Competition of 1923 (source: *Adolf Loos* by H Kulka, 1931, Schroll, Wien).

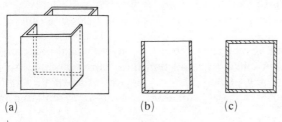

(a)   (b)   (c)

Figure A.3.3. Three-dimensional objects represented in two-dimensional media.

format of the representation in figure A.3.4. Let us consider it a correct representation in terms of syntax and one that is intended to represent a real object with planar faces. In this case, representation is inconsistent because of its contents. Parts of the representation contradict the plausibility of other parts. For example, each pair of corners of the triangular shape requires that the third corner should *not* be the way it is.

Figure A.3.4. 2-dimensional representation of depth.

A.3.4 Functionality
Representations, being products of the intellect, are intended to serve a purpose. Language, for example, allows communication among species. Graphic representations, on the other hand, are communicated most efficiently visually, and a verbal description conveying the identical scene can take pages of prose and still be 'incomplete'. 'A picture is worth a thousand words'. Similarly, a word is worth a thousand pictures. Each representation, by virtue of the properties of the reality that it represents and the nature of the consistency it has among its parts, serves certain purposes, or functions, better than others.

For example, a section such as the one in figure A.3.3 is a useful representation for designing the profile and internal makeup of an object on the section-plane rather than orthogonal to the section-plane. This is because it contains all the topological information pertaining to the profile of the object and very little information pertaining to the parts of the object orthogonal to the section plane. However, with the deliberate selection of where in the object the cross-section would pass, one can maximize or minimize the amount of useful information. Consequently, any given representation has definite implications about what can be accomplished with it.

A.3.5 Abstraction
Another property of representations, one that makes them a significant intellectual tool, is abstraction. Although realities are singular in the dimension of time – space and contain open-ended information, representations allow us to focus on a subset of these properties. This helps us produce generalized versions standing for many individual realities. In this fashion, we have the convenience of talking about large numbers of realities all at once, devising tools to deal with many

instances of the same generality, and we increase, manifold, our capacity
to deal with complexity of real life. Or alternatively, we have the
opportunity to articulate specific aspects of realities, excluding all
information extraneous to our task.

Clearly, many intellectual endeavors are not possible without the
ability to abstract[65]. First, through abstractions we can aggregate many
things into one. Second, we can select only those aspects of a reality
that we wish to talk about. Third, we can manipulate the representation
without bothering with realities, until we thoroughly understand the
effects of our manipulations and how they may affect realities.

A.3.6 Organization

A central factor in all four properties of representations, especially
abstraction, is organization. The extent of organization present in a
phenomenon will determine the success with which a generalized
property can be abstracted and around which representations can be
built. This in turn will determine the success with which the
representation will serve its function.

Take the example of motion-picture technology as a type of
representation. The central concept of organization here is the
frequency with which static images must be presented to the eye. The
film strip with its series of images strung up one after the other and the
process of flashing each image with split-second intervals produces a
representation of real images almost as powerful as the reality itself.
Of course, with the aid of today's sophisticated electronic and optical
wizardry this effect can be made even more powerful. However, the
critical factor of organization in all such cases is the $\frac{1}{24}$ second interval
between two subsequently flashing images which does not allow the
perceptual system to see the discontinuity between them. Through this
predictable attribute of human perception we can successfully represent
moving images. When the time interval between two images is greater
than a certain value, that is, when the central organizing factor for this
representation is disturbed, the representation does not work any more.
We begin perceiving something like frequently flashing slides. This is
when the organization underlying the representation breaks down and an
inappropriate representation, or one that assumes a very special meaning
(analogous to special movie effects) is produced.

[65] The ability to represent realities in abstract terms has been identified by
Piaget and Indler (1969) as one of the fundamental development stages during
adolescence.

References

• Reference not specifically quoted in the text but of particular relevance to this book

Akın Ö, 1978a, "Architectural inference making" in *Third International Conference and Exhibition on Computer Engineering and Building Design, CAD-78* (IPC Science and Technology Press, Guildford, Surrey) pp 506–521

Akın Ö, 1978b, "How do architects design?" in *Artificial Intelligence and Pattern Recognition in Computer-Aided Design* Ed. J-C Latombe (North-Holland, New York) pp 65–104

• Akın Ö, 1978c, review of *The Architecture of Form* edited by L March *Environment and Planning B* **5** 122 127

• Akın Ö, 1979, "A style named post-modern" *Architectural Design* **49**(8–9) 224–226

Akın Ö, 1980, "Perception of structure in three-dimensional block arrangements" IBS report 8, Department of Architecture, Carnegie-Mellon University, Pittsburgh, PA

Akın Ö, 1982a, "Instructional criticism in architectural education" in *Design Theory and Practice* Eds R Langdon, P A Purcell (Whitefairs Press, Tunbridge Wells, Kent) pp 90–96

Akın Ö, 1982b, "Representation and architecture" in *Representation and Architecture* Eds Ö Akın, E Weinel; Information Dynamics Inc., 111 Claybrook Drive, Silver Springs, MD 20902; pp 1–26

Akın Ö, 1984, "An exploration of the design process" in *Developments in Design Methodology* Ed. N Cross (John Wiley, New York) pp 189–208

• Akın Ö, Chase W, 1978, "Quantification of three-dimensional structures" *Journal of Experimental Psychology: Human Perception and Performance* **4** 397–410

Akın Ö, Reddy R, 1977, "Knowledge acquisition for image understanding research" *Journal of Computer Graphics and Image Processing* **6** 307–334

Alexander C, 1964 *Notes on the Synthesis of Form* (Harvard University Press, Cambridge, MA)

• Alexander C, Ishikawa S, Silverstein M, 1977 *A Pattern Language* (Oxford University Press, New York)

Anderson J R, 1981 *Cognitive Skills and their Acquisition* (Lawrence Erlbaum Associates, Hillsdale, NJ)

Bachus J W, 1960, "The syntax and semantics of the proposed international algebraic language of the Zurich ACM-GAMM Conference" in *Information Processing* (UNESCO, Paris)

Baer A, Eastman C M, Henrion M, 1979, "A survey of geometric modelling computer aided design" report 58, Institute of Physical Planning, Carnegie-Mellon University, Pittsburgh, PA

Baylor G W Jr, 1971 *A treatise on the Mind's-eye: An Empirical Investigation of Visual Mental Imagery* unpublished doctoral dissertation, Department of Psychology, Carnegie-Mellon University, Pittsburgh, PA

• Beittel K, 1972 *Mind and Context in the Art of Drawing* (Holt, Rinehart and Winston, New York)

• Bhaskar R, Simon H A, 1977, "Problem solving in semantically rich domains: an example from engineering thermodynamics" *Cognitive Science* **1** 192–215

• Bobrow D G, 1968, "Natural language input for a computer problem-solving system" in *Semantic Information Processing* Ed. M Minsky (MIT Press, Cambridge, MA) pp 146–226

• Booker P J, 1963 *A History of Engineering Drawing* (Chatto and Windus, London)

Boulding K, 1969 *The Image* (University of Michigan Press, Ann Arbor, MI)

• Braid I, 1975, "The synthesis of solids bounded by many faces" *Communications of the ACM* **18** 209–216

Broadbent G, 1973 *Design in Architecture* (John Wiley, New York)

Buchanan B, Sunderland G, Feigenbaum E A, 1969, "Heuristic DENDRAL: A program for generating explanatory hypotheses in organic chemistry" in *Machine Intelligence 4* Eds B Meltzer, D Michie, M Swann (American Elsevier, New York) pp 209–254

Chase W G, Simon H A, 1973, "The mind's eye in chess" in *Visual Information Processing* Ed. W G Chase (Academic Press, New York) pp 215–282

Clark H H, Chase W G, 1973, "On the process of comparing sentences against pictures" *Cognitive Psychology* **3** 472–517

Collins A M, Quillian M R, 1969, "Retrieval time from semantic memory" *Journal of Verbal Learning and Verbal Behavior* **8** 240–247

• Dansereau D F, 1969 *An Information Processing Model of Mental Multiplication* unpublished doctoral dissertation, Department of Psychology, Carnegie-Mellon University, Pittsburgh, PA

Davis G, Szigeti F, 1980, "Comparative listing of systems for planning, management and utilization of facilities: Public Works Treasury Board Secretariat and OGD's" The Environmental Analysis Group Ltd, PO Box 1088, Station B, Ottawa, Ontario KIP 5R1

deGroot A D, 1965 *Thought and Choice in Chess* (Mouton, The Hague)

• deGroot A D, 1966, "Perception and memory versus thought: some old ideas and recent findings" in *Problem Solving* Ed. B Kleinmuntz (John Wiley, New York) pp 19–50

deKleer J, 1977, "Multiple representations of knowledge in mechanics problem solver" in *Proceedings of the Fifth International Joint Conference on Artificial Intelligence* Department of Computer Science, Carnegie-Mellon University, Pittsburgh, PA, pp 299–304

Eastman C, 1968, "Explorations of the cognitive processes in design" Department of Computer Science report, Carnegie-Mellon University, Pittsburgh, PA

Eastman C, 1969, "Cognitive processes and ill-defined problems: a case study from design" in *Proceedings of the International Joint Conference on Artificial Intelligence* Eds D E Walker, L M Norton; The Mitre Corporation, Bedford, MA 01730, pp 669–691

Eastman C, 1970, "On the analysis of intuitive design processes" in *Emerging Methods in Environmental Design and Planning* Ed. G T Moore (MIT Press, Cambridge, MA) pp 21–37

• Eastman C, 1972, "Logical methods of building design: A review and synthesis" *DMG-DRS Journal: Design Research and Methods* **6**(3) 79–90

Eastman C, 1973, "Automated space planning" *Artificial Intelligence* **4** 41–64

Eastman C, 1976, "General purpose building description systems" *Computer Aided Design* **8** 17–26

Eastman C, 1978, "Representation of design problems and maintenance of their structure" in *Artificial Intelligence and Pattern Recognition in Computer Aided Design* Ed. J-C Latombe (North-Holland, New York) pp 335–366

Eastman C, Henrion M, 1979, "GLIDE: a system for implementing design databases" *PArC 83: Proceedings of the International Conference on Computers in Architecture* (Online Publications, Pinner, Middx) paper 44

Eastman C, Henrion M, 1980, "GLIDE: a language for interactive design" in *Tutorial and Selected Readings in Interactive Computer Graphics* Ed. H Freeman; IEEE Computer Society, Long Beach, CA; pp 183–192

• Eastman C, Lividini J, Stoker D, 1975, "A database for designing large physical systems" in *Proceedings of the 1975 National Computer Conference* American Federation of Information Processing Societies Inc., Montvale, NJ 07645, pp 603–612

Ericsson K A, Chase W G, Faloon S, 1980, "Acquisition of a memory skill" *Science* **208** 1181–1182

Erman L D, Lesser V R, 1975, "A multi-level organization for problem solving using many, diverse, cooperating sources of knowledge" in *Proceedings of the 4th International Joint Conference on Artificial Intelligence* The AI Laboratory Publications Department, 545 Technology Square, Cambridge, MA 02139, pp 483–490

Farley A M, 1974 *VIPS: A Visual Imagery and Perception System; The Results of a Protocol Analysis* PhD thesis. Department of Computer Science, Carnegie-Mellon University, Pittsburgh, PA

Feigenbaum E A, 1961, "The simulation of verbal learning behavior" in *Proceedings of the Western Joint Computer Conference* National Joint Computer Committee, Association of Computing Machinery, 2 East 63rd Street, New York, NY 10021, pp 121–129

Feigenbaum E A, Feldman J, 1963 *Computers and Thought* (McGraw-Hill, New York)

Flemming U, 1978, "Wall representations of rectangular dissections and their use in automated space allocation" *Environment and Planning B* **5** 215–232

Foz A, 1973, "Observations on designer behavior in the parti" in *The Design Activity International Conference, volume 1* Printing Unit, University of Strathclyde, Glasgow, pp 19.1–19.4

Freeman P A, Newell A, 1971, "A model for functional reasoning in design" in *Proceedings of the Second International Joint Computer Conference on Artificial Intelligence* British Computer Society, 13 Mansfield Street, London W1M OBP, pp 621–640

Gilmartin K, Simon H, 1973, "A simulation of memory for chess positions" *Cognitive Psychology* **5** 29–46

• Goumain P G, 1973, "Design methods and designer's methods" in *The Design Activity International Conference* Printing Unit, University of Strathclyde, Glasgow, pp 23.1–23.8

Grabrijan D, Neidhardt J, 1957 *Architecture of Bosnia* (Drzavna Zalozba Slovenije, Ljublijana)

• Graves M, 1977, "The necessity for drawing: tangible speculation" *Architectural Design* **47** 384–394

• Gregg L W, Simon H A, 1967, "An information processing explanation of one-trial and incremental learning" *Journal of Verbal Learning and Verbal Behavior* **6** 780–787

Guzman A, 1968, "Computer recognition of three-dimensional objects in a visual scene" MAC-TR-59, Project MAC, Massachusetts Institute of Technology, Cambridge, MA

Hanks K, Belliston L, Edwards D, 1977 *Design Yourself* (William Kaufmann, Los Altos, CA)

Hauser A, 1951 *The Social History of Art* (Routledge and Kegan Paul, Henley-on-Thames, Oxon)

• Hawk M C, 1962 Schaum's Outline of Theory and Problems of Descriptive Geometry (Schaum, New York)

• Hayes J R, Simon H A, 1974, "Understanding written problem instructions" in *Knowledge and Cognition* Ed. L W Gregg (John Wiley, New York) pp 167–200

Henrion M, 1974, "Notes on the synthesis of problems: an exploration of problem formulations used by human designers and automatic systems" master's thesis, Department of Design Research, Royal College of Art, London

Herot C F, 1974, "Context in sketch recognition" master's thesis, Department of Architecture, Massachusetts Institute of Technology, Cambridge, MA

• Hewitt C, 1972 *Description and Theoretical Analysis (Using Schemata) of PLANNER: A Language for Proving Theorems and Manipulating Models in a Robot* PhD thesis, AI-TR-258, The Artificial Intelligence Laboratories, Massachusetts Institute of Technology, Cambridge, MA

Hofstadter D R, 1979 *Godel, Escher, Bach: An Eternal Golden Braid* (Vintage Books, New York)

Hunt E B, 1975 *Artificial Intelligence* (Academic Press, New York)

Jenks C, 1978 *The Language of Post-modern Architecture* (Rizzoli, New York)

Jones C J, 1970 *Design Methods* (John Wiley, New York)

Katona A, 1940 *Organizing and Memorizing* (Columbia University Press, New York)

• Klahr D, Siegler R S, 1978, "The representation of children's knowledge" in *Advances in Child Development and Behavior, Volume 12* Ed. H Reese, L Lipsitt (Academic Press, New York) pp 61–116

Krauss R I, Myer R M, 1970, "Design: a case history" in *Emerging Methods in Environmental Design and Planning* Ed. G Moore (MIT Press, Cambridge, MA) pp 11–20

Latombe J-C, 1977, "Artificial intelligence in computer-aided design: the TROPIC system" in *CAD Systems* Ed. J J Allan (North-Holland, New York) pp 61–121

Lenat D B, 1976 *AM: An Artificial Intelligence Approach to Discovery in Mathematics as Heuristic Search* PhD thesis, Computer Science Department, Stanford University, Stanford CA

Lenat D B, 1983a, "Theory formation by heuristic search. The nature of heuristics II: background and examples", *Artificial Intelligence* **21** 31–60

Lenat D B, 1983b, "EURISKO: A program that learns new heuristics and domain concepts. The nature of heuristics III: program design and results", *Artificial Intelligence* **21** 61–98

Lindsay P H, Norman D A, 1972 *Human Information Processing* (Academic Press, New York)

Lobell J, 1975, "Design and the powerful logics of the mind's deep structures" *DMG-DRS Journal: Design Research and Methods* **9**(2) 122–129

• Marcus S H, 1977 *Basics of Structural Steel Design* (Reston Publishing, Reston, Manitoba)

• Marples D L, 1974, "Argument and technique in the solution of problems in mechanics and electricity" CUED/C-Educ/TRI, Department of Engineering, University of Cambridge, Cambridge

Michie D, 1974 *On Machine Intelligence* (John Wiley, New York)

Miller G A, 1956, "Magical number seven, plus or minus two: some limits on our capacity of processing information" *Psychological Review* **63** 81–96

Miller G A E, Galanter E, Pribram K H, 1960 *Plans and the Structure of Behavior* (Henry Holt, New York)

• Mitchell W, Steadman J P, Liggett R S, 1976, "Synthesis and optimization of small rectangular floor plans" *Environment and Planning B* **3** 37–70

Moore G T, 1972 *Emerging Methods in Environmental Design and Planning* (MIT Press, Cambridge, MA)

Moran T P, 1970, "A model of multilingual designer", in *Emerging Methods in Environmental Design and Planning* Ed. G T Moore (MIT Press, Cambridge, MA)

Neisser U, 1976 *Cognition and Reality* (W H Freeman, Salt Lake City, UT)

Newell A, 1968, "On the analysis of human problem solving protocols", in *Calcul et Formalisation dans les Sciences de L'Homme* Eds J C Gardin, B Jaulin (Centre National de la Recherche Scientifique, Paris)

Newell A, 1970, "Heuristic programming: ill-structured problems" in *Progress in Operations Research, Volume 3* Ed. J A Arnofsky (John Wiley, New York) chapter 1 pp 360–414

Newell A, 1973, "Production systems: models of control structures" in *Visual Information Processing* Ed. W G Chase (Academic Press, New York) pp 463–526

Newell A, Shaw J C, Simon H A, 1957, "Preliminary description of the General Problem Solving program I (GPS I)" WP7, Carnegie Institute of Technology, Pittsburgh, PA

Newell A, Simon H A, 1965, "An example of chess play in the light of chess playing programs", in *Progress in Biocybernetics* Ed. N Weiner, P Schade (Elsevier, Amsterdam) pp 19–75

Newell A, Simon H A, 1972 *Human Problem Solving* (Prentice-Hall, Englewood Cliffs, NJ)

• Norman D A, 1969 *Memory Attention: An Introduction to Human Information Processing* (John Wiley, New York)

Novac G S, 1976, "Computer understanding of physics problems stated in natural language" TRNL-30, Department of Computer Science, University of Texas, Austin, TX

Ohlander R, Reddy R, Akın Ö, 1976, "An experimental system for knowledge acquisition in image understanding" in *Working Papers on Image Understanding: I* Department of Computer Science, Carnegie-Mellon University, Pittsburgh, PA, pp 26–37

Piaget J, Indler B, 1969 *The Psychology of the Child* (Basic Books, New York)

Poincaré H, 1952 *Science and Method* translated by F Maitland (Dover, New York)

Popper K R, 1972 *Objective Knowledge* (Oxford University Press, Oxford)

Posner M I, 1973 *Cognition: An Introduction* (Scott Foresman, Glenview, IL)

• Quillian M R, 1968, "Semantic memory" in *Semantic Information Processing* Ed. M Minsky (MIT Press, Cambridge, MA) pp 227–270

• Raman P G, 1973, "Form models and design synthesis" in *The Design Activity International Conference, Volume 1* Printing Unit, University of Strathclyde, Glasgow, pp 15.1–15.6

Rapoport A, 1969 *House Form and Culture* (Prentice-Hall, Englewood, Cliffs, NJ)

Reddy R, Newell A, 1974, "Knowledge and its representation in a speech understanding system" in *Knowledge and Cognition* Ed. L W Gregg (John Wiley, New York) pp 253–286

Reiger C J III, 1975, "Conceptual memory and inference" in *Conceptual Information Processing* Ed. R C Schank (American Elsevier, New York) pp 157–288

Reitman J, 1976, "Skill perception in go: deducting memory structures from inter-response times" *Cognitive Psychology* **8** 336–356

Reitman W R, 1964, "Heuristic decision procedures, open constraints and structure of ill-defined problems" in *Human Judgements and Optimality* Eds M W Shelly, G L Bryan (John Wiley, New York) pp 282–315

• Rubin S, 1978, "The ARGOS image understanding system" technical report, Computer Science Department, Carnegie-Mellon University, Pittsburgh, PA

Shank R C, 1975 *Conceptual Inference Making* (American Elsevier, New York)

• Sheppard R, Metzler J, 1971, "Mental rotation of three-dimensional objects" *Science* **171** 77–110

Simon H, 1944, "Decision making and administrative organization" *Public Administrative Review* **4** 16-31

Simon H A, 1969 *Sciences of the Artificial* (MIT Press, Cambridge, MA)

Simon H, 1970, "Style in design" in *Proceedings of the Environmental Design Research Association Conference* Department of Architecture, Carnegie-Mellon University, Pittsburgh, PA, pp 1-10

Simon H A, 1973, "Structure of ill-structured problems" *Artificial Intelligence* **4** 181-201

Simon D P, Simon H A, 1978, "Individual differences in solving physics problems" in *Children's Thinking: What Develops?* Ed. R S Siegler (Lawrence Erlbaum Associates, Hillsdale, NJ)

Steadman J P, 1983 *Architectural Morphology* (Pion, London)

• Stiny G, 1976, "Two exercises in formal composition" *Environment and Planning B* **3** 187-210

• Stiny G, 1981, "Grammar of form'" unpublished manuscript, copy available from the author at Graduate School of Architecture and Urban Planning, University of California, Los Angeles, CA

• Studer R G, Stea D, 1971, "Architectural programming, environmental design, and human behavior" *The Journal of Social Issues* **22** 127-136

Sussman G J, 1973 *A Computational Model of Skill Acquisition* PhD Thesis, Department of Mathematics, Massachusetts Institute of Technology, Cambridge, MA

Taggart J, 1975, "Sketching: an informal dialogue between designer and computer" in *Computer Aids to Design and Architecture* Ed. N Negroponte (Petrocelli, New York) pp 147-162

Turing A M, 1950, "Computing machinery and intelligence" *Mind* **59** 433-450

• Voelker H, 1974, "An introduction to PADL" Production Automation Project, University of Rochester, Rochester, NY

• Vygotsky L S, 1971 *The Psychology of Art* (MIT Press, Cambridge, MA)

Wade J W, 1977 *Architecture, Problems and Purposes* (John Wiley, New York)

• Weinszapfel G, 1973, "It might work, but will it help?" in *The Design Activity International Conference, Volume 1* Printing Unit, University of Strathclyde, Glasgow, pp 16.1-16.4

• Winograd T, 1972, "A program for understanding natural language" *Cognitive Psychology* **3** 1-191